FROM CABBAGE
TO CAULIFLOWER

From Cabbage *to* Cauliflower

Memoirs of an Obscure Academic

WILLIAM G. MONAHAN

with *Jane N. Monahan*

LUMINARE PRESS
WWW.LUMINAREPRESS.COM

From Cabbage to Cauliflower
Copyright © 2021 by W. Gregory Monahan

All rights reserved. This book or any portion thereof may not be reproduced or used in any manner whatsoever without the express written permission of the publisher, except for the use of brief quotations in a book review.

Printed in the United States of America

Luminare Press
442 Charnelton St.
Eugene, OR 97401
www.luminarepress.com

LCCN: 2021915834
ISBN: 978-1-64388-761-6

TABLE OF CONTENTS

Preface ix

Forward 1

CHAPTER I
Education and the Chance to Become 3

CHAPTER I: ADDENDUM
Pauline Tabor's House of Ill Repute 58

CHAPTER II
The Military Times 62

CHAPTER III
The Academy: Then and Now 99

CHAPTER IV
On Becoming an Educator 131

CHAPTER V
The Bureaucratic Interlude (1956-1958) 161

CHAPTER VI
The Professorial Years: Michigan State University and
Oklahoma University (1958-1965) 191

CHAPTER VII
The Professorial Years: University of Iowa (1965-1972) 224

CHAPTER VIII
West Virginia University (1972-1996) 240

CHAPTER IX
Rewards and Recognition 271

CHAPTER X
The Later Years (1996-2011) 287

APPENDIX A
Your Billy: Letters From A Nineteen-Year-Old Soldier 304

APPENDIX B
The Death of Robert "Sonny" Monahan, Jr. 330

Index 343

Preface

My father published his last scholarly book (with co-author Ed Smith) in 1995.[1] By that time, he had already been at work for some time on this autobiography, which he finished and had bound for members of the family in 1996. I never found the original digital version, so I have decided to retype the entire manuscript. That is fine, because it has enabled me to read it more closely, and to add some materials, particularly photographs, but also occasional tidbits from surviving letters he wrote at various times in his life as well as emails I received from him after he had finished. He claimed later to have "noodled around" with further chapters, but a thorough search of his computer after his death in 2011 revealed no further work. As a result, I have taken the liberty of writing a final chapter that chronicles his life after he finished this work in 1996. I have also added a short supplemental chapter on his "connection" to a local house of ill-repute in Bowling Green and two appendices, one containing passages from the extensive number of letters he wrote to my mother while he served in the army in late 1946 and 1947, and the other on the death of his brother Sonny during the Second World War.

In editing my father's memoir, I have chosen not to make any changes in his wording or the structure of his occasionally long sentences, since these do a fine job of relaying his voice. That said, his punctuation could be quite "original," and I have chosen to correct it where the grammar of his sentences demanded it and to fix the occasional typo or misspelling.

---

[1] *Leading People: What School Leaders Can Learn from Military Leadership Development* (New York: Scholastic, 1995). It culminated a lifetime of publishing that included four other books, three of them co-authored and one edited, and a very large number of articles and papers.

Where he refers to a particular historical event or person (including me), I have occasionally inserted a footnote, and all captions for photographs are by me. Editing and enhancing my father's work has inspired me to write my own memoir once this one is published. More should be remembered of us in the generations after our deaths than a few character traits that may or may not have had any grounding in reality. Of course, no memoir is in any way "objective." We all reconstruct our pasts, but at least with this work, future generations can understand something of my father's life the way he saw and experienced it.

Original bound Memoirs with blue cover

"Training is everything. The peach was once a bitter almond; cauliflower is nothing but cabbage with a college education."

—MARK TWAIN, Pudd'nhead Wilson[2]

---

[2] Mark Twain, *Pudd'nhead Wilson and Those Extraordinary Twins* (New York: Harper Brothers, 1894), p. 37. The passage begins Chapter 5 in all editions and is attributed by Twain to "Pudd'nhead Wilson's Calendar."

Forward

It is said that when Noel Coward went off to Jamaica to write his memoirs, a friend asked him whether he had an abundance of notes and records. Coward said no, that he had a memory like an elephant. "In fact," he said, "Elephants consult me!" In trying to put down the events and circumstances of a lifetime which this small volume reports, I too have relied primarily on recollection. Elephants do not consult me! But I think I have remembered it well, and if I might have left out some of the worst of it, that's what a kind of family memoir ought to do, for I'd like all of those who come after me to think reasonably well of me.

Now, while I have written the most of this thing, and it tries to chronicle my own professional career, it is truly "co"-authored with Jane. As with most of almost anything I have ever written, she "edited" it, telling me here and there that "this" didn't sound right, or "that" needed this or that! And that is why the title page carries both our names. In truth, every "title" page of anything I have ever written should also more properly have included her name, for she has been the heart of anything I have ever done or accomplished.

I am now at the edge of seventy years old, though except for rheumatoid arthritis and an enlarged prostate, I don't feel much differently than when I was thirty (although in *that* case, my memory may *not* be so exact!). Nevertheless, I should like it noted that what is included in these following commentaries is certainly not the end of me and Janie. We fully expect that down the road a ways, we could probably add at least another several chapters. In truth, life does indeed go on, and it is only the pace and the pattern that changes, and as one enjoys these halcyon days of relaxed retirement (given a nice check monthly from TIAA!), there is considerable truth in an old song that I enjoyed teaching to my granddaughter during one recent summer visit: "Life is just a bowl of cherries…." I'm sure that with a little coaxing, she could finish it.

Jane and I have often wondered what the lives of our own parents and grandparents were like, for apart from the things that we were the most familiar with about them, there is so much more that we will just never know. Of course, they gave little thought to such a notion, and other than brief and dimly remembered conversations, we know all too little at all of what they or their world were like. We simply wanted our own children and grandchildren to know a little of what our lives were like across many years of reasonably good fortune and fairly hard work (plus a really adventurous spirit) that took us all across this marvelous country: in Kentucky, from Marion to Murray, from Murray to Frankfort, from Frankfort to Michigan State, and from there to Oklahoma, Iowa, and West Virginia.

We hope that Greg and Rita, and Joe, will one day add their own memoirs to this kind of record, for it is a rather good thing to pass on to those that come after us. But in the meantime, and so far as this piece is concerned, it's been one hell of a ride! And it ain't over yet!

WILLIAM G. AND JANE MONAHAN
Morgantown, WV
November 1996

CHAPTER I

Education and the Chance to Become

When one reflects on it even in passing, the circumstances of life that somehow result in any of us finding something we can do reasonably well and genuinely enjoy in the process constitute a rare and remarkable thing. That it happens at all anywhere is curious, I suppose, but I am convinced that it happens more often in the American way of things than in any other culture. Moreover, I think that it happens even in America less frequently than is often pretended.

In a sense, that is a more substantial affirmation of the American "equal opportunity" ideology than it is of the more romantic *Horatio Alger* kinds of myths that have tended to distort and exaggerate the so-called American dream. By that I simply mean that, though not too long ago there was a rather clear pattern in one's life space whereby his or her chances were pretty much fixed, the great consequence of the developing Western idea of egalitarianism and particularly its distinctly American version has been that traditions of privilege, of birth and class and other kinds of fixed entitlements, have been largely canceled out. And I say "largely" because advantage will always remain to some people, and there is no way to put all such circumstances aside. But the fact remains that one has greater choice still today in these United States to find one's way through life with satisfaction and achievement than in most any other society anywhere or anytime.

Moving Up: A Little Luck,
A Little Work, and...the G.I. Bill

In my own case, this American circumstance is nicely illustrated.

If the idea of luck has much to do with it, for me it was simply a matter of being born at a ripening time. When people say—and it is an accurate observation—that luck and chance play a more significant function in our lives than most of us are willing to admit, an antecedent principle is implied: that it is something in the nature of the system itself that makes it possible for chance to work. If it were not for the system itself, what chances would there be? Without belaboring the point, there is ample evidence to prove the idea that what the American version of polity has made possible is a genuine chance. Of course, that chance is invigorated by our marvelous system of schools and law and a broad belief in equity, but, in retrospect, a real chance is about all even the best system of government can really try to ensure. Certainly, the odds change, and they are not the same at the outset for everyone, but they are there all the same—there *is* the chance! There is that, at least.

For thousands of persons of my generation, our chances were enhanced further by the GI Bill of Rights.[3] It is moot as to whether or how many of us would have gone off to college otherwise. Unquestionably, many probably would not, but the point is that so many did indeed take advantage of that entitlement. Accordingly, the cumulative consequences of the GI Bill are incalculable, and there is no question that it constituted a particular kind of revolution and reflects one of those rare events in the life of a national culture of which legends are fashioned. Probably as well, it had much more to do than we might suppose in contributing to the increasingly common expectation today that some kind of post-secondary education for almost everyone is almost presumed. Thus today, the idea of going

---

[3] Officially called the "Servicemen's Readjustment Act of 1944," it was pushed hard by the American Legion and signed into law by FDR on June 2, 1944. Benefits included dedicated payments of tuition and living expenses to attend high school, college, or vocational/technical school, low-cost mortgages, low-interest loans to start a business, as well as one year of unemployment compensation. It provided one of the greatest boosts to college/university enrollment in the history of the United States.

to college is almost generally taken for granted, and the extent to which the academic culture is now familiar to so many high school youngsters is itself in remarkable contrast to the notions so many of those of us in the forties and fifties had about college life.

It is occasionally worth remembering that despite the emergence during the late thirties of our society as just beginning to emphasize a welfare policy, the idea of "going to college" remained an option still perceived even into the late war years of the forties as mostly reserved for the more privileged among us. There is probably much to support the hunch that those perceptions had already begun to change somewhat as a result of our painful experiences during the war years of '39-'45. In its turn, that remarkable period of great change provided significant embellishment to emerging notions of social justice that were somehow anticipated by early thrusts of the New Deal itself.[4] The remarkable thing about so much of FDR's New Deal policies was the presumption that, given any kind of "equal chance," even the least of us had a shot at the *good life*. The coming of World War II merely, though painfully, emphasized that equity.

Perhaps also, that contributed in some way to the fact that the Congress of the United States somehow had the wisdom to see, even perhaps only dimly then, that a more lasting contribution to America's growing status in the world would be much better served by the beneficence of subsidized education than by those historically more conventional devices like Old Soldiers' Homes and Veterans' Bonuses. Consequently, for whatever reason or happy accident, the Congress enacted something called the GI Bill of Rights. Certainly, there was some of that other stuff too, i. e., Veterans' Homes and Bonuses. When we servicemen were discharged, for example, we received a modest stipend from the government for almost a year which was sort of aimed at transitioning us from the military into civilian endeavors. Far be it from me to put any

---

[4] "A New Deal for the American People" was the slogan used by Franklin Delano Roosevelt in his election campaign of 1932. Following his inauguration in 1933, he and a large Democratic majority in the Congress elected with him enacted a number of laws that established new government agencies to put the unemployed to work, regulate the financial system, and ensure some measure of economic security for millions of Americans. These laws and agencies are often summarized under the term, "New Deal."

of that lightly. After all, government benefits for those who had served their country well and had sacrificed much in the process showed that they surely deserved to be taken care of.

But it was the GI Bill of Rights that most surely revolutionized America in the immediate aftermath of World War II. It brings to my own mind something almost as memorable in the development of American stature as was the Emperor Augustus Caesar's ability to extend the life of the Roman Empire at the beginning of the modern era. When I say that the idea of going to college was a quite different proposition for those of us who trekked into colleges and universities by the thousands in the late forties and fifties, I am trying to evoke an image that is not easy to fashion with convincing persuasiveness. But I think my own situation is a fairly generalizable case in point.

A Little Background

My grandparents on both sides came from Ireland and emigrated during the latter stages of what historians now characterize as a prolonged potato famine.[5] On my mother's side, they were stone masons and quarrymen. On my father's, railroaders. It could be asserted that the Irish represented the second great infiltration of low born ethnic stock into the American continent after the Blacks. The latter came much earlier and almost universally not of their own choice, of course.

The Irish, on the other hand, came mostly at their own choice such as it was, for it was a choice least among almost any other alternatives. They either came or they stayed and starved. There were many other differences, of course, between these two large cohorts of immigrants. Though both groups came impoverished, the Blacks came as slaves unprepared in any way for immersion into even the most remote

---

[5] "The Great Hunger" or great potato famine actually struck both Ireland and Germany between 1845 and 1852, though it appears to have been worse in Ireland, where English ownership of much of the land and divisions due to inheritance forced peasants to live off progressively smaller plots of land. Potatoes could be grown in large numbers on small plots, but a blight in these years ruined the crop and led to mass starvation and emigration. Also, it turns out that my father's grandfather was born in this country very soon after *his* parents immigrated, though my father did not know that.

aspects of Western culture such as it was in the early seventeenth century. The Irish came, on the other hand, with a well-developed sense of culture and openness.⁶ And despite significant obstacles and setbacks, they also brought with them an established tradition of myths and a long and internalized history. They were almost universally Roman Catholic, and they were almost universally poor. Yet, they came with a remarkable spirit and a conviction of their own ability to prevail over any adversity. Only European Jews may have surpassed them in that attitude of single-minded tenacity.⁷

The Irish displayed that attitude because, though they were a mystically religious people, they also had come to grips with the ultimate recognition that almost nothing could be worse than what they had already endured. It not only provided them with the strength to be mobile, but it enabled them also to take an ironic view of life, of themselves, and of their new circumstances. Their religion provided them with absolution for their sins (and some of them—especially the menfolk—sinned with joyous abandon and terrible guilt), but no people ever loved life more nor feared the consequences of dying still more so. Accordingly, despite their almost obsessive dependence on their religious indoctrination, no people anywhere have ever held more "this world" doubts about the "other world's" rewards. Probably it has been this strain between reality and skepticism that has contributed to their almost universal and indomitable faith.

The whole history of the Irish people is one of hardship and turmoil, and since the eighth century, they have had to struggle to sustain their identity as a people. For at least the last three centuries, they have endured a continuous resistance against what can only be felicitously referred to as "Anglicization," and while the land is

---

⁶ Of course, slaves did come with a "well-developed sense of culture," parts of which they eventually shared in various forms with a wholly undeserving white population, but much of their culture was unhappily crushed beneath the dreadful weight of bondage.

⁷ My father's pride in his ancestry is certainly understandable, but other ethnic immigrant groups would certainly qualify here, from the Italians who came late in the nineteenth century to Hispanics from a wide variety of countries in the Americas who continue to come today.

beautiful ("...sure a little bit o' heaven fell out of the sky one day..."[8]), it is not bountiful. The Irish had to emphasize a faith in the glories of everlasting contentment, for there was so little of it *here*! It is said that the strength of a people is ultimately honed by its ability to take adversity without too much lasting seriousness. Thus, for the Irish, there has always been a special affinity not so much with the New Testament as with the Old. There is, in Revelation 7:14, an almost Irish Creed:

"Those are they which came out of great tribulation and have washed their robes and made them white in the blood of the lamb."[9]

So they came, these buoyant people. They were, long before the words were written and cast at the base of an image, "the tired, the poor huddled masses yearning to be free...."

The Monahans and the Murphys

My father's people were railroaders. They had done well and moved up into positions of trust at the shop level in that enormous industry. My mother's folks were stone masons and quarrymen. They used their talents to dig limestone from Kentucky hills, and they cut it, and they built with it, and they fashioned it according to the designs of American architecture. Like my father's people, who did not design railroad locomotives, they did not design the buildings nor have much at all to do with the policies or purposes which caused them to be built. They merely provided the material and the labor. Labor and work and contentment with the opportunity to provide it were not only necessary to these people but were enough even in an America which, in the late nineteenth century, heard outrageous things being said about the glories of what is now clear to us was a very corrupt and exploitative kind of Capitalism.

---

[8] My father here quotes the first line from the old Irish song "A Little Bit of Heaven" by J. Keirn Brennan and Ernest R. Ball.

[9] The Book of Revelation is actually in the New Testament, but one could argue that it is the most "Old Testament" book in the New!

John Joseph "J. J." Monahan, my father's grandfather

They provided the stone, and they made the railroads work. Ironically, while they were intensely Catholic, they believed as strongly in much of the Protestant Ethic as anyone else. They took a curious, almost caste-like attitude toward their well-being and generally expected their children to do much as they had done with one important exception: In every Catholic family everywhere and at one time or another, there was the fervent hope that when some male child showed some brilliance and sensitivity beyond that which seemed otherwise to characterize the normal style of the family, that he indeed might become a priest. The Roman Catholic priesthood was the ultimate avenue for a kind of cultural exception. To have a son become a priest represented such a complex of mystical, sacred, and status phenomena as to defy explanation. Suffice only to say that it brought to any such family an abundance of glory beyond understanding.[10] It took a while, but America changed much of that too, for here it became increasingly apparent that one could become something else, and if not as mythically noble as priesthood, "not bad" in any case.

In the case of my family, that widening of opportunity was most fortuitous since it surely *was* obvious that none of the progeny demonstrated any presumed priestly qualities nor certainly any inclinations to a life of abstinence and celibacy!

---

[10] A similar, if "lesser" honor accrued to women becoming nuns. My father's sister Joan contemplated that choice for some time before turning to nursing instead. She eventually married and mothered a child, my cousin Nan.

My parents married in 1920. My father was then almost 34; my mother had barely turned 20.[11] That was the pattern in those times. He had sowed his wild oats, as the saying has it, and she was about of marriageable age. At that time, he had moved up the explicit and narrowly prescribed sequence of the railroad industry's hierarchical labor pattern. As was the case with most industries, railroading was darkly immersed in those notions of *efficiency* and *scientific management* so popular still in the first quarter of this century. He had served a six-thousand-hour apprenticeship in the "shops" and was by the time they married, a first level machinist. His father was the Yard Master of the Louisville and Nashville ("L&N") Railroad in Bowling Green, Kentucky, a position just barely beneath honest-to-God corporate management, and in that position, he was responsible for scheduling freight, making sure that trains were made up properly, where they were to go, when, and that they were in first-class operating condition.[12] His function was vital to the railroads and somewhat analogous to that of a Master Sergeant with the Army, and it paid much better.

All of my grandfather's sons—there were four of them—were in the shops in various cities served by the L&N, and he was

---

[11] Robert Eugene Monahan (1886-1949) married Anna Catherine Murphy (1899-1983) in 1920.

[12] There is some question as to where John Joseph "J. J." Monahan, father to Robert Eugene, was actually born. His nephew Gus maintained he was born in Parkersburg in what is now West Virginia, but census records indicate Maryland (probably Baltimore). In any case, he was American, born shortly after his parents, Dennis and Mary, immigrated from Ireland. His wife (my father's grandmother) was named Johanna Sullivan, about whom little is known save that she had a sister named Theresa Massey. John Joseph went to work for the L&N Railroad in 1870, barely eleven years after it had completed its first line from Louisville to Nashville, thus its name. He had several siblings, including one older brother, Dennis (born in Ireland), who joined the Westward migration as a private in the 51st infantry, was stationed briefly at Fort Apache in Arizona (from which he wrote a surviving letter), and mustered out in Alaska in 1875, after which nothing more is known of him. Likewise, my father errs in calling his grandfather a "yard boss." In the only extant letter we have from my father's cousin Gus, who also worked all his life for the railroad, the latter pointed out this error, and noted that their grandfather was always a master machinist, an occupation in which his sons followed him.

apparently quite proud of them.¹³ By 1927, the year I was born as the third living child (there were two miscarriages and a daughter who followed in 1929), my father was earning a monthly salary of a little over $500 per month and was surely already well on the way to becoming a full-fledged member of the emerging laboring middle class.¹⁴ He was good at what he did, enjoyed it, was universally liked by the people with whom he worked, and had a marvelous sense of humor. He was renowned as a singer of Irish ballads in a high, sweet tenor voice, could drink with the best of them, was a raconteur of the first order, and knew as much about the idiosyncrasies of big steam locomotives as about anyone in the whole of the L&N operation. That, at least, was a child's perception of him and was, in general, apparently rather accurate.

In 1929—the reasons are somewhat obscure—he was "let out" as the expression had it at the time. There is some reason to believe based on information provided by others, that there were some labor troubles, either a strike or an effort to unionize, or some such set of events of similar nature.

---

[13] Besides Robert Eugene, there were William, or "Will," Frank, and John Thomas, as well as a sister, Julia. Frank and Julia had descendants. My father's cousin Joseph "Gus" Monahan, followed *his* father Frank in working for the L&N, as did Gus's son, Michael, so that at least four generations of the family worked for that railroad, prompting a 1966 article in its magazine titled "There'll Always be a Monahan."

[14] My father's siblings were Robert Eugene, Jr., Frank Spencer, and Joan. I wonder about my father's memory of his father's income. $500 in 1927 would be over $7,600 today (in 2021), for a yearly income of $91,200! According to the U.S. Department of Labor's *Union Scales of Wages and Hours of Labor 1927-1928*, the hourly wage for a Railroad Machinist averaged $0.75. Assuming the twelve-hour day my father indicates below, that would amount to $45 per week or around $200 per month (https://fraser.stlouisfed.org/files/docs/publications/bls/bls_0476_1929.pdf) In 2021 dollars, that would constitute around $3,000 per month, or $36,000 per year. Of course, a master machinist probably made more, and it is likely they worked more than five days per week, but $500 per month seems a bit high!

From Cabbage to Cauliflower

L&N Locomotive

Because my father went along with his father, who was a rather benevolent authoritarian who believed that loyalty to the "company" was an important dimension of gratitude, my father supported the company in the dispute. The workers won, my father lost. He had begun work part time with the L&N when he was fifteen. He had limited schooling, having attended an academy of sorts in Nashville when his father, Mr. John (Grandpa J.J., as he was known to those of my cousins who remembered him at all, for he had passed on a few years after I was born) worked there. Truth be known, all my father knew so far as earning a living was concerned was the railroad, or more explicitly, its engines. From the time he was born in 1886, he had never really known nor presumed that he needed to know anything else.

My father's education, such as it was in the Nashville Academy, began in about 1895 when he was maybe eight or nine years old, and it was already assumed that in time—when he turned fifteen or so—that he would go to work in the shops. His elementary education (referred to in those days as "Grammar School") had been reasonably instructive and, all things considered, as satisfying as any such compulsory restrictions on youthful exuberance could have been. On dimly remembered occasions, I can recall that he had related to us that he suffered the poetry and short stories with some enjoyment, was passably interested in math but hated

Latin, and was much fascinated in discussions about science. In the latter area, he told us when we were children that he thought he was learning much more about science when he went with his father and his older brothers to the "shops." We didn't know then—it was much later in life that I came to realize in fact—that what he was really talking about was technology rather than science.

In any case, my father's formal education ended abruptly in about 1902 or 1903 when he, like many of his contemporaries among the Irish railroading subculture, probably looked at his own mother with mixed emotions as, at five o'clock on some forgotten morning (he used to tell us these stories with a twinkle in his eye), she handed him a two-quart leftover Lard Bucket—his badge of belonging—which contained a couple of biscuits with bacon, a small wedge of cheese, hard-boiled eggs, and because it was his very first day of work, a special piece of cornbread apple cake and a chicken thigh that she had thoughtfully saved from the Sunday dinner. With an older brother, he headed off for his first full day of work, and I'd guess his mother watched him go off on that day with both sadness and pride.

*Original L&N Railroad Depot,
Bowling Green, Kentucky, now a museum*

I've heard my father talk about that initiation into the world of work on a number of occasions, and he always talked about it in terms which remind me of all the other kinds of "firsts" that all of us at one time and another must endure, with both excited anticipation and anxiety. His day began at six in the morning and ended at six at night. He was an apprentice machinist, a particularly distinctive opportunity which was owed to the considerable influence of his own father and of his father's special affection for him among many of his contemporaries. More mundane railroad work was all that was available. Incidentally, my father also mentioned several times that few of his working associates and contemporaries ever were involved with the passenger services of the railroads, and he and his chums often expressed envy of the "Negro" porters who were able to serve on the *crack* passenger trains and were thus able to see so many exciting things and visit exotic places. Most of those of his generation never rode on any of the trains they serviced nor ever knew much about any of the places either freight or passenger trains went. Their world was very circumscribed and parochial.

Confronting the Different

It is impossible for me to imagine what it must have been like to have worked in a system that most surely was presumed to last forever and to have done so faithfully from the time one was fifteen years old until one was almost thirty-five, and then to come to work one day and be advised that you were through. How devastating that must have been. One day you are earning $500 every month, and the next day you are dismissed. What can you do? What are you prepared to do? What skills do you have?

There were no employee benefits, no cushions. Those sorts of things came much later after organized labor began to have some political power, and government assumed responsibility for equity under law. How can you go to anybody and tell them that there is nothing that you don't know about a steam locomotive and nothing much that you really know about almost anything else? Someone tells you that Scottish manufacturers are making the best steam locomotives in the world and that they need machinists, but even given the possibility that you might hire on, can you imagine working for the Scots? Of course, they wouldn't hire you anyway; you're an Irish American.

*First known picture of my father, aged four,
with his sister Joan, aged two, in 1931*

You have four children, a wife, a most satisfying set of relationships with a whole group of friends and associates, but in one fell swoop, you are out on the street. Deep down, you had reservations about the Company's responsibility to its workers. You had seen too much to convince you that there had not been capriciousness and heavy-handedness, that the workers had not been treated well and fairly, nor had they been justly paid. But you had a responsibility and a debt. You owed your father respect and commitment to his principles, so you felt that you had to support the Company even if you did so without conviction. But in the final analysis, all of that made no difference. Interestingly, you were the only one of all the brothers who was let go. Your father himself was secure, and not many years thereafter retired. He had earned his retirement, and the ubiquitous gold watch and little over a year after that, in about 1930, he passed away.[15]

I have no substantial information on the precise timing of this set of events. Apparently, the issue was protracted and drawn out over as much as six months as it was reviewed and discussed. But the fuzzy insights that came along afterward cause me to believe that the final decision was made in the late summer of 1929 before my young sister was yet even a year old (she was born on March 13, 1929).[16] All the world knows what happened in October of that fateful year: the black Friday stock market "crash" and the beginnings of the Great Depression of the 30s.

Because the Irish have always been a political force in numbers, interest, and energy, "public work" has also claimed them. Accordingly, my father was fortunate to be known and liked in small city and county politics, and he was able to get some work with the city.[17] Patronage has always been a pejorative footnote in the history of American politics at

---

[15] Actually, John Joseph Monahan died in 1929.

[16] This timing may indicate that John Joseph, who had officially retired from the L&N in 1924, or his other sons, who continued to work for the railroad, were able successfully to prevent the ultimate firing for a time, but there is no hard evidence of that. Though my father makes no reference to any such efforts, it would be surprising if there had been none.

[17] My grandmother Anna Catherine was particularly active in local precinct politics and may have played a significant role in securing the city patronage job for her husband.

all levels, but it saved my father and our family. The job he was able to secure wasn't much, but it turned out to be more than was available to most others out of work at the time. He was hired as a Park Keeper and reservoir supervisor. What that meant very simply was that the city's water works were partly sustained with two modest man-make pools, and these were situated such that the immediate grounds surrounding them had been fashioned into a modest recreation facility. These facilities consisted of about forty acres of pleasant meadows and woods situated on a prominent hill and included about a half dozen clay tennis courts, some picnicking paraphernalia, a small sheltered pavilion, and some playground equipment like chain-linked swings and slides which were almost always in a state of disrepair owing to heavy use and no funds for maintenance. My father's job was to more or less supervise these facilities in addition to his more technical responsibilities with reference to the water parks.

More importantly, with the job came a rather pleasant house, rent free. My father's salary was $75 a month, and by "moonlighting" (the term was not known then) as a substitute city police officer, he was able to add sometimes as much as fifteen additional dollars monthly.[18] His work consisted in monitoring certain rather technical aspects of the reservoir system—checking the pump house and periodically chlorinating the pools—and doing rounds through the park several times daily. In the latter case, there was usually a final walk through the grounds around nine or ten o'clock at night in the company of a *huge* flashlight. My father was also authorized to carry a sidearm because his duties involved some kind of law enforcement with power of arrest. He had to spend his own money to purchase a small caliber handgun—a 32 as I recall—which he carried in a holster attached to his pants belt. I remember clearly based on a frequent lecture to us kids, that he had great fear and respect for such weapons and a great distaste for being required to carry one. He solved that issue merely by never inserting any bullets in the thing, and on very rare occasions when he was required to fire it for practice, seemed to take humorous and self-deprecatory pride in the fact that he couldn't

---

[18] As my father indicates earlier in this chapter, his father had been making a good wage with the railroad, so his new job represented a substantial loss of income.

hit the side of a barn! I can remember clearly that he joked with some of his intimates who knew about his unloaded gun to the effect that bullets were too expensive to waste on shooting at real people whom one had no equally real responsibility for hitting. It made perfectly good sense to me.

In the late fall and winter, as a child, I loved being permitted to make his evening "rounds" with him in the Reservoir Park. I was the youngest boy, and probably he took me for that reason as much as any other. My two older brothers had chores and school work to do, so I had my father to myself on those thirty or forty-minute excursions. There was no part of the park I didn't know, and he would entertain me with adventurous stories about Civil War skirmishes that had been fought from our hill across to another ridge of hills where the College now stood. In retrospect, of course, his stories were pure fantasy, but he was a good storyteller.[19] He would show me how the Confederate troops defended their positions and was totally convincing as he explained that the black spots and marks on the limestone outcrops were the bloodstains of wounded soldiers. We never talked as I recall as to what the issues were and which side was in the right of things. It seemed to suffice for him that we were on the side of the South, and I perceived, probably like most other children of similar circumstances, that there was more glory in defeat than in victory, and that the South had fought for principle and democratic sovereignty against Big Business and northern industrial corruption. My father tended to see the railroads and their ruthless power as synonymous with the "Yankee" cause, and that was sufficient for me. We never talked about slavery or any of the issues truly related to the conflict so far as I can remember, and it was almost as if the Civil War had nothing at

---

[19] As was my father. The history of the Civil War is often a "gateway" to an interest in studying history, and I have often wondered if these walks with his father first ignited an interest in that field, since he would later major in Geography and History in college. In fact, there *was* some action around Bowling Green during the Civil War. The town was the "capital" of Confederate Kentucky in 1861 and the heart of the Confederate defensive line for a time. Three forts were begun there by the Confederate forces and subsequently finished by the Union army when southern troops were forced out in February, 1862. One of them, Fort C. F. Smith, was indeed located in what became Reservoir Hill Park, so perhaps his father's stories were not as far off as my father assumed!

all to do with that. For him it just seemed to be little people against powerful people, and he was such a hero to me that even at seven or eight years old, I was somehow aware that he had been wronged, and that the "big" and "powerful" people were responsible, so I rooted for the South! I guess it was years afterward before I realized all of this was a piece of the history of egalitarianism, and that the South was clearly wrong all along.

Long after I had started school and even until the time around 1937 that we moved from the "hill," I still occasionally made rounds with Pop, and he would tell me things about the geography of the place that turned out to be remarkably accurate. Sometimes, too, in the summer when I was nine or ten, he would take me along with him when he would get small extra compensation by acting as a guard, to take "work gangs" of county prisoners out into the countryside. The prisoners involved were men who had committed minor offenses—mostly "drunk and disorderly"—and would work off their sentences in public reclamation kinds of chores. On these occasions, my mother would pack us a lunch, and I would play and explore the creek beds and enjoy the companionship of my father and his friends. I recall that the prisoners liked him, and he took pains to point out to me that they were for the most part decent men who had merely got into trouble. The underlying lesson was that they were victims of the circumstances of poverty and ignorance, but people who deserved civil treatment.

One of my early remembrances of the reservoir hill house was the day it caught on fire. We were walking home from school that day. It was about three o'clock on an unseasonably warm day in the afternoon in late March or early April as I recall. As my brothers and I took our routine shortcut and came onto the large open field just below our house, we could see smoke and flames coming out of the roof. It was a terrifying sight, and we began to run! Now, as was typically the case, I was wearing hand-me-down corduroy knickers that I'd inherited from my older brothers, and the "crotch" hung down well below where a reasonably well-fitted pair of pants should ordinarily have hung, and (I'd guess I was about seven years old), the excitement was a bit much, and I peed in my corduroy pants! Trying to dash up that hill with the flames coming out of the roof, yelling and crying, and with wet corduroy pants dragging along, I must have been a really miserable kid! Fortunately, my father's sister (Aunt Julia) was visiting, and she heard the yells of my older brothers and got everybody out of the house and also called the fire department. The house suffered considerable damage, but not anything like as much as me! Needless to say, I was *mortified*!

St. Joseph's Catholic Church, Bowling Green, Kentucky

My father began more and more to be involved with law enforcement simply by the nature of things, and, in about 1937, he was ready when a new city administration resulted in the loss of his job at the park. That year, we moved from the house on the hill to my grandfather Will's [Murphy] house on Scott Street in the south of town. Near to St. Joseph's Catholic Church, Scott Street was part of a large neighborhood of Irish Catholic families in what was known in those days as the "Church Street" section. Across the street from us lived Grandpa Will's brother, uncle John and his family, J. J. (he was the oldest of Uncles John's children), Loretta, and "Red" (whose real name was Bernard) and Regina (the youngest), who could really play the piano. She would always buy the latest popular sheet music, and accompanying my older brother Bobby who had a great singing voice, they would together entertain us often.

Directly across the street lived my mother's sister, my aunt Madge (we always called her "Meemie"—I have no idea why) and her husband, uncle Billy Daugherty and his family—our cousins Joe Billy, Mary Ann, and Jimmy. Down the street a couple of houses away, lived another of my Grandpa's brothers, Uncle Pete, and around the corner and up a couple of blocks, almost right across from the Church itself, in a handsome stone house lived another brother, Uncle Tom and more cousins! Also in that "Church Street" neighborhood were the O'Hearns, the O'Rourkes, and the O'Connors, and down the street a ways (in the less fashionable "end" of the neighborhood) were the O'Sheas and the Keoughs. In a sense, this was the kind of rather nice Irish ghetto in those times although we had no notion about such things then. Today, that entire area has badly deteriorated and is little more than a slum. In truth, it isn't even *that* nice![20]

---

[20] The area is now African-American. When my father visited the site of his former house, which had been torn down some time before, the people living in a newer house on the site were very welcoming. Poor people often lack the resources to keep up older houses, and I occasionally chided him about this remark in his memoir.

Grandpa William Murphy, my father's namesake, in the 1930s

Anyway, in about 1937 or so when I was ten years old and certainly soon after we'd moved down to the Scott Street house, my father secured a job as a deputy sheriff, and again due to some political relationships, and after about a year or so, he became a regular policeman with the city. Soon thereafter, he was promoted to Assistant Chief of Police and a few years after that, was named Chief of Police. His pay in the latter position, in 1940, was $175.00 per month.

When we moved into the Scott Street house, my grandfather Will, after whom I was named, was at that time in his early sixties, although, in retrospect, he seemed much older to me. He was a fairly good businessman, or had been, and was co-owner with a brother of a then (1937) declining stone quarry.[21] During the previous twenty-five or so years, the business had enjoyed considerable success. My grandfather had traveled rather extensively throughout the region bidding on jobs and contracting for the purchase of his oolitic limestone, the qualities of which, as a building material, were that it tended to get whiter as it got older, and that was a prominent selling point. In addition to the quarry itself, there had been an impressive stone-cutting mill, and during the teens and 20s, it was not uncommon for his firm to ship out many tons of precisely cut and specified building stone on flatbed railroad cars. Based on information I've had from my mother, the firm employed as many as thirty men in the early 20s, but the Depression had taken its toll on that too, and by the time we moved in with him, his business was struggling and declining. The quarry was operating only part time, and by 1939, the cutting mill was unused and in disrepair and was subsequently sold for a pittance.

Of eight children, only one of his daughters still lived with Grandpa Will when we moved in with him, and it was clear that the move was good for both him and for us. He needed my mother to look after the house and to take care of him since the younger daughter—my mother's young sister was then still in her early twenties—was not capable of that responsibility. His wife, my grandmother, had died early of diabetes, and I never knew her.[22] Grandpa himself was both loving yet stern, and we kids never quite knew how to take him. I am certain as I look back on it that four youngsters must have been a very trying experience for him. He usually drove a fairly new automobile, and although his business was in apparent decline, he still required a car for his several trips to various nearby cities.

---

[21] Actually, he had co-owned the "Murphy Brothers Company," founded in 1886, with three brothers, John J. (called "J. J."), Peter, and Thomas. Their stone was used for several buildings still standing, including the State Street Methodist Church and the Burton Memorial Baptist Church in Bowling Green, both of them entirely sheathed in white limestone.

[22] Jennie Spencer, said to be the seventh child of a seventh child, but non-Catholic (and not of Irish ancestry either) until she converted on her marriage to William Murphy. Her father was a farmer in Larue County, home to several stone quarries, and it certainly seems possible that one of them was owned by her future husband's company.

That house had an entry hall into a small room which we called the parlor and was adjacent to the living room.[23] It was a common pattern in those days. Such a room sort of introduced people into the house itself and was followed by a long hall that led directly into the middle-back of the house and into what was then the dining room. In the 30s this was our radio room where we listened to our favorite radio programs: "Amos 'n Andy," "Lum 'n Abner," "Fibber McGee and Molly," "Edgar Bergen and Charlie McCarthy," and "Allen's Alley," among many others. My father particularly liked "Gangbusters" and other "crime" shows.

Coming in the front door, this parlor was just to the right of the rather spacious living room. It was separated from the living room by a rather elaborate set of sliding doors which, in my youth, were just never used. I suppose that the original idea was to be able to sort of close off that living room for whatever purpose might have seemed appropriate. In any case, all of the major rooms, i.e., that living room and all the bedrooms, had their own fireplaces (though we referred to them in those days more accurately as "grates") since we did not enjoy anything like what came to be known as "central heating."

Coal Scuttle from the 1930s

---

[23] This paragraph and the three that follow formed part of emails my father sent me in May 1998 and January 1999. Because these descriptions fit so well here, I have chosen to add them to the memoir.

Heat was totally supplied by the grates. In winter, fires were built in each room's grates and coal scuttles were filled and set beside the grates. We burned coal—"lump coal"—and Uncle John, my father's somewhat retarded brother, always made sure that the scuttles (which were curious-looking special buckets specifically designed to hold coal) were always filled and handy. Among the chores that we boys were required to perform was to go into our "coal shed" and regularly fill the scuttles with coal. It was not too pleasant! These were *not* fireplaces in any real sense of the word. Coal was placed in the iron holdings, ashes were cleaned out regularly, and the fires were "banked" every night. This was all the heat we had. In about 1939 or so, we were able to install a central-heating coal-burning furnace. From then on, no more coal scuttles had to be filled. It was a glorious time!

Everyone we knew still used "ice boxes" as refrigerators, and there were ice merchants who had horse-drawn ice wagons. In those days, my mother would put out a little diamond-shaped sign in an observable window of our house which indicated to the Ice Man whether she wanted twenty pounds of ice or ten pounds.

The number that showed in the top of the diamond-shaped card told the ice man how much ice we wanted delivered. The ice wagon came around every morning regular as clockwork. As children, in the summer, we used to chase it (the horses didn't run too fast!), and we'd catch the wagon and capture small pieces of the ice that had been chipped off—very refreshing! In about 1937 we were able to buy our very first refrigerator. We bought a Kelvinator because it came fully stocked. All kinds of goodies were included.

1937 Kelvinator Refrigerator

My grandfather Murphy had friends who lived in the country, and when they'd kill hogs, we would get a lot of fresh country sausage (a lot of sage in it for preservation) and it was very good! So breakfast was a big meal with us—eggs, sausage, homemade biscuits which my mom could whip up in jig time[24]—and we canned a lot of our own jellies, jams, pickles, preserves, peppers, tomatoes, and just about anything else that could be canned. We ate a lot of corn meal bread. My mother cooked the best fried cornbread "batty cakes"—mostly corn meal and water which she fried in a big iron skillet with bacon grease. She also cooked a lot of northern beans and turnip greens and kept them in big pots in a warming oven atop an old coal-fired kitchen range. Many times after I walked home from school, I would have a bean sandwich—soup beans on a cold biscuit. I once really embarrassed my mother when I was about eight years old and we accompanied my better-off aunt on a short trip up to the Nazareth Academy where her daughter was in private school and stopped at a restaurant. I had never been in a restaurant in my life, and when asked what I wanted, I said that I'd like a bean sandwich. She was mortified!

Even as children, we were aware of the automobile as a symbol of some status, but as well, we were also aware that Grandpa was an absolutely terrible driver! He always "slipped" the clutch so that his cars made grinding noises as he went through the gears, and increasingly, he would depend on his sons—my several uncles—to do the driving when he had a longer than usual trip to make for one of his business appointments. These trips usually consisted of a drive to Louisville or Nashville, and on rare occasions, I was able to accompany them. I remember those trips as very exciting prospects, for the drive from Bowling Green up to Louisville on the "Dixie Highway" was a good three hours and took one by the big army installation at Camp Knox by way of Elizabethtown where one of Grandpa's sisters lived, and we would always stop there for a brief time to visit.[25]

Grandpa Murphy was an inveterate pipe smoker. My earliest memories were of his use of small clay pipes favored by some of

---

[24] "In jig time" derives from Irish dance, the "jig," which was a fast dance.

[25] Much of the original road still exists as Federal Highway 31W, though some of it has been overpaved by I-65, upon which modern traffic mostly moves.

the Irish, but for some reason, he changed to hickory pipes, heavy-handed things with a bowl tapered from a piece of hickory wood with a long cane-like stem that fitted into the base of the bowl. I remember these pipes vividly because they were so completely awful! He fashioned his own tobacco mixture for these pipes from large "hands" of cured leaf tobacco that some friends surely must have provided and then combined it with "store-bought" sacks of "Red Cap" and mixed it all together with a small quantity of sorghum molasses. Altogether, this produced the most absolutely oppressive manifestation of air pollutant known to human experience! He carried a plentiful supply of this admixture loosely in one of his suitcoat side pockets and enjoyed sitting in his own special rocking chair on our wide and favorable front porch while puffing away. Needless to say, we had little problem with house flies or mosquitoes, for no breed of insect could survive those clouds of noxious poison. It was only when the summer breeze was decidedly downwind from us that anyone could enjoy his presence on the porch. Interestingly though, on those frequent occasions when we were close to him—when he would take us on his lap—I don't remember any particularly distasteful reminders of his awful pipe.

Grandpa wore good suits tending toward conservative dark blues and browns, but they always seemed to me in retrospect to be rumpled and unkempt. But the most marvelous aspect of his appearance was a unique gold watch chain with a small, oval-shaped "fob" attached. I now know that it was a specially fashioned and skillfully jeweled piece of pyrite, or "fool's gold," It fascinated us children, and he told us over and again an exciting story to the effect that the man who gave it to him had found it in Alaska and had thought it to be real gold, and that this poor nameless Irishman had come back from his adventures in the Klondike penniless and ill with little more than some "fool's gold" and a "steel bright glint in his eyes" as his only possessions. Grandpa used the fob for a "moral" to us: "I keep this shiny piece of worthless rock to remind myself that the poet Longfellow knew what he was talking about when he said that 'life is real and life is earnest'" he would tell us, and although the quotation is inexact, that was the gist of it.[26] He would advise us to know that hard work and honesty and a willingness to be happy with the smaller things in life ought to be sufficient for God-fearing people. But he would also—and often—admonish us to be aware that America was a great nation, and that any one of us could grow up to be great. And then he would tell us about some of his contemporaries who had indeed enjoyed such good fortune.

Often when Grandpa related these stories, he would conclude by giving us several pennies. These were precious keys to youthful indulgence, and we eagerly went off to the neighborhood grocery store on the corner of our street to shop for candy and chewing gum. Our response to my Grandfather Murphy was always largely one of affectionate respect. We were, all of us kids, including my cousins, but especially my brothers and sister, a little anxious in our relationships with him, for he could be unpredictable, and while we somehow knew that he held us dearly, even we perceived without knowing the ways to denote it, that he was the authority, and we were living in his house and at his pleasure. But if that was any source of difficulty for my father, it was never known to me at least.[27]

He [my father] was "Pop" to us and continued to be our best friend and our hero. He was clearly admired by all who knew him, and his ability to exert a reasonable tolerance of all of those unfortunate persons who came under his jurisdiction at one time or another provided him with much influence. As a law enforcement officer, he even had a few episodes in the late 30s with some of that era's real desperadoes,

---

[26] From Longfellow's "A Psalm of Life":
Tell me not, in mournful numbers,
Life is but an empty dream!
For the soul is dead that slumbers,
And things are not what they seem.
Life is real! Life is earnest!
And the grave is not its goal;
Dust thou art, to dust returnest,
Was not spoken of the soul.

[27] William "Grandpa" Murphy died in December 1945. Since my father's family stayed in the house, his daughter (my grandmother) presumably inherited the house, or at least, the right to continue living in it. She did leave and move to Mississippi after the death of her husband (my grandfather) in 1949, taking his disabled brother John with her.

From Cabbage to Cauliflower

those "most wanted" kinds of reprobates who robbed banks and killed people. I can still vividly remember one night when, with a group of other officers, he was able to capture some now nameless desperado of that ilk after traipsing about the countryside near creeks and streams. We were in bed by the time he came home, but at breakfast the next morning, he recounted much of the episode in thrilling fashion. He did the same the morning after he and my mother went to the movies, which was fairly rare, retelling the movie story to us in brief but satisfying details at breakfast. We were enraptured by these narratives, for he was indeed very good at it.

In those days too, radio was at its zenith, and among our favorite programs were "Gangbusters" and "Mr. District Attorney." We also thoroughly enjoyed the comedy shows like "Edgar Bergen and Charlie McCarthy," "Fibber McGee and Molly," and "Allen's Alley." In the afternoon after school and just before supper, we kids would listen to "Jack Armstrong: All American Boy," and the whole family listened attentively to "Amos and Andy" and "Lum and Abner." After chores and homework were done, we all enjoyed sitting together in a kind of small room at the end of a long hall in Grandpa's house to listen to the radio. This activity was enormously enhanced when, in about 1939, one of my uncles presented us with a handsome new Philco Console radio with the most mellifluous sound one could imagine.

Philco Console Radio from late 1930s

Sometimes also, we would gather 'round a big kitchen table and play "Old Maid" cards. Among those who really loved that was one of my father's brothers, Uncle John, about five years younger than Pop. He had suffered a serious case of Scarlet Fever when he had been in his early forties, and it had left him somewhat mentally debilitated, so after that, he had become a sort of helper around the house. He was fully capable of self-reliance in most things, but in certain dimensions of mature reasoning was somewhat childlike and unquestionably disabled.[28]

My father's mother with Uncle John in Mississippi

He was of essential support to our household though, and after my mother decided to work full time as a deputy county court clerk, his role was even more important. As I look back on it, both of my parents were immensely supportive of him and solicitous of his well-being. They did not treat him condescendingly but knew well what he was and wasn't capable of. It is characteristic of that generation's sense of family solidarity that even after my father's death in 1949, my mother insisted that Uncle John go with her when she then moved to Mississippi to live near my younger sister, and John still faithfully carried out his own sense of responsibilities as her helpmate and a contributing member of our family until he also died in 1953.

But back to the point of our card games: Uncle John loved to play

---

[28] I wonder about this particular diagnosis. Scarlet fever was primarily a childhood disease, and none of the literature I have seen indicates that it would result in intellectual disability (mental retardation). The most likely cause of that might be meningitis, which can also cause a skin rash. Since penicillin was not yet used in large amounts, whatever fever John suffered was presumably left untreated by any kind of antibiotics.

"Old Maid," and that was superb family entertainment for us. Pop was particularly good at it, ensuring that all of us including John could enjoy something so delightful together. In those games, he was the "conductor," and he orchestrated the excitement with wit and suspense. He would love to have the "Old Maid" in his hand and then push up a single card such that it protruded well above the remainder of the cards in his hand. It might or might not be the old girl, and he would sort of urge John to draw it. John, on the other hand, clearly knew the nature of this gambit, but like all of the rest of us, how could he be *sure* that Pop was bluffing? John would agonize over his decision, and that in itself would delight him and us. Sometimes, he laughed so much that he had to pull out his handkerchief to wipe his eyes, and all of us would agonize with him. Then, just as he had about made up his mind, Pop would switch the card and put *that* one carefully over at the very end of the extended "hand" and push up still another card. It was great fun, and whenever Uncle John chose correctly and avoided picking the "Old Maid," all of the rest of us would enjoy Pop's exaggerated, crestfallen face and Uncle John's giggle of triumph.

Robert E. "Pop" Monahan as Chief of Police

What a lovely man was my Pop. Certainly, he had a quick Irish temper, and sometimes it got the better of him, and woe betide anyone who might have unwittingly triggered it, but it was always over in a flash, and as he grew older, he controlled it even better. Yet with it all, there was never a time that he struck any of us in anger, although all of us could be very trying. There were times when my mother told us that we were certainly going to have to endure a licking from Pop when he got home for some terrible thing that we had done, and sure enough, when she so informed him, he would make a big show of carrying out this doleful duty but would always find a way to escape that responsibility which both she and we knew would be the case, though she was certainly more sure of it than were we. On the whole, from childhood on, I always knew my father as affable and supportive, fun loving and gentle. Almost everyone who knew him even remotely held him in affection.[29]

The Winds of Change

It was clear to us by 1939 that a war was coming. Europe was already caught up in turmoil, and we followed that closely. For some reason, even when very young, I had followed world events rather closely, and although we knew little nor thought much about events on the other side of the world, I had always been fascinated by what I knew was happening in Europe, and our parents' experiences during the first world war had sharpened their own interests in such events. Thus, as a family, I think we were surprisingly well-informed about what was happening in Europe, and we were intensely patriotic. Pop had served in the fledgling Army Air Corps during the First World War, and although he never was called for overseas duty, he was nevertheless an ardent soldier and had remained active in the American Legion. The modest Veterans Bonus authorized by the Congress in about 1935 or so had also served us well. I'd guess that he tended too much to romanticize war, and yet, he was particularly anxious about events in Europe as those became increasingly ominous. So, the nightly news on the radio preoccupied us in those times. Our favorite

---

[29] My mother shared that opinion. She occasionally had some mild conflicts with her mother-in-law, but she always remembered "Pop" with nothing but affection.

"commentator" was a chap named Gabriel Heater, and our least favorite was Mr. Kaltenborn.

Father Charles Coughlin

At the same time, being a traditional Roman Catholic family, we were caught up in the growing controversy that began to surround a radical radio priest named Father Coughlin. As kids, we understood little of the context within which this man ranted and raved, but only that opinions and attitudes about him often resulted in much heated debate around our Sunday dinner table.[30]

In the late 30s, our Sunday mid-day dinners seemed, to we youngsters, too much dominated by this priest's intrusions, and, as was the case with most other families, we picked up a copy of the syndicated church newspaper *Our Sunday Visitor* after Mass, and in those days, it too was filled with comments about him. Father Coughlin's radio program was broadcast every Sunday afternoon, and it was almost universally listened to. Thus, without knowing the nature of the ideology involved, we resented this priest's

---

[30] Father Charles Coughlin (1891-1979), a charismatic priest born in Canada, was an early supporter of Roosevelt's New Deal, but felt betrayed when the President did not consult him, and turned hard against it after 1935. As the war approached, Coughlin's early anti-Semitism became explicit, and he opposed any entry by the United States into the war, arguing that the war was a combined Jewish and Communist conspiracy. His influence declined sharply after Pearl Harbor, when he still opposed American entry into the war.

imposition of heated political debate on our Sunday relaxation. In order to appreciate our resentment, one needs to understand the ways that we perceived these familial functions. At our Scott Street house in Bowling Green, Kentucky, it somehow came to be accepted after my mother became the mistress of Grandpa's house, that everybody came to Sunday dinner there. Certainly, that was the case with most of her brothers, who were, for the most part, bachelors. Sometimes, too, some of my mother's sisters also came, and we kids enjoyed that because we liked being with our many cousins, the Doughertys and the Brashears. These were my mother's sister's families, and all of the children were of generally similar ages. I guess my favorite among these was Mary Ann Dougherty, since she and I were of about the same age and enjoyed similar things.

Mary Ann Dougherty in the mid-1940s

This developing tradition of Sunday family get-togethers was not, however, without some small difficulty. For me, one of the worst was that I, my younger sister Joan, and my brothers (though the older brothers seemed somehow to manage to avoid most of our chores!) had to spend a good portion of our precious Saturday afternoons boiling chickens and picking off feathers. (Joan was young enough not to have to endure the worst aspects of this set of chores.) None of us could bring ourselves to carrying out the act of executing the hen. My mother had to do that herself, and as we would watch with both admiration and chagrin, she simply grasped the bird by the head and neck and "wrung" it about until the head twisted off. She did it with aplomb, and after the poor beast quit flapping about, one of us had to capture the carcass and put it in a washtub of boiling water. After some appropriate time, we then had to pick off the feathers. It was a smelly and most distasteful chore, but it was being carried out all up and down our street on those Saturdays.

With as many as twelve people sitting down (first) to dinner, we usually required at least three good sized hens. All of the children went "seconds"—which means that there wasn't room at the table the first time around, and that there wouldn't be much of the best part of the chicken remaining. But my mother always made certain that some was saved for us, and there were always lots of vegetables, and she must have peeled and mashed five pounds of potatoes and could manufacture the biggest flakiest buttermilk biscuits ever known.[31] These Sunday dinners were a cultural celebration. There was lively conversation, occasionally delicious gossip, and a lot of good-natured ribbing and joking. Some of that got a little raunchy and elicited expected but only half-hearted objections from the women. My father sat at the head of the table—my grandfather had earlier suffered a leg injury and had gotten used to taking his meal in his room. Regardless of relationship, Pop was always "Uncle Bob" to all there assembled, and he loved these Sunday affairs. God, how proud we were of him and how unquestioningly we admired him. He seemed to us so easily to endure, and it never occurred to me that he wouldn't live forever.

---

[31] That my father never cooked much shows in his estimation of how many potatoes they prepared. It would have taken considerably more than five pounds of potatoes to feed such a large group! My grandmother continued into old age to be able to whip up a classic chicken/potatoes meal in no time at all, though she was famously unkind to her pots and pans, and the noise from her kitchen was formidable.

In those days, we were only dimly aware that times were so terribly harsh. For most of us—children of the Depression as sociologists would now describe us—we knew no other alternative existence. We did not think of ourselves as poor because we knew so many others who *really* were. By the same token, we knew clearly who in our town were the well-to-do, and we all had our fantasies about being rich one day—maybe winning the Irish Sweepstakes—so even very young, we had a well-developed appreciation for the value of money. We assumed that we had to wear what someone older outgrew, and though we knew we were not to eat meat on Fridays for obvious reasons, we didn't always understand why we didn't have meat on so many other days. We listened and learned much from the incidental talk about the need for working people to organize into strong unions, and we accepted the prevailing conventional wisdom that one didn't look *too* far forward because life was not very predictable nor optimistically promising. There were other patterns in our lives that reflected the economic difficulties of the times, but we attached no special significance to them. For one example, [as I wrote previously] we heated the house with coal-filled "grates." We bought the coal from "Coal and Ice Merchants" in lump form, and whenever it was time for delivery of a load, some of us with Uncle John would have to help get it into the coal house at the rear. In most cases, one could not shovel it because of the size of the "lumps," so we had to do much of it by hand. There are innumerable people of my generation who remember how the fires were banked at night by covering them with ashes, and what it was like on winter mornings to climb out from under warm quilts and blankets to dress quickly in front of the fire, first turning to face it, then turning away. Sometimes, when we thought about what it might be like to be wealthy, it consisted of the pleasures of central heat.

There were four of us children, each of us born about two years apart—my two older brothers shared the same birth date.

Frank Spencer Monahan, aged three, and Robert "Sonny" Monahan, Jr., aged five, on their birthdays in 1928

We were fairly close when we were younger, and my sister and I were, and remain, very close. As children, we had no scarcity of playmates and amused ourselves with all kinds of games and activities. When the weather was favorable, a favorite game in the evenings was "kick the can"—an improvisation on hide and seek, and we often manufactured our own playthings. One activity that occupied us often was "rubber gun" fights. We would fashion these notorious weapons by taking a piece of wood of appropriate size, fasten to the butt of that a clothes pin of the type with a spring, and then cut strips from a discarded tire innertube, and by stretching these strips from the barrel end of the piece of wood and clasping the other end into the clothes pin, the weapon was properly loaded. To fire it, one merely released tension on the pin, and the huge rubber band flew across maybe ten feet. At close range, these things could have been dangerous, and this was an activity not approved at all by our mother. Another activity that was quite innovative had to do with our roller skates. These were "street" skates in that they had steel wheels and were attached to the shoes with a clamp and a strap, and we used these skates heavily—I have skated all over the entire town where we lived. But when the skates no longer functioned properly, usually because one or more of the steel wheels wore out (but other wheels were still good) we would fashion a couple of three-foot two-by-fours together to form a right angle, take the skates apart (the front and rear of a single skate came apart since they were designed to be adjustable to any size of foot), and then we would nail the front and back portion of the skate to the front and back of one of the two-by-fours, nail a handle to the top of the other board, and, voila! We had a "skate-scooter." Of course, tearing down the street on one of these things and suddenly encountering even a small stone could result in disaster.

We also had a lot of impromptu games. We played baseball and football (tackle, not touch!). We'd go to the hardware store (which was the only place to buy any kind of sports equipment) and buy a cheap baseball for fifty cents. We'd hit it a few times, and it would start to come apart, so we'd tape it up with electrician's tape, and we'd use it for another twenty games or so. We got old footballs the hard way. Someone would go up to the stadium when Western Kentucky [State Teachers College] played football, and when they'd kick an extra point, one of our friends would be there waiting and when he caught it, he'd run like hell! We managed to "requisition" a number of footballs that way![32]

---

[32] This paragraph comes from the same May 1998 email that supplied further details earlier in this chapter and, again, seemed an appropriate addition to this section of the memoir.

Bicycles, though not uncommon, were nevertheless not so much in evidence as today. My oldest brother won the first one any of us enjoyed as one of the prizes when he won the first ever soap box derby race held in our town. Later, because there was a local promotion of some sort by which bicycles were given away in a drawing at one of the local movie houses, we won another one. I was able to get my own first bicycle when I secured a job as a newspaper delivery boy. I bought it with money I earned delivering papers and paid for it "on time" making payments regularly on an installment plan.

Robert "Sonny" Monahan, Jr. winning the first soap box derby race in Bowling Green, July 1938

We enjoyed enormous freedom as children, and we were seldom bored. We learned to swim in a creek on a farm owned by friends of our family and were taught by an older cousin. Thereafter, we often swam in the river and loved to follow and bob in the wake of the steamboats (tugs) that traversed it. Even younger than that, it was not uncommon during the summer vacations for me to leave the house soon after breakfast and not return until the evening meal. There was no part of the town and little of the countryside that I didn't know intimately. In the language of sociologists, we had an expansive "life space" in which to grow up.

Educational Awakening

No one in my family had ever gone to college. The idea of it was beyond realistic expectation, although my mother had attended business school for a short course in better times. In truth, our general family attitudes had hardly even accepted the growing recognition that high school graduation itself was easily to be presumed.

Eighth Grade Graduation. My father is top row, far left

I was the first in my own immediate family to complete high school, and I had to do it after having "dropped out" for over a year. My sister finished right on schedule, but she was better prepared for it, was more disciplined than we boys, and the expectations for girls were more circumscribed than for boys. She was also a lot smarter than the rest of us. Certainly, it was our parents' hope that we would attend and graduate from high school, but there was tolerance of the circumstance of drifting off into the world of work—for large numbers of kids like us, it was the rule rather than the exception.

Joan Monahan's graduation photo

I had always worked hard all though the high school years in a variety of odd jobs. I worked with some of my uncles—my mother's brothers—in the so-called "concrete business" when I was no more than fifteen by "feeding" a cement mixer, shoveling sand, gravel, and cement into the thing for seven or eight hours a day. I wasn't stout enough to manage the heavy wheelbarrows into which the mixture was deposited. I was always happy with the money I earned but looked forward to school as a respite. Inevitably, though, I became bored with the confinement and though much like many of my contemporaries, that I was pretty much a waste of time.

Frank Spencer Monahan in uniform

By the time I entered high school, the "great war" was in full sway, and nothing seemed stable as a consequence. By 1943, both of my older brothers were deeply involved. Frank, the brother next to me in age, was an infantryman serving with the 34th infantry division in North Africa, and Bobby, my oldest brother, an Air Corps cadet who had been subsequently reassigned to gunnery training aboard B-24 bomber aircraft.[33] Being still too young myself, I was all the more impatient to become a part of that enormous set of unfolding events. By late 1944, the tide had clearly begun to turn in favor of the allies, and I began to badger my parents unrelentingly to let me become a part of it. Finally, I persuaded them to let me join the U.S. Merchant Marine. In retrospect, that must have been a terribly agonizing thing for them. At that time, my soldier brother had once been reported missing in action though he later turned up ok, but my eldest brother had been killed in a mission over the Ploesti Oil Fields in Romania. Ironically, he was very near the end of his designated

---

[33] Frank Spencer Monahan was injured in action during the Cassino campaign in Italy in 1944 and sent back to the United States. He later served in Korea. On Bobby's service, see Appendix B.

number of missions and was, like so many thousands of others, carrying out what has become somewhat well-known in textbook studies of military strategy as a "command decision," the commitment of low level massive air strikes on the major source of fuels for the German armies. Incidentally, that policy cost most dearly, and its ultimate value remains moot. When he was shot down, he was only a couple of missions shy of the number required for rotation back to the States.[34]

Robert "Sonny" Monahan receiving his wings

---

[34] My father may be mistaken here, since it appears he still had quite a few missions to fly. See Appendix B.

"Bobby"—named after my father—was a most personable and talented young man who could do so many things so easily. An incurable romantic, he was touched with a need for adventure from earliest childhood and had read all of the Tom Swift books by the time he was no more than thirteen. As a youngster, he was always busily engaged in all kinds of curious activities and loved doing innovative kinds of things. As one example, I can remember he and a friend building a huge kite and trying to ride it, and once he nearly broke his leg jumping off our barn with a homemade parachute! He was obsessed with airplanes, had built dozens of models that he flew, repaired, and flew again, and when I was very young—no more than nine or so—he and I would hike out to our rather primitive airport just so he could be there and watch and talk with "seat-of-the-pants" flyers who seemed always to come in from God-knows-where. Occasionally, some unique plane came there like a Ford Tri-Motor or a fancy Waco Monoplane, and Bobby would always manage to ingratiate himself with these men, and on numerous occasions talked them into letting him go up with them while I remained on the ground, terrified for both of us. It was no surprise to anyone when he enlisted in the Cadets, though subsequently deprived of pilot training because of some minor physical problem. He was remarkable in many other ways as I now think about it. He wrote to me occasionally and always advised me that I should take advantage of my chances for an education. He kept a diary, which I still have, and he was committed to his own chances after the war to go on to college and make something good of his life.[35] He was a sensitive, handsome and popular, and intelligent and mature young man and had an enormous love and appreciation for life. What a tragic waste that he had to die so young and so savagely.

---

[35] It was a training diary, and he made the last entry in January 1944 not long before he "shipped out" to Italy. The dramatic letter from a survivor detailing his last mission and death is reprinted in Appendix B.

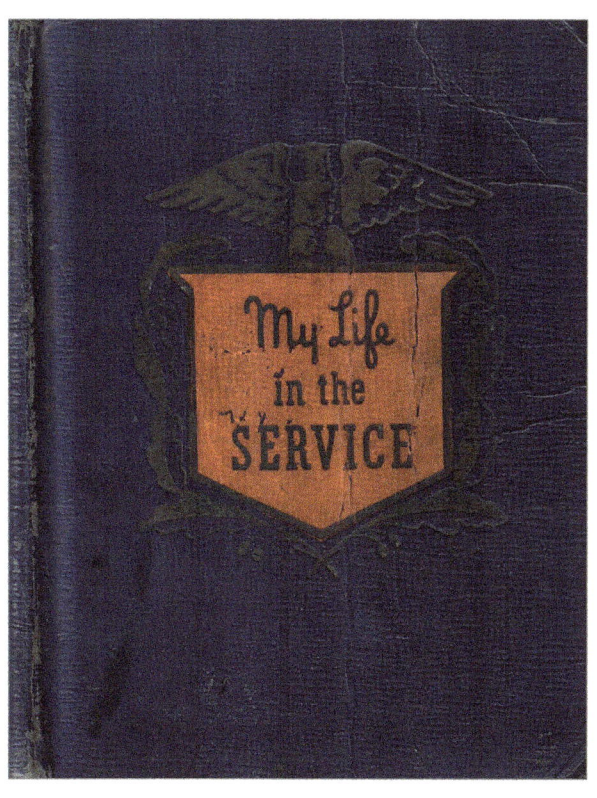

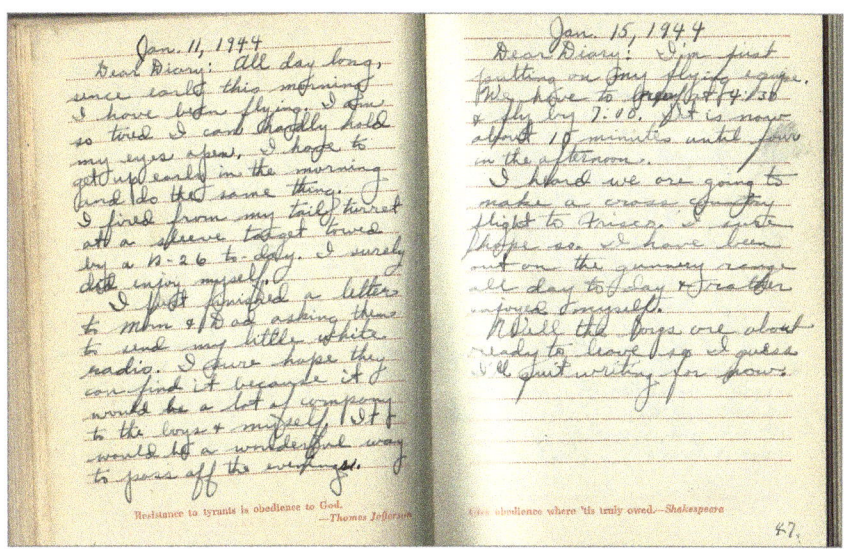

Sonny's War Diary: Cover and last entry

From Cabbage to Cauliflower

Given these realities, it must have been a painful thing for my parents to endure my badgering to be a part of the war before it all ended, but relent they did, and off I went to New York to begin brief training as a merchant seaman. That's another story, however, and I'll save it for another place.

Concluding the Beginning

Suffice to say at this point merely that for me as one who entered the academy after the war with so much perturbation and genuine insecurity, it is passing curious that except for a few important and rewarding years in public school teaching and administration, I have spent my life in universities. It is almost as if paradoxically, once I got the "hang" of it, I never really got the "hang" of anything else. So, to conclude these comments, I come back to the point where I began: where else than in America and especially in the America of my generation could such events as these have been possible? I have had reason often to think about that across the passing years, and some words engraved on the marker of the tomb of Wendell Willkie in Rushville, Indiana seem to express this complicated relationship between chance and opportunity better than anything else I could say:

> I believe in America because in it we are free—free to choose our government, to speak our minds, to observe our different religions. Because we are generous with our freedom, we share our rights with those who disagree with us. Because we hate no people and covet no peoples' lands. Because we have great dreams and because we have the opportunity to make those dreams come true.[36]

Like Mr. Willkie, I believe in it too. Profoundly. In no other place that any God ordained has there ever been a better chance to become.

---

[36] My father here excerpts the "American Credo" by Wendell Willkie, first published in an article, "Why I Believe in America," *North American Review* 248, No. 2 (Winter, 1939-40).

There were many bumps and bruises along the way, but my stars seemed mostly to have been in some propitious orbit and not least of all those happy chances for me were two circumstances: First of all, growing up the way I did in an extended family with much support and "togetherness," yet with remarkable independence for a kid to explore his world on his own initiatives. And secondly—and more importantly—marrying Jane Newcom when both of us were probably too young under any presumed standards about that sort of thing for anybody to have guessed that such a marriage would have ever worked out. At that time, she was barely nineteen and me barely eighteen, but here, too, single-mindedness in behalf of our making something of our chances was the basis for everything good that's happened to us. I never could have done any of it left to my own devices, and with her, it has all seemed to be just about right.

Jane's Background

Jane had grown up in different circumstances. Most of her childhood and later school years had been in small towns, first in Morganfield, Kentucky and later in Marion, which was only some forty miles away. Her mother was one of seven girls! Her maternal grandfather who had emigrated from Canada, had been quite well off, having owned and operated a very successful lumber company in Morganfield.[37] In point of fact, he owned one of the first automobiles in Morganfield, had built

---

[37] Adolphus James "A.J." Thornton (1860-1924) emigrated from Ontario to Dyersville, Tennessee, where he met and married his wife Kittye Thornton (1869-1938), born Mary Catherine Ballard. He partnered with his brother to form Thornton Brothers Lumber and they together operated at least four lumberyards (two in Henderson, Kentucky, one in Owensboro, one in Morganfield). One Henderson yard went to his nephew, the Owensboro yard was destroyed by fire, and the other Henderson yard and the Morganfield yard went to his eldest son-in-law, Thomas Gatlin. The graves of Adolphus and Kittye enjoy a very prominent place toward the front of Morganfield's oldest cemetery, and their house still stands. Indeed, in January 1917, according to *The Lumber Manufacturer and Dealer*, he was chosen by the city council of Morganfield as mayor of the city, an office in which he served until at least 1920. Of their seven daughters, only Tommie C. Thornton Thompson (1902-1983), who married but had no children, is buried in Morganfield in their family plot. There is some circumstantial evidence that Pearl and her father did not get along. She kept no photographs of her father, and he forced the annulment of an earlier marriage. Also, her marriage to Clarence Newcom took place barely three weeks following her father's death in 1924.

a handsome house in Morganfield's most fashionable neighborhood [which still stands (ed.)], and provided his large family with all the good things that the times prescribed.

Six of the seven sisters (Virginia, the youngest, was not yet born.) Pearl is far right

The sisters were and remained, close throughout their lives, and several of them, including Pearl [Pearl Ballard Thornton (ed.)], Jane's mother, married men who were also subsequently to enter the lumber business. Typical for the time, the Great Depression took its toll, and when Jane was no more than four or five years old, her family moved to Marion where her father's people had lived for more than a hundred years.[38] Her father, C. J. (Clarence Joseph) Newcom, was an energetic and disciplined man who worked hard at several jobs through the depression years to sustain his family, which included another daughter, Jane's sister, Ann, who was born about 1932.[39] In the late 30's, Clarence joined the Boston Lumber company in Marion as a kind of overall manager, and he remained with that firm until he retired in his early 70s.

Jane and Ann, ca 1931

I think that these circumstances were somewhat trying for Pearl, who, in later years somehow came to be known to all of us as "Minnie."[40] She had grown up in well-to-do circumstances, had wanted for nothing, and enjoyed the life of a daughter of a fairly wealthy family in a small town. This happy situation ended rather abruptly in the 30's, and there is

---

[38] Well, sort of. The family was actually from the tiny town of Repton, several miles from Marion, albeit in the same county (Crittenden). Several are still buried in that now-vanished town's small cemetery.

[39] Actually, Ann Rutledge Newcom was born on March 31, 1929. My mother, originally named "Virginia Jane Newcom," was born March 8, 1926. She was named "Virginia" after the youngest of her mother's seven sisters but never used that name.

[40] Our assumption was that the nickname came from the famous country singer and comedienne, Minnie Pearl. We always knew her as "Minnie."

no question that things were difficult for the Newcoms in Marion for a time.[41] But much of this was not apparent to Jane and Ann. They enjoyed the affection of their paternal grandparents who subsequently lived with them.[42] Her paternal grandfather had been a school teacher, was lively and intelligent, and was an important influence on her scholastic life.[43] The Newcoms prospered in Marion after a time, and Jane enjoyed some status among the town's "better" families, but this was not such as to prevent her from being something of an adventurer nor from enjoying all of the freedom and fun of growing up in a small town. She was always one for independent thinking, and, like me, would take off on her bicycle on summer days for hours on end.

Yearbook photo of my mother when she briefly taught high school

---

[41] Clarence Newcom supplemented his income by hustling pool at the local pool hall. He was by all accounts very good at it!

[42] Clarence and Pearl Newcom purchased a house at 130 North Main Street in Marion in the 1920s and added several rooms on to the back, probably with the fairly substantial cash bequest from Pearl's father. Their daughter Ann moved into the house after the death of her mother in 1986 (Pearl) and lived there until she moved into an assisted care facility in 2012. Her father lived in the house in rooms that had been made into a separate apartment until he developed dementia, moving into a care home for the last few years of his life (dying in 1993). The house was sold after Ann moved out of it but was still standing as of this writing. I hope to treat our many visits to this house in my own memoir.

[43] Clarence Rutledge Newcom (1863-1948) taught school and sold insurance. He married Henrie Howerton (1865-1942) in 1897. The Howertons enjoyed a reputation for fierce tempers, and Henrie Howerton Newcom was apparently a formidable woman. The "Howerton Temper" has become a character trait in the family ever since, a subject I will treat in my own memoir.

She was smart and industrious, and when it came time to decide on what to do after high school, she decided to apply for study at Bowling Green's then quite famous Business University—and, of course, that's how we met.[44]

*Old postcard showing
Bowling Green Business University*

Our meeting occurred as a consequence of the familiar blind date. Friends of ours who were deeply involved with each other needed transportation, and I happened to have access to my father's 1939 Chrysler, so they "fixed us up."[45] The rest is history.

As I write this, that bright though chilly October 18th day in 1945 when we married is still fresh in my mind. She drove up to Bowling green from Marion, Kentucky with her parents in her dad's 1941 Plymouth (it was a two-toned maroon and grey!), and we married in the rectory of St. Joseph's Church at one o'clock in the afternoon with Father Spaulding officiating. (He was, as I now think it, a stiff-backed, narrow-minded, conservative cleric who sort of believed

---

[44] Bowling Green Business University merged with Western Kentucky University in 1963.

[45] My father noted in a letter to my mother marking the first anniversary of their meeting that it had taken place on August 3, 1944.

that anyone who married "out of the Church" (which meant, in his view—not marrying anyone who was not a Catholic) surely doomed one to questionable status in the hereafter.) And one must remember that Jane was a "Protestant" [actually, a Methodist (ed.)] and in those days, so, accordingly, we could not be married in a Nuptial Mass. As was also required, poor Jane had to endure a number of sessions of "instruction" prior to our marriage, and this narrow-minded priest just totally turned her off in the process to anything that had much genuine meaning about Catholicism.[46] But she endured it, albeit with a stiff upper lip, and on that glorious day in October, we tied the proverbial knot.

My own father was my best man—but he had always been my best man in any kind of circumstances, and at that time, he was still lively and full of mischief.[47] My mother's brother, Bill Murphy, was also there, and he was always very close to us, and there were just a few others. Jane had carefully selected a lovely, soft powder-gray suit and wore a big, fancy hat with a marvelous feather, and she was STUNNING! She had previously helped me to pick out a brown suit, and after the ceremony, we'd arranged to have pictures taken at a local studio, and those still show us as bright eyed and bushy tailed!

And then we caught the three o'clock "pan American" passenger train and went off to a marvelous weekend honeymoon in the big city of Louisville, Kentucky. After all, wartime conditions still prevailed, and we were lucky to even be able to go to Louisville. Moreover, we had little money—my dad had given me a hundred dollars, and Jane's folks had given her a little money, so, at least we anticipated that we could enjoy our honeymoon weekend in "style." And we did!

---

[46] My mother remained hostile to Catholicism for the rest of her life, a factor that resulted in a bit of coolness between her and her mother-in-law. She was less than enthusiastic about my own wife's Catholicism, but attended our Catholic wedding with her usual good grace in 1976.

[47] Interestingly, it appears from a letter my father wrote only one week before the wedding that his brother Spencer was originally slated for this role, but Spencer had to leave (he doesn't say why) before the wedding, so he asked my mother if it would be all right if his father filled the role. "He'd sure get a kick out of it, and so would Ann." She apparently said yes!

"Official" wedding photograph, retouched, as was occasionally the practice with black and white "portraits," to add some color

ED. NOTE: In an email written in October of 2010 remarking that it would have been their 65th wedding anniversary, my father remembered more about that day and the very brief honeymoon: "I so well remember that it was a lovely autumn day, about 55 degrees, and after we tied the knot—maybe about 2 PM—we went to a studio and had some pictures made, and then we went down to the train depot. We had tickets on the L & N 'Pan American' non-stop to Louisville. Our families were there to wish us off. Uncle Bill, Mom's brother, was a cut-up, and he kidded around and took some more pictures—have no idea what happened to those. I remember that I had on a top coat so it might have been a little cool. I also remember that I had written a note to the Seelbach Hotel in Louisville reserving our room, but when we got there they had no record of it. You must remember that this was just at the end of the war, and there was a lot of activity at the hotel, but they took pity on us—your mother had rice dropping off her hair. How totally naive of me to send a letter to reserve a room! The room was small and spare but we felt lucky to have it. We had a lovely night on the town—dinner at a fancy place and a movie. The best of the night was a little awkward as I recall, but it was just fine. It is just hard to believe that that day and night was 65 years ago!! We were just SO young, just kids really, and I don't think anybody gave us half a chance. She was reasonably well-off, and I was poor as a church mouse. We really had not all that much going for us except we cared a lot for each other. It was kind of difficult, and it was a tough adjustment, and it took a while for things to sort out."

Thus began a long journey together that despite a little trouble here and there along the way has lasted all these more than fifty years. Who'd have thunk it!

Original hotel bill for my parents' honeymoon in Louisville, Kentucky

CHAPTER I: ADDENDUM

Pauline Tabor's House of Ill Repute

by Greg Monahan

One of my father's best childhood friends in Bowling Green was a young man named Billy Tabor. They hung out together on many occasions since Billy lived close by on Clay Street.

My father and Billy Tabor, ca 1942

Where Billy lived, fascinatingly, was a house of prostitution operated by his mother, Pauline Tabor. In 1971, Pauline Tabor wrote and published her own autobiography with the Touchstone Press in Louisville. How much of what she wrote was factually true is difficult to tell. The book is chock full of remarkable stories of the "houses" that she ran, of her associations and run-ins with various authorities, and efforts by organized crime families to take over her profitable enterprise. Thrice-married, she regaled the reader with tales of running off would-be thieves with her shotgun, and especially of efforts by the "Holy Joes" to shut her down.

Of course, my grandfather ("Pop") was chief of police of Bowling Green while she ran her house, and my father maintained that his father fought to keep her open because she ran a "clean" house, and rates of venereal disease inevitably sky-rocketed whenever she was forced to close. In her book, she discussed a large-scale military raid during the war that forced the closure of many such places, including hers. She wrote that, six months after the closure of her house, the mayor of Bowling Green saw her on the street and invited her up to his office. "'Pauline', he said, 'we need you back in business.' 'What's the problem now', I asked. 'I thought the military bosses ruled that screwing is off limits.' The mayor cursed heartily. Since the military crackdown, he said, the town's venereal disease rate had risen to alarming proportions—and the same thing had happened at the military posts."[48]

Interestingly, she never used any names in her book, preferring to refer to authorities by their positions—mayor, sheriff, police officer. And not once did she refer explicitly to the "chief of police." When she did discuss the police of Bowling Green, it was with some affection: "I never had to make a payoff to law-enforcement officials. If I had operated in larger cities, I'm sure I would have been forced to buy protection from crooked cops, but I was lucky to be able to work with honest, decent lawmen in Bowling Green."[49] Of course, she also noted that several police officers were regular customers! Was my grandfather one of them? That seems doubtful, but she did note that the local sheriff was a loyal customer as were several unnamed state officials.

Only once in her book did she refer to her sons and then with some regret: "As far as my immediate family was concerned, I know I caused them much grief and humiliation. But never once did they turn their backs on me. My sons, growing up in the same town, had more than their share of scraps defending me against the jibes of their school-mates. But I stayed as close to them as possible in my role as a "part-time" mother. Both matured into good, law-abiding men with fine families and profitable businesses."[50] My father never spoke of his friend Billy Tabor with anything

---

[48] Pauline Tabor, *Pauline's: Memoirs of the Madame on Clay Street* (Louisville: Touchstone Publishing Company, 1971), p. 207.

[49] Tabor, *Pauline's*, p. 191.

[50] Tabor, *Pauline's*, p. 215.

but affection and even inferred now and then that he had actually been with his friend to the house, though not, given their ages, as customers! When the Clay Street house was demolished after it closed in 1968, bricks were sold as souvenirs, and some of his friends got together and got my father—then a dean of the College of Human Resources and Education at West Virginia University—one of those bricks. I have no idea what happened to it, but I do wish I still had it.

A brick from the Clay Street House

Pauline Tabor's book is a fun read, and my father took a certain amount of gleeful pleasure in the fact that he was even remotely associated with one of his hometown's more notorious "small businesses"!

The infamous House on Clay Street

CHAPTER II

The Military Times

Responsibility and Immaturity

In 1944, I was looking forward to my senior year in high school. I had made the varsity football team, and life was pretty good. And then, almost out of the blue, my father asked me whether I would like to go to work for the Federal Bureau of Investigation. Pop had little appreciation for football, and I'd guess he'd never seen a game, so all of that sort of thing that had so much appeal for me meant little to him. As chief of police, he had many interactions with the FBI people, and it being wartime, the Bureau needed people. Certainly, it had some appeal to a sixteen-year-old; I would work in Louisville and be paid a rather nice salary.[51] I would attend Louisville Male High School during the day and then would have to work the 4 pm-midnight shift as a clerk. I agonized over this turn of events much more than anyone knew, but ultimately decided to do it, and, I think—in retrospect—I did it as much to please Pop as for my own interests.

It turned out to be something of a disaster. I went on to Louisville, got a room where other FBI people lived, enrolled at Male High (which, incidentally, was our "foe" in our first Bowling Green High football game that year, and I felt much the traitor in that regard!) and went about the business of getting my work organized. The work itself was routine and often boring. I did enjoy reading old files about famous gangsters, but, all in all, the work itself was something anyone with half a brain could do.

---

[51] His father might also have hoped that it would keep my father out of the war, given that one of his brothers had been killed and the other injured.

Old Louisville Federal Building

But it was difficult to get up very early on my own, catch a streetcar to school, endure classes, and then hurry home to change clothes (suit and tie was mandatory) and report to work at the Federal Building. Increasingly, I found I was late to school, so I just "skipped" my first class (where no one ever called a "roll" anyway), and after a month or so, I'd just skip the whole day. Needless to say, that caught up with me rather quickly, and the "Special Agent in Charge" (SAC) called me in one day and said he didn't think I was quite ready for all this, and he was quite right, so I resigned and came home.

A 1939 Chrysler Windsor

Unfortunately, I was too far behind to get back in school, so I went to work at this or that job and just sort of wasted most of the rest of the whole year.[52] In about February or March I met Jane, and we started dating rather regularly. She didn't know all that much about my circumstances, and I was increasingly at "loose ends." We'd met on a blind date because a friend of mine who was dating a friend of hers had no transportation, and I did have access to my Pop's '39 Chrysler Windsor. Actually, our friends were already secretly married at that time, but of course, we didn't know that. They "set us up" because they wanted to be able to go here and there, and I did have fairly free use of the car. Jane and I sort of hit it off, and we continued to see each other, and it began to be a bit more than just dating.

The Merchant Marine

In the spring of 1945, I finally persuaded my folks to let me join in the "Great War." I was increasingly convinced the war would be over before I had any chance to be a part of it, and since I wouldn't be eighteen and eligible for the draft until August, I knew too that by then I would be totally at the whim of the draft, and who knew what *that* would entail! Since I'd had two brothers in service, one who'd already been killed in action and another who'd been reported missing in action (but who later turned up ok), the regular Services would not accept me as an enlistee, so I joined the Merchant Marine.

I had to report at Cincinnati, Ohio, and my uncle Bill Murphy drove me up there and went along too, to sort of provide a little moral support.[53]

---

[52] The irony that my father, who later became a high school teacher, professor of Education, and a college dean, was for a time a high school dropout, was never lost on him. It simply reinforced his belief in the value of public school education.

[53] My father may be misremembering here. In a letter he wrote to my mother from the Palace Hotel in Cincinnati, he indicated he'd taken a train, writing "I have never seen such a big place in my life as that train depot here…You would have died laughing at me if you could have seen me on the "Esculator"—you know—an elevator that walks. I damn near fell off of it 3 different times." In this very sweet letter, he closed "I'll love you with all of my heart for all of my life." Keep in mind that he was only seventeen years old. He signed most of these very early letters "Your Irish," that being my mother's nickname for him at the time.

I went through the processing there, and two nights later, they put me on a train for Sheepshead Bay, New York, where I would undergo six to ten weeks of training. Even though I was really quite excited about this turn of events, I can only now appreciate the agony that this must have put my parents through, but I was really at loose ends with no prospects, and this seemed a reasonable temporary solution. Also, the war was winding down, and there was not anything like the danger of submarine attacks that had characterized the Merchant Shipping Service in the first several years of the war.

I had a pretty good time as a Merchant Seaman although my first weeks away from home were very melancholy. I was terribly homesick, among people and circumstances I'd never imagined, and with all kinds of immunization shots, and everything else, had gotten very sick for a while.[54] Those first couple of nights were really difficult, for I don't think in all my life before or since have I ever felt more totally alone. Gradually, however, I began to perk up. The training was interesting, and we were issued uniforms and marched to our various classes together. So, when we'd completed about five weeks of training, we were allowed "leave," and after a couple of wonderful weekends in New York City, I began to look forward to shipping out.[55]

Jane and I had begun a lively correspondence during this time, and I really sort of thought of her as my "girl." And then, in April 1945, I was shipped to Norfolk, VA, where I reported to the Union Hall to be assigned to a ship. As it turned out, my ship was a fairly new "Liberty" made in the Kaiser yards in California, and it had just returned from its maiden long voyage to Murmansk in Russia.[56] I reported aboard as an OS (Ordinary Seaman) on about April 20, 1945.

---

[54] So sick he had to be hospitalized, according to one of his letters to my mother.

[55] In May 1945, he indicated he'd hooked up with the base orchestra as a singer and hoped to do that during his service, but there were no more mentions of it. He spent his first leave May 18-19 at the Dixie Hotel near Times Square (now the Carter Hotel) and went to see Charlie Spivak and his Orchestra. He complained that it had cost $1.97. "Things are awful high up there."

[56] Over 2,000 inexpensive "Liberty Ships" were mass-produced in the United States during the war, each one taking about 42 days to build. Women played a substantial role in their construction at various shipyards around the country.

From Cabbage to Cauliflower

Merchant Marine Identification Card

World War II liberty ship

Life Aboard Ship

We departed Norfolk Navy Yard on the evening tide after three or four days taking on cargo.⁵⁷ It was a very mixed bag. We had one entire "hold" in our forward unit of about three thousand cases of a very bad Connecticut beer called "Red Fox," and it must have been provided by some kind of government contract, for it surely must have been the absolutely worst beer man ever invented. We knew that because among the crew I sailed with, there were some old grizzled, career sailors who assumed that whatever we carried was fair game for "testing," so not more than about four days out, they managed to "capture" several cases of this instant laxative, and we spent pleasant sundown evenings on the foredeck sampling several cases of this terrible brew. In other "holds," we carried various kinds of machinery, boxes and boxes (*thousands* of boxes) of paper, which only confirms the idea that even in military affairs, the military functions on paper rather than bullets. In our after-holds, we carried a mixed cargo of guns, clothing (mostly "fatigues" and a zillion pairs of combat boots, and whatever else, I have no idea about).

⁵⁷ My father served aboard the Stephen T. Mather, which was not scrapped until 1966. Several pay stubs survive from his service, as well as his discharge papers.

My work was terribly routine, and the most arduous had to do with getting us underway—managing the lines and handling them (these big ropes weighed heavily and handling them was no small thing). At sea, I quickly learned that I was the "rookie," and thus, I was assigned the *worst* watches—the 4-8 (afternoon) and 12 (midnight) to 4 am, and on the bow. The bow watch in earlier years was a crucial "watch" because that was the place where sightings of submarines were most likely, but by our time, the threat had significantly subsided, and because the midnight to four watch was so deadly, it was typically assigned to a neophyte. In truth, though, I liked it. Though I often had a really difficult time keeping awake during those lonely hours, the sea was beautiful on those long moon-filled nights as we sailed from Panama toward Hawaii. Porpoises played along the bow, and phosphorescent fish danced about. Except for a few nights, the moon provided remarkable illumination, and with the *very* strong coffee provided from our mess, I managed nicely.

My afternoon watches on the bow were also pleasant; it was here that I really learned to read, and we had a fairly good library on board, and I read all kinds of things. Sitting on the bow plate (a triangular piece of sheet steel about four square feet in mass and with my legs twined about the bow mast—a small stanchion with its end turned toward aft and a pulley at its zenith for the purpose of helping to move deck cargo or whatever) this served nicely as a platform on which to sit and relax. I could still manage the small "green-lighted" phone in the small alcove below me (i.e., it was green-lighted when I was being called from the bridge, which was almost never!).

When I was not on watch, like others (when I was not sleeping), I spent much of my time scraping paint, painting (ships are almost constantly in need of painting because of the damage from the salt-sprayed air) and doing other kinds of ship-shape chores: checking lines, storing things properly, "policing up" and, of course, doing our laundry. The latter was mostly a matter of merely tying our dungarees on a line and dangling them over the side. The salt water and the buffeting of the ship's movement dashed the jeans about, and they dried out from the deep navy blue and harsh texture of their newness to a soft bleached whitened look which marked anyone who wore them as a genuine "old salt."

The crew's quarters on a ship are referred to as the "foc'sle" (or, more properly, the "forecastle"), but on a Liberty Ship, crew quarters were a bit spread out. Since several of us were "rookies," we were assigned sleeping quarters on an inside space just above the engine room; thus, the constant temporal rhythm of the engines was omnipresent. Though there were no portholes, we nevertheless learned to enjoy the regular beat of the engines, and it lulled us, though typically, we were so tired, we needed no incentive to sleep. Among my four "mates" was a chap from Indiana named White. He was a Steward's Mate (a "Messman" whose work was mainly to serve food in the crew's Mess). Actually, this was good duty, since, typically, at the end of a voyage, the Messmen, whether in "Crew" or in the Officers' Salon, usually received a handsome tip. (No such gratuity for those of us who worked on deck, but there was just a little more status for the latter.) White and I were to enjoy a subsequent adventure together at the end of our voyage. More about that presently.[58]

The Canal and Beyond

After about seven days at sea, we approached the Panama Canal. It was about nine or ten o'clock in the morning, and we confronted a Navy LST boat just absolutely *loaded* with sailors, and suddenly, it became a kind of contest as to which of us could get into the channel first. After all, getting through the canal was a terribly time-consuming chore, and if we were able to get in first, we'd be able to get through in the same day while the other ship would have to wait. It turned out to be a big race, and unfortunately, we had a modest collision. So we had to anchor out on the other side for a couple of

---

[58] In a later chapter, my father mentions his service as a messman aboard ship, and there are several surviving documents among his papers proving that he began his service in the Merchant Marine in that role. In addition, he wrote in a letter to my mother that he had been rated a "Steward's Mate 1rst," and described the Mess in detail, noting that he worked three hours at breakfast, three at lunch, and two at dinner, with a lot of spare time. "It is my restaurant, and I run it," he wrote. As he notes in that later chapter, he transferred out of the Mess, and his descriptions of his duties in this chapter focus exclusively on that later period.

days while there as a general "inquiry," but this gave us an opportunity for shore leave in Colon.[59] We had a real good time, and it was the most foreign-looking place I'd ever imagined.

The General Route

At the outset, we had no real notion of our destinations, nor were we told very much. But secrets are hard to keep aboard ship, and we learned that we were bound for Pearl Harbor where we were to discharge most of our current cargo and take on something else. The voyage from Panama across to Hawaii was totally uneventful—the seas were calm though with magnificent big Pacific swells. The sun shone almost every day, and we endured only one brief storm. We arrived at Pearl Harbor and docked between two huge US Navy ships—an aircraft carrier over on one side of us and a huge heavy cruiser on the other. I never knew the name of the carrier, but the cruiser was the USS Cincinnati. (I'd later learned that my future brother-in-law Harvey Hill had served on that cruiser, though I don't think he was aboard at that time.)

We enjoyed shore leave in Hawaii and rode the famous little train from Pearl into Honolulu. We had a good time, but I had no money to speak of, so couldn't buy anything much, but we did walk the beach at Waikiki (it wasn't much of a beach!) and had a good time.[60] And following the advice of my more experienced shipmates, I spent almost all of my "draw" (we could draw on our earnings from the ship's purser) for a "high-powered" uniform consisting of navy-officer "grays"—pants and shirt and a neat garrison cap with the fancy maritime gold medallion pinned to its front. This looked for all the world just like the uniform of a naval officer, and since we

---

[59] Colon sits on the eastern coast of Panama, consistent with the ship transiting east to west through the canal. Interestingly, in his letters, he does not mention Colon but says they did have shore leave on the other side of the canal in Panama City. It is, of course, entirely possible that they had both. He writes that some of the "boys" came back from shore leave in Panama City with "a certain disease" that had to be treated with penicillin!

[60] He did write to my mother to say he had bought her a pretty bandana with a hula girl on it and the words "Aloha Hawaii!" It is long lost, alas. That said, he took several pictures of various sights which he kept in a photo album that is still extant.

My father in his "fancy" dress uniform of the Merchant Marine

were awarded "ribbons" indicating our "service," the appearance was altogether quite jaunty. It all cost me only about thirteen dollars, but it proved to be most useful. Incidentally, "high-powered" was the term for such outfits, and some of our most *ordinary* seamen could dress themselves up to look for all the world like admirals!

There was real purpose in this idea. The Merchant Marine was not looked upon with much respect by the regular military people. They thought (erroneously) that we made too much money and had life too easy. In the latter case, the criticism was probably justified—we certainly ate better! But we didn't really make much money. I was paid $60 monthly and was able to earn a little extra money doing overtime painting and scraping. Some of our cohorts did earn extra money selling stuff on the black market—booze and bed sheets and so forth—but none in our crew did any of that. We were also paid extra when we were in "war zone" waters where we would be completely at the mercy of Japanese kamikaze suicide planes or when we were involved in supporting an island invasion. In point of fact, we received additional pay a few days after we'd docked in Pearl because they sent us out into the harbor and loaded our two aft holds with hand grenades! The idea, all glorious, was that if we blew up in the process, we'd be out there where we wouldn't hurt anybody else.

But we normally enjoyed none of the regular privileges of the other uniformed services. Curiously, we were often reviled by regular army and navy personnel when we went about in our old regular blue maritime uniforms. Moreover, for example, we were not normally allowed to frequent "canteens" or USO clubs that were available to the regular service personnel, apparently because we were actually employed by steamship companies rather than by the government. Neatly, those who'd gone before us had somewhat solved some of those issues, albeit surreptitiously, and had passed on that intelligence through advice to secure those "high-powered" uniforms. And I'll tell you, it worked very nicely—we were able to get all the free donuts and coffee that our counterparts in the other services enjoyed! (And I guess I ought to acknowledge that I took considerable satisfaction in the frequent times that some GI or enlisted sailor saluted me at Pearl Harbor or in Guam mistaking me for some naval bigwig. I loved it!)

On to Guam

We departed Hawaii and steamed almost directly to Guam. When we'd taken on the hand grenades, we'd also taken on about four or five big semi-truck flatbed trailers (no trucks, just the trailers), and we'd had a hell of a time trying to figure out how to anchor those big rigs down on our decks. We'd finally tied them down with heavy chains and hooked those into small hook retainers that we'd welded into the steel decks. But those stupid trucks caused us all kinds of problems in the next ten days or so because they were never *quite* secure to the satisfaction of our Bosun, and we had then endured just about the worst weather anyone could imagine. We were constantly convinced that those big rigs were going to break loose and be like gigantic battering rams. All the way out to Guam, our crew was tense and irritable, and this was *not* a crew that one enjoyed even when they were at peace with themselves, much less when they were anxious.

The Crew and the Great Storm

Our crew for the most part were long-time experienced seamen who mostly lived in coastal Virginia around Norfolk when they were not at sea. They were hard men, they drank a lot, fought a lot, and could intimidate me with just a look in their eyes. If they told me to jump, I'd have jumped over the moon—now, I mean, these were the kind of men that would have made Long John Silver nervous. But they were also marvelous at their craft, and if they told me to do something on deck, I learned that it was the right thing to do no matter how I might have felt otherwise. In truth, the Japanese may have been our mortal enemy, but they didn't really scare me half as much as these guys. And two days after we'd steamed out of Guam headed back toward Pearl, I really learned how much one owes to experienced seafarers, because that was when we got caught up in the great Okinawa typhoon of 1945. Thank God we were only in the outer edges of it, but I'll tell you, it was about the most terrifying experience I've ever endured, and although, afterward, we all sat around and enjoyed reliving the experiences of having endured it, I'd absolutely never want to do anything like that again! It was only owing to the skillful seamanship of our captain and first mate and of that very experienced crew that we came out of it in one piece. And incidentally, it was the same storm that just totally sheared off the entire bow of the USS Washington, a huge battleship, and it didn't hurt us one bit, and we were much more in the thick of it than the Washington.

Calm Confusion before the Storm

I don't remember much about the harbor at Guam. We'd had to anchor off a ways since we still had all those hand grenades aboard. Typically, if a ship that was anchored out had any personnel going ashore, a "taxi" came out to pick people up, and they flitted about like water bugs. A navy guy who had become a good friend of mine and who was in our complement of "armed guards" (these were regular navy personnel assigned to all merchant ships who were supposed to protect us by manning our fore and aft 3-inch 50 caliber guns, but who couldn't hit the broad side of a barn) decided we would go ashore together given the opportunity.

We'd been anchored out for almost an entire day before a big barge showed up, and it was manned by marines with big "P's" on the backs of their fatigues—i.e., they were "prisoners"—stockade guys who'd been court-marshalled for this or that kind of offense, and "stevedoring" was apparently their work duty. Our first mate wasn't too thrilled by this, but he was also anxious to get rid of those hand grenades. These marines unloaded the big trailers, loaded the beer onto them, and took off, and we didn't see anybody for another couple of days. Meantime, my navy friend and I got shore leave, and we went happily off to Guam to see what it had to offer, which, as it turned out, wasn't much.

That's where he and I ended up getting our now (in)famous tattoos—big ugly black panthers on our upper arms. In truth, there just wasn't much else to do.[61] We couldn't even find a bar to get a drink or a beer, and he and I figured that we were surely the only guys left in the whole fleet who didn't have a tattoo, and we wanted something a little different! The big woman who did them was naked to the waist with ponderous breasts, and under one, she had tattooed the word

---

[61] The tattoo resulted in a very guilt-ridden letter to my mother.

"sour" and under the other "sweet"! It was a really uncomfortable experience, and after she'd completed her work, she just wrapped our bleeding arms in some kind of wax paper and said don't wash that in salt water for two or three days! She also told us that the tattoo would probably fade away in a few years. That was more than fifty years ago, and that thing is as clear and bright as it was the day she did it! I have no idea whatever happened to my friend, but there has never been a day in my life that I have not regretted getting that tattoo.[62]

Marines Return and Storm Gathers

We heard lots of rumors about a big storm that was developing in the Sea of Japan or the China Sea, or wherever. We'd heard all this sort of thing before—for example, we'd been told that we'd surely be under constant bombardment from Japanese suicide planes—we never saw a one (but anytime a small squadron of our own planes flew over, we dived for cover!). So, after a couple of days, we became very blasé about all this stuff, but we did begin to notice that of the more than 200 ships in the area, many of them were putting quickly out to sea. But we still sat waiting for the marines to return to finish unloading us, and we then also had to wait to be re-cargoed with God-knows-what!

In truth, the weather was bountiful. It was most pleasant, and we passed time by diving off the ship and swimming about in the beautiful lagoon-type water despite our tattoo wounds and which seemed not to make much difference. We sat around deck, had a beer or two, and listened to the old salts tell marvelous stories about other voyages. And it was altogether very relaxing while we waited for the marines to do their bit.

Finally, five big barges came along, and they loaded us with tons and tons of boxed canned goods or boxed rations or whatever—the

---

[62] He always bought longer short-sleeve shirts that stretched down to his elbow to hide the tattoo, though he did occasionally play a game with kids and grandkids where the panther would "jump" and growl if they touched it. They were enchanted, but he did hate having it.

rumor again was that these were supplies that were to be used for the invasion of Japan, but that someone had decided that they were not to be needed. Of course, as it turned out, that was indeed the case. Also, this turned out to be excellent cargo. All of these cases fitted nicely into our several holds, and they weighted us down deeply in the water, but our biggest problem was a half dozen beat-up light tanks that we had to secure on our deck. These had been only slightly disabled, and our job was to return them to Pearl where they could be easily rehabilitated. But no matter how secure we could make them, the idea of having heavy vehicles straining against their holds in a really severe storm gave us much concern—could one imagine what it might be like for a two-ton tank to come loose and slide around our deck?[63] I almost suddenly appreciated the metaphor about "loose cannons on a deck"! It would just sink us as surely as if we had been hit by a torpedo, so I was clearly aware that our "old salts" had an uneasy feeling about this deck stuff and particularly so when, by the time we hauled anchor and set sail for Pearl Harbor, we were already aware that the weather was not at all good.

We'd already heard rumors about the big typhoon, but it didn't really matter too much to us. We were very pleased, first of all since we'd missed the invasion of Borneo where, apparently, we'd been originally assigned, because our ship—the Stephen Mather, by the way—couldn't do eleven knots! I guess that a ship participating in an invasion as a support vessel had to be able to do at least eleven knots—now I *know* that ship could have done eleven knots although top speed for the best of the Liberties would have been no more than thirteen knots. I still privately believe that our chief engineer knew a lot more about our safety than anyone would have credited him. So, setting sail back to Pearl was in and of itself enough to give us much relief, and, accordingly, we could have cared less about some little piddling storm!

We sailed out of the harbor at about dusk, and before dawn of the following day, the weather had worsened. We sailed as far north of

---

[63] He had more ample cause to be worried than he indicates here. A fully loaded Sherman tank from that era weighed over thirty tons, not two!

the predicted pattern of bad weather as our heavily loaded old boat could go, and at about eight knots wide-open, we couldn't expect to outrace even a mild front, and this was a raging typhoon. Our mate's notion was to see whether we could get to the outer edges of it, for surely (as he told us at a brief meeting in the Officer's Salon) if we happened to somehow get caught in the midst of it, we'd be torn up like a piece of flotsam.

That first night was not so bad, but it gave us time to make some preparations. It rained like cats and dogs, and the sea was nasty, but I was told that it was mild compared to what we'd endure in the next couple of days. Now, I was totally new at this—my experiences as a seaman had been altogether mild. I had no notion of what it might be like to endure a raging storm, but our old hard-nosed bosun got us together and gave us a point-of-fact lecture. The gist of it went something like this: We'll string lines all over the deck, he said, and if you're out there, you damned well better hang on to them, or you'll be washed away! You'll wear your foul-weather gear, and you'll always be within reach of one of your mates, and if you get sick, which some of you will surely do, you'll *not* let it get in the way of your job. And what is your job? Your job is to make sure that deck cargo doesn't stray. If the deck cargo breaks away, this ship is doomed! *Do you understand that*!! We did. I was scared to death!

Our biggest problem was the wind. If we were in anything like the meat of the storm, the wind would be totally unpredictable, and it could swirl us around like a child's spinning top. He told us that there's nothing we could do about the wind except to hope that we could keep the ship into the face of the huge waves that would be about us. I again was assigned to the bow, and that was good for me—I wouldn't have to worry about traversing a very slippery deck holding to lines—I just needed to try and see where the big waves moved and advise my mate. By ten o'clock in the morning, the sea was remarkably heavy. We'd be sixty, seventy feet up one minute looking straight down at a gaping cavern of water, and a half minute later, be sixty or seventy feet down looking straight up at an impossible wall of water. We were indeed like a big cork on the water and just rolled with it. It was crazy. And it went on like that until about four in the afternoon. Fortunately, the worst was during the daytime.

Somehow, that seemed better—to endure that during the day seemed better to me than were we to have to endure it at night. And then, almost all of a sudden, the strong winds subsided. The seas were still huge—big swells that took us way up and then dropped us way down sometimes with our propellers spinning noisily totally out of the water, but the old boat just bobbed along, and by six o'clock, it was all over. The seas continued to swell, but nothing like during the storm, and we just rode it. Turns out, we were only at the very edge of the typhoon, but some other ships weren't so fortunate.[64]

In late July, four or five days later, we had steamed uneventfully into Pearl, discharged our cargo, and in two days had taken on an entire cargo of raw sugar! We didn't even have time for leave and left for San Francisco. About three days out, we heard a report on the radio that the U.S. had dropped some kind of strange bomb on Japan that had just about wiped them out. A couple of days later, we heard a report that we'd dropped another one, this time on Nagasaki. We had no idea where that was.

War's Over—Home Beckons

We streamed into the mouth of the Sacramento River at San Francisco at about five o'clock in the afternoon headed up to Stockton where there was a sugar refinery and where we were supposed to discharge our cargo. Although it was August, I was quite cold and had on my pea jacket, and as usually was the case, I was on the bow watch.[65] We had entered the bay, and just under the famous bridge, a tanker was steaming out, and he hooted at us a couple of times. I remember that I shivered a bit, and my little green light came on. It was the Mate. "What's wrong with the tanker? He asked. "Aren't we well away from collision?" "Oh yeah, no problem so far as I can tell," I said, "I don't know what's wrong with that guy." And then after about thirty seconds, the green light comes on again, and the Mate says, "Monny,

---

[64] A total of 12 ships were sunk, 222 grounded, and 32 severely damaged.

[65] Mark Twain is credited with saying once that the coldest winter he had ever spent was summer in San Francisco!

I know what his problem is. He was telling us that it's all over. The Japanese have agreed to surrender unconditionally. The war is over!"

I just sat there. It was hard to believe, but I remember that I didn't feel any particular elation. I was cold, and I was hungry, but then something else began to occur to me. I wanted to go home. I came off watch about forty minutes later, and our captain announced that the ship would be refueled and readied for a trip down to San Diego where it would be cargoed for an immediate trip to China, and that all personnel were "frozen" to jobs. Not for me, I thought. I'm going home. A chap named White whom I've mentioned previously who was a steward's mate had similar feelings. To make a long story short, we conspired with the chief steward's mate who managed to secure our overtime records so that we could ultimately be paid for what was owed us, packed our sea bags, secured our records in wax, water-proof paper, and dived off the bow of that ship into the coldest water I've ever endured and swam about two hundred meters to the shore.[66] We changed clothes on the beach, hitched a ride into San Francisco and had the most wonderful time of our lives celebrating the end of the war right in Market Square. Then, the next day, I wired my dad for money to come home, caught a bus, and three days later, I was back home in Bowling Green, Kentucky.[67]

The Army Awaited and a Wedding was Planned

Unfortunately, being in the Merchant Marine Service did not exempt me from being drafted into the regular military services. A merchant seaman was seen more as "government employment" rather than as military service, even though many merchant seamen died heroically during World War II. So, once again, I was at loose ends, but by this time Jane and I had developed considerably more than just a steady relationship. In the early fall of 1945, I spent almost as much time in Marion as she did in Bowling Green, and we talked constantly on the phone, so quite

---

[66] The fact that my father's best friend was a messman, and that the chief steward's mate had access to his pay records, further confirms that he was, in fact, a messman too, at least in the first months of his service.

[67] V-J Day (Victory over Japan Day) was August 15, 1945.

soon, it became apparent that the best thing for everybody was for us to get married. Otherwise, our folks would have to take out loans to pay the phone bills! I reported to my draft board and informed them that I was going to return to complete my high school education, and that I was planning to be married. They gave me a twelve-month deferment.

A Modest Wedding and a Wartime Honeymoon

Jane and I were married on October 18, 1945 in the Rectory at St. Joseph's Catholic Church in Bowling Green, Kentucky at about one o'clock in the afternoon, and at about 3:00 pm departed for Louisville for a week-end honeymoon. (I think I've mentioned salient aspects of this event elsewhere!) But, God, how totally naïve we were![68] But we had a good time, and then, we had to make some plans. I went back to school and graduated in June 1946, and then we had to consider the pros and cons of being drafted or enlisting.

Welcome to the US Army

We decided that it was probably best for me to enlist in the regular army for an eighteen-month "hitch." At that time, that was a special enlistment choice since so many people were being discharged that the army needed recruits to fill their needs if only on a rather short-term basis. It was fortunate for us: Most draftees had little choice about their circumstances, and at least this meant that I would know the limits of my service, and, moreover, it would provide me with twenty-seven months of GI Bill collegiate education were I to opt for that. Both Jane and I fully intended to take advantage of that benefit, and that was the primary incentive for my enlistment.[69] Had

---

[68] As he noted in the previous chapter, they were teenagers. That the marriage lasted as long as it did (55 years until the death of my mother) really is remarkable.

[69] My father reinforced this idea in a later letter to my mother in September 1946, in which he noted that "most of the guys" were in the army for "the college they'll get out of it," adding that he looked forward to the day when "I would be a graduate of college with a degree which will entitle us to a life of comfort and opportunity."

I waited to be drafted, for example, I might have had to serve only a year or maybe even three years. Who knew? This way, we knew what we could count on.

In the Service

There were several guys I knew from high school who also enlisted at the same time, and following the usual pre-assignment routines in Louisville where we underwent physical examinations and all kinds of written stuff, we were herded onto a train and sent to Fort Benjamin Harrison near Indianapolis, Indiana.[70] There, we were further "processed," were provided new uniforms and *big* new combat boots, and after about a week or ten days, we were put on a troop train and dispatched for "basic training." No one knew where we were going, but it was soon apparent that it was somewhere in the south because that was the way the train was headed.

After about twenty hours on the train, we arrived at Camp Polk, Louisiana, out seemingly in the middle of nowhere. We were assigned to various "training companies," and our eight weeks of basic training began. All in all, it wasn't that bad. I met a lot of guys, many of whom I served with throughout my entire hitch. We had to do all the usual things recruits had to learn how to do: close-order drill, "retreat parades." Every day when the flag was lowered (which is referred to "retreat" on base), we had to parade across the grounds with the band playing, and it was all quite impressive.

---

[70] More specifically, he underwent his physicals at Fort Knox, just south of Louisville, from which he wrote my mother several surviving letters, including one in which he noted that he and his fellow initiates got into a small amount of trouble for taking part in a pillow fight. It's useful to remember that he was only nineteen at the time! As for Indiana, he may once again be misremembering, as his letters are addressed from Camp Atterbury, near Edinburgh, Indiana, and not Camp Benjamin Harrison. His confusion may arise from the fact that the Induction Center for Fort Benjamin Harrison was transferred to Camp Atterbury in August 1944, and one can well imagine both personnel and documents from the former using its name after they were transferred to the latter. Camp Atterbury is still operating as of this writing as an Indiana National Guard installation.

On payday during basic training in Louisiana, upper left

We had one weekend of leave toward the end of our training, and several of us went over to Shreveport, which was the largest town accessible, and we had a good time just being away from army routine. And then, almost all of a sudden, our training was about to end, and we were curious as to what our next assignments might be.[71] We knew that we would be going overseas *someplace*! The two most likely assignments were either Japan or Korea. Very few people from Polk were assigned to the European Theatre which, of course, was the most preferable duty.

---

[71] Early in his basic training, he wrote my mother that he thought he might be sent to a "tech" school to be trained as a medic, allowing him to stay in the United States, but hopes for that goal faded as his training continued. He had finally gotten his first monthly pay check—for $28—from the army on October 10 and wrote that he had spent almost all of it at a carnival while on his pass to Shreveport. That was actually the first of two trips to that city during his basic training.

Fortunately for me, it had been announced that the camp would close at the end of our training period, and they needed a number of volunteers to help round up livestock, for there were open-range laws in Louisiana, and both pigs and cattle often strayed onto the installation. Normally, this wasn't much of a problem, but with the camp scheduled to close, a lot of work was involved in boarding up barracks, and all kinds of things that had to be done when a big facility like that closed up, and not least was to round up all the livestock and then make arrangements for those who owned it to come into the camp and claim it. (Incidentally, Polk didn't remain closed too long. Some politician had its designation changed from a "camp" to a "fort." "Forts" are permanent installations, while "camps" are not, and even today, Fort Polk is still operating.[72])

They advised us that they needed volunteers who knew how to ride horses to round up these stray animals, and I volunteered. I didn't know beans about riding a horse, but my drill sergeant whom I'd gotten to know pretty well had told me that those who did this kind of work had a much better chance of getting reassigned somewhere in the U.S. rather than overseas, and that appealed to me. Moreover, I'd seen the horses, and they were just old, docile animals, and I thought what the hell—I can do that! As it turned out, I *couldn't* do it. I had no trouble riding the horse, but I didn't know how to make the stray animals go where they wanted them to go, so after a couple of days, they reassigned me to helping to board up buildings, and that was easy work.[73]

All of the guys I'd gone through "basic" with had received orders and were provided ten days of "en route leave" and had been shipped out about two weeks previously. Subsequently, I also was reassigned and also granted ten days of "delay-in-route" leave. Jane was waiting for

---

[72] Named for a Confederate general (and not the U.S. president of the same name), Fort Polk today operates the "Joint Readiness Training Center" including such sites as a realistic Iraqi village. Its 198,000 acres are home to as many as 11,000 soldiers at any given time. Like other bases controversially named for Confederate officers, it may at some point be renamed.

[73] Oddly, there is no sign of this volunteer sojourn in his letters to my mother. They break just before he left for his en route leave and pick up again on the train to Camp Stoneman in California.

me in Bowling Green, and we had a good time for a little while. I still had no idea of what my "orders" were except that I was to take a regular train to Kansas City, Missouri where I was to catch a Troop Train. I didn't know where it was to go, but when I got there and boarded the train, the rumor was that we were all going to Korea. Not me! Because of that little sojourn at Polk, I was assigned to the 19th Infantry Regiment, 24th Infantry Division in some obscure place called Beppu, Kyushu, Japan! Japan! Boy! That beat the hell out of cold Korea where just about every single guy I went through basic training with ended up, including the three or four guys I enlisted with from Bowling Green.

We boarded a big troop ship in California, and it was a very long trip to Korea, which was our first stop.[74] That voyage took twenty-three days, and we unloaded the Korea troops onto barges, since there was no pier that could handle that ship.[75] And then, we sailed on to Yokohama, Japan, where the rest of us disembarked and were assigned to a unit called the 5th Replacement Depot. This was a *very* temporary station merely to get arrangements worked out for those of us who would thence be shipped to all kinds of units in Japan from Sendai up in the North where the 82nd Airborne Division was stationed to the several other divisions situated throughout Japan. The 25th Division was in Honshu with its three regiments and a "Divarty" (Division Artillery) unit, and the 24th was situated at four different locations in Kyushu—its three regiments and its Division Artillery unit. The 19th Infantry was in Beppu way down on the southern part of Kyushu, and it turned out to be an altogether quite pleasant locale.[76]

---

[74] He wrote my mother that he was glad to leave California, where he stood in endless lines for various forms of bureaucratic "processing." He also expressed amusement at all the worrying from his fellow soldiers about a voyage at sea, one area, at least, where he was something of a veteran! According to his letters written aboard ship, he managed not to get nearly as seasick as many of his fellow soldiers.

[75] Rather than continue footnoting passages from the substantial body of letters he wrote my mother during this period, I have appended a separate Appendix to this memoir devoted to them, beginning with his sea voyage to Japan.

[76] Beppu sits on the eastern side of Kyushu, the southern-most of the Japanese main islands, south even from Hiroshima and Nagasaki, though not too far from those unhappily infamous cities.

The Nature of the Circumstance

There were more than 1,800 of us who were assigned to the 19th. Needless to say, we sort of filled up the Regiment, which was, I suppose, the intent. Accordingly, with almost a full complement of personnel, the idea was to whip us into shape as quickly as possible. The regiment was also, understandably, very low on "ranked" personnel. When we arrived in Beppu, there were only a very few NCO's and officers, and among all of these, not many were at the ranks normally appropriate for their jobs. Thus, a company commander was supposed to have the rank of captain, but our company when I arrived had a first lieutenant as commanding officer. Each platoon was supposed to have a "tech" sergeant commanding, but in almost all of our companies, there were mostly "buck" sergeants with only an occasional "staff sergeant" here and there.

In the regular "TO&E" (Table of Organization and Equipment), a regiment was to be commanded by a full colonel, and each of its three battalions, by a lieutenant colonel (of which there were three in a regiment). The battalion HQ was to be commanded by a major, and the function of the HQ unit was mostly administrative: each "line" company by a captain, each platoon by a first or second lieutenant, and a platoon sergeant who normally held the rank of tech sergeant (three chevrons and two rocker arms on the bottom), and each squad in a platoon, of which there were three, by a staff sergeant (one rocker arm on the bottom). In each company, too, there were particularly special personnel who held the rank of ("buck") sergeant—three chevrons, no rockers. This, incidentally, turned out to be my ultimate rank as the company communications NCO.[77]

---

[77] At the same time he was writing this memoir, my father was working on co-writing a book with his colleague Edwin Smith on the ways in which military leadership models could inform educational administration, and it seems likely that that work informed this section of his memoir.

In addition to the "line" companies which were really the basic combat units, there was also an HQ company which had to look out for feeding, transporting, and all of the myriad of management concerns which keep a military unit functioning. There was typically only one headquarters company for each regiment, and those who made that unit function had considerable influence.

When we joined the regiment, there were almost none of these ranks filled, so a part of our early work in training was to determine who among us would be promoted to these important positions, at least among the enlisted personnel. So, our first two months or so, we endured the most vociferous and exhausting training one could imagine. It made our basic training seem like child's play. We marched miles and miles up and down mountains, slept in the field in terrible conditions, and had to endure the "honey-bucket syndrome." This last concern was ever-present. You see, we were in a very rural part of Japan, and farmers cultivated every absolute square inch of available land, and they fertilized with human manure! Somehow, they gathered this stuff and stored it in shallow wells (we called them "sh__ pits") usually in a remote corner of a field, and one had no notion of where these holes were until he fell into one![78] On our marches in the heat of the day, a honey-bucket cart (two-wheeled things pulled by either very old horses or oxen) would pass us by, and the odor was devastating, and when one of us

---

[78] I've kept my father's somewhat old-fashioned (and, I think, charming) spaces for this rarely used (in this memoir) four-letter word!

on maneuvers fell into one of the pits, he would be a total outcast forever! Most happily, I never endured that experience.

As members of the 24th Infantry Division, our shoulder patches exhibited a bright green leaf on a red field [pictured (ed.)], and our own regimental identity was a small lapel enameled pendant that we were issued soon after arriving there. Our 19th regimental installation at Beppu was called "Camp Chicamauga," which was derived from some rather famous historical battle that the unit had endured in Tennessee during the Civil War.[79] The facilities had been rather recently constructed and occupied about a hundred acres of what was probably the best land in the whole province. The buildings were all of a sort of cream-colored stucco which the Japanese had built according to some military specifications, and each of the larger buildings housed one complete infantry company. We also had a fairly nice enlisted men's club, an NCO club, and an Officer's club. In addition, there was a kind of all-purpose gymnasium, and there were adequate "open areas" for parades and games. The buildings themselves were very basic and not too fancy inside, but certainly a bit fancier than anything similar would have been in the States. All in all, it was rather nice as far as army conditions went.

[79] Fought on the border between Tennessee and Georgia in September 1863, the Battle of Chicamauga was a Confederate victory won by Braxton Bragg, whose name still graces Fort Bragg in North Carolina, headquarters of the 82nd Airborne Division.

Luck and Circumstances Again

We'd trooped down to Kyushu on those curious, small narrow-gauge railway trains that were typical of Japan in those times, and even though I was only of about average size, only about two of us could occupy a seat. The trip was long and slow down from Yokohama and took the better part of two days. We were very tired when we arrived in the middle of a night but were quickly assigned to barracks and were allowed to settle in for most of the rest of the next day.[80]

On base in Japan

Not long after getting settled, someone advised that we required a "company clerk" who needed to know how to type. I volunteered, and it turned out to be a good job. First of all, being a clerk, I earned the rank

---

[80] As his letters to my mother indicate, he arrived on Christmas Eve. See Appendix A.

of corporal but also as a consequence, was privy to information about almost anything new that was needed, and that's how I came to attend Communications School where I graduated in about six weeks with the rank of sergeant. (I held that rank throughout my tour in Japan.)

With his radio equipment

In that responsibility, I had mostly to look after our communications and radio equipment (which was very primitive by today's standards) and had to shoulder a *very* heavy radio pack that was to be available to the company commander at all times. Thus, I was always close to whatever was going on, and although it almost killed me to carry that thing up and down mountains on our many maneuvers, I came to be well thought of by most of our officers. During these times, I remained as company clerk, and when, a little later, a call went out for tryouts for the Regimental Glee Club, I was ready!

The TDY Champion

Joining the Regimental Glee Club meant that I would be put on "TDY"—the army's designation for "Transfer of Duty." It was always a temporary designation, for the presumption was that whenever any "TDY" assignment concluded, one automatically returned to his previous assignment. But I learned a lot about "TDY," and for most of the remainder of my tour in Japan, I was *always* on "TDY"!

Singing outdoors with the Glee Club

The glee club was very special. We had a marvelous young director who'd graduated in music from the University of Illinois, and there were about twenty-five voices in the group. We had guys from all over—California, Indiana, Georgia, New York, Kansas—everywhere, and we were pretty good. In fact, we were so good that we were singled out to provide the opening and closing numbers for a special GI show that was to premier at the "Ernie Pyle Theatre" in Tokyo. It was the grandest theatre in the entire Far East, and we performed there![81]

We also served as the choir for all the weekend services—Protestant, Catholic, and Jewish—and we also wrote and performed our

---

[81] While in Tokyo, he attended the War Crimes Trial of Japanese leaders. See his letters in Appendix A.

own special show for our own regiment.[82] It was a blast. In one of our various trips around Japan performing here and there, we were able to spend a couple of days in Nagasaki City where the second atom bomb had been dropped (on my birthday as a matter of fact: August 9, 1947). We walked all around the area and even took some pictures at precisely the point where the bomb supposedly hit.

A fellow sergeant posing on the spot where the bomb fell

---

[82] Attending Protestant services caused him to begin reconsidering his Catholicism, as excerpts from his letters in the appendix show.

The spot was marked by a huge and rather primitive arrow, and I remember taking photos of some of our glee club members at that very spot. We also visited a nearby medical school that had been totally devastated by the explosion as well as an old, rather famous Catholic church. Typical of the Japanese, however, there was also a huge machine gun factory and several other important military targets nestled in among these other facilities. But, I can remember that I was particularly impressed by the very widespread devastation that the bomb had wrought. Incidentally, it never occurred to us at the time that any of all of this might still be radioactive. We walked about the entire area without any thought of danger.[83]

When my work with the glee club ended because too many of our members were shipped out for home, I then again went on "TDY" to join the 19th Infantry football team. I'd played only one football game in high school because I'd been ruled ineligible for having transferred from one high school to another, and then in my senior year, had gone off to work for the FBI before our season began, but I'd practiced diligently and felt I had a halfway good chance of making the regimental team. I was in very good physical shape at the time. I weighed about 165 and had worked out with weights with several other members of our glee club, and I was as hard as a rock. I could run very fast (if not too far), and I was very "shifty," which had always been my talent in high school. I did make the team, and that again kept me from the drudgery of regular duty until it was just about time for me to ship out for home.[84]

The one most memorable experience I had with the team was in a run-off championship game against the 25th Infantry Division team at a place called Sasebo. We'd beaten five other regimental teams and had also lucked out against our own division artillery

---

[83] My father did have a cancerous tumor removed in the late 1960s, and I have often wondered whether that resulted from his visit to still-radioactive Nagasaki twenty years earlier. For more on this trip, see his letters in Appendix A.

[84] This section does bring a smile. At the time, my father was very skinny—about 5'10 and 162, according to one of his letters. I figure the team must have needed small guys who could run fast! It's interesting also to note the considerable work my father went to to avoid standard duty in the army!

team, which angered some nameless colonel, for had he thought any regimental team was that good, he'd have drafted its players for the Division! We went up to Sasebo to play in the quarter-finals for the Far Eastern Championships, and had we won that game, we'd have been in the semifinals in Tokyo in late November 1947. Well, we lost that game, but not too badly as I recall. Anyway, we had an End on that team who'd been a freshman star at UCLA, and he could catch a pass anywhere near him, and he'd done very well, but after a while, was being double- and triple-teamed. I was the substitute at the other end, and when the regular guy got hurt, I got to play, and, of course, no one paid any attention to me. We had a quarterback who was an old captain who'd played football for West Point, and we're in the huddle, and he looks at me and says something like, "If I throw it out to you in the flat, can you catch it? They seem to be dropping off of you." And I said, "Well, no one seems to even think I'm on this team, so if you throw it out there where I can get my hands on it, I'll catch the damned thing." And that's what we did, and I could have almost *backed* into the end zone!

It was the first time I'd ever played against blacks (though we called them "negroes" in those days). The 25th Infantry Division was the *only* integrated unit in the entire U.S. Army at that time, and it was a curious experience to see "negroes" in ordinary army activities.[85] For the most part, most of the black people in those times were either cooks or bakers or served in HQ companies in very servile kinds of functions. That was not at all the case with the 25th Division, and it had enjoyed an enviable reputation for its excellence. But for me, that football game was just about the first time I'd ever encountered black people in any similar context, and this big dude across from me had been hammering me all day (needlessly, I might suggest), so when our guys finally got back on offense after the other team had gone down the field and scored on a long, time-consuming drive, we took to the field again, and that was the first time I'd ever heard the word "honky" when this big black guy said to me on that very first play, "Honky, this is your last play!" And it was! I knew

---

[85] He was perhaps forgetting that he had sung with African-Americans on board the ship going to Japan. See his letters in Appendix A.

he was going to cold-cock me, so I thought I'd just give him a little fake and ease by him, but he hit me with a forearm and almost knocked my headgear off. And he was correct. I had to be carried off the field, and I didn't feel good until the next day. So much for my athletic career. Still, I did score a TD, and it kept me away from drills and maneuvers, and when I returned to Chicamauga, I learned that we'd be shipping out for home almost a month sooner than expected. With luck, it seemed very likely that I might even be home for Christmas.

A Photographic Record of It All

During our time in Japan, we were paid in "Occupation Scrip" or "funny money" as we referred to it, for it looked for all the world like Monopoly money.

It was only good at American installations, so if one wanted to "deal" with the Japanese, one had to utilize "Yen." When I first went to Japan, the exchange rate from occupation dollars into yen was modest—about twenty to one—but inflation was rampant, and on the black market, a carton of American cigarettes which cost us about $2.50 at the PX could be sold for 550 yen. No more than a couple of months after I'd arrived, exchanges were cancelled entirely.

The PX at Camp Chicamauga in Japan

Thus, one either participated in the black market or just didn't buy any Japanese goods except through our own army PX system. I didn't have much money, but I did buy a Japanese 35 mm camera for the equivalent of about ten dollars. It wasn't a very good camera, but I did take a lot of pictures, and somewhere, I have all of them in an album.[86]

I also purchased a very special tea set of Noritaki china through the PX that we still own. I guess it might be rather valuable now, and at the time, I think I must have paid about fifty dollars for it, and I also bought Jane a marvelous pair of pure silk oriental pajamas with the high neck button top and which, incidentally, she never wore nor cared too much for—not her style! But had I been more enterprising, as were some of my buddies, I could have made a lot of money on the black market, for I'd known of some guys who put back a very nice bundle of cash through skillful management of the "market." In my own case, I always just sort of knew that had I engaged in

---

[86] The album survives and is the source of several photos in this chapter. Interestingly, because he was often the one taking the photos, there are very few of my father in his own album!

any of that, I'd probably get caught and sent to Ft. Leavenworth for the rest of my natural life. It was enough for me to just know that I would soon go home free and clear.

Others Never Came Home

Sadly, some of my best old friends from the 19th with whom I'd shared my last month or two in the comfortable NCO rooms that were set aside in the big barracks for some of those of us who'd enjoyed some status had subsequently to accompany our 24th Infantry Division into combat in the Korean War. These guys were highly respected by officers and enlisted personnel alike and were thus accorded much deference because they'd been through the thick of battles in both the European and Pacific theatres. They'd all signed over to spend their final "hitch" in Japan so that their retirement pay would reflect a final overseas assignment. They were all staff, tech, or master sergeants who were career army veterans having joined up during the 30's and who entertained us with marvelous stories of their times in the army, and no one enjoyed their remembrances more than I did.

The 24th was the first division into combat in the Korean War, and the entire division was at low ebb at that time. Moreover, my own unit—the 19th Infantry Regiment—was the first of the 24th Division's units to fight in that melancholy war, and too many of those of us who had made it a fairly combat-ready unit had been rotated back home, so the Korean War caught everybody off guard. *All* of those good guys I'd shared that big room in "I" Company with were killed in the early months of that war.

These included S/Sgt. Wesley Sandel, who had been "busted" from M/Sgt for some kind of impropriety and had worked himself back up and who had a very close compatriot during my last weeks in "I" Company, T/Sgt "Dusty" Rhodes, who'd served all through that Battle of the Bulge, and our own company commander, Captain Keyes, who had been subsequently promoted to major and was the Battalion executive officer.[87] (I learned about these details in a letter I

---

[87] I can find no photos of "Dusty" Rhodes. For a picture of Captain Keyes, see Appendix A.

received sometime in 1950 from a guy named Molasky who was our Company Artificer and with whom I shared a room during one period of my service with "I" Company.[88] Since our names followed each other [alphabetically], we'd been together from the beginning in the Company.) I never knew what happened to him. I never heard from him again. What a waste! The division was simply not combat-ready. Its TO&E [Table of Organization and Equipment (ed.)] was low, and most of those who'd been well-trained had been rotated back to the States. The old veterans had to endure the brunt of the pressure, and the division, as with other units that were pressed into action so quickly, took a hell of a beating. What a waste!

Wesley Sandel

---

[88] The term "artificer" was new to me. Wikipedia defines an artificer as "an appointment held by a member of the armed services who is skilled at working on mechanical devices in the field," but most references are to much earlier periods or to other armies. I can find no reference for the term being used at this time and can only guess it was a colloquialism among soldiers of the period?

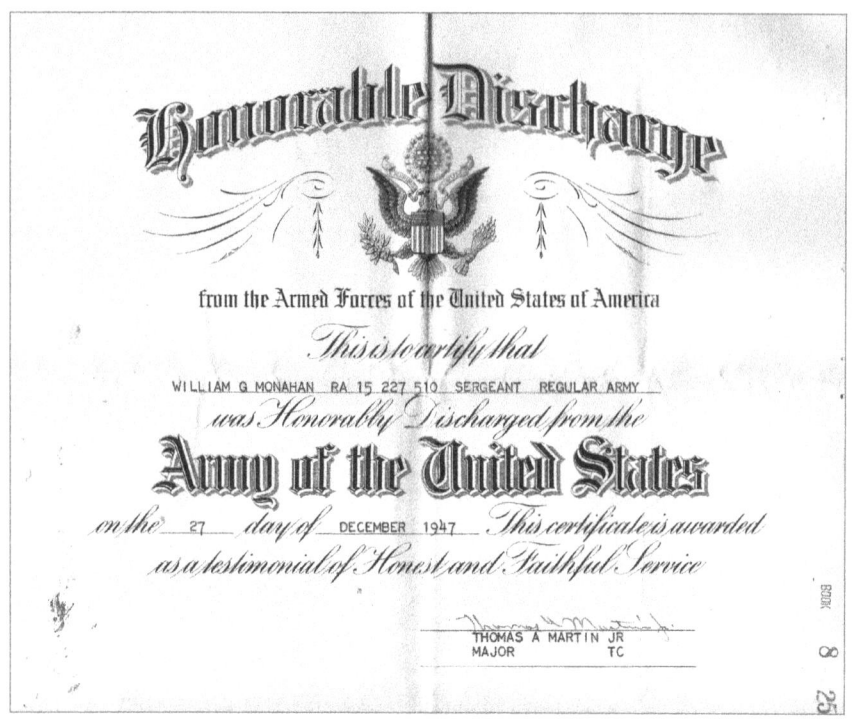

Coming Home

As it turned out, I didn't make it home for Christmas. We sailed from Japan for California in early December and disembarked for discharge processing at Camp Stoneman, California just outside San Francisco on December 20, 1947. But by the time they got to the "M's" in the alphabet, it was the day before Christmas Eve, and everything stopped. It was a particularly lonesome kind of Christmas, since we were all in a very strange place even by military standards and were allowed no leave. I spent Christmas with several guys from the old regiment whom I knew on base at Stoneman. We had a very nice Christmas dinner courtesy of the U.S. Army, and I was then discharged on December 27. I left for home on the train the next day, and Jane and her family were waiting for me in Evansville, Indiana on December 29th.

Home again and ready for whatever might await.

CHAPTER III

The Academy: Then and Now

When I think about trying to write something of what the college experience was like for me forty years ago, and in the process reflect on how things have changed since then (and as I have changed with them), comparisons with the contemporary nature of the academy seem almost pointless. Nonetheless, in these comments, I'll try to make some such comparisons. But since I want to try to remember what it was like for me and what my world was like when I went to college back there in the late 40s, my perspective is obviously one-sided. (Or, as I think about it just a little, perhaps "then-sided" would be a more exact metaphor.) In any case, I'd guess that any view from the student perspective is *always* one-sided. All college students then and now experience only a very transient set of images and experiences so far as the complexities of the academy are concerned.

College students are *in* the academic culture but not nearly so much *of* it, at least not so much as any student might believe. In a way, that is what one of my former colleagues at the University of Iowa observed during the great student upheavals in the late 60s. His notions may now seem more than a little cynical, but at that time (and even still, to a large extent) were remarkably incisive. He said the faculty don't really care all that much about what happens in the institution so long as they have a parking space, nor do the alumni so long as their teams win more than they lose, but students care, and we should care about them. Unfortunately, he said, students graduate!

I found his comments about students to be particularly the case in the early 70s when I began what turned out to be a ten-year tenure as a university academic dean. Because students had been so visible and intensively involved in so much of university affairs during the latter half of the previous decade, all of us in administrative roles who came into those roles in the early 70s were very sensitive to ensuring that students had ample opportunity to participate in the kinds of decisions that might directly affect them. Accordingly, as dean, I made certain that any college committees that dealt with such matters included student representatives. What I quickly learned was that the students we had in the late 60s, years still so closely linked to the revolutionary period of unrest consequent to the Vietnam fiasco and the celebrated Chicago riots and culminating with the Kent State tragedy, were not at all the same kinds of students we had in September of 1972 when I assumed the deanship at West Virginia University. Those more activist and militant students had graduated!

So, I learned that the students coming into the university in 1972 and most of those already there didn't want to commit their time to the kinds of issues and activities that preoccupied their immediate predecessors, at least not by way of serving on and attending academic committee meetings. Apparently, even then—that soon—a different cohort had arrived with different concerns. Or perhaps they had merely concluded that we, too—faculties and administrators—had learned some important lessons and that we could now be trusted to meet by ourselves, yet still consider their interests. More likely, as is typical of college students, they were simply "into" something else.

In retrospect, I think I sort of intuited some notions about "context" and the rather powerful idea that there is something to this age cohort set of notions that Matilda Riley and some of her Sociology colleagues have been studying closely in recent years. Their focus on social and cultural dynamics as "embodiments of long-term fluctuations in the values and meanings that shape human lives" is a compelling idea when one thinks seriously about it.[89] It helps to explain much of what is reflected in experiences with institutional

---

[89] Matilda White Riley, "On the Significance of Age in Sociology" in Matilda White Riley, ed., *Social Change and the Life Course, Vol. 1: Social Structures and Human Lives* (Newberry Park: Sage, 1988), 27.

culture from quite different time perspectives. Thus, a student, even in a single new *class*, can be quite remarkably different in many ways from similar students in a previous cohort. And not so surprisingly, the same is true of the faculty and the administration and even of those influential persons external to the institutions who help to govern it and make policy for it. Old Heraclitus was right on when he observed that a man cannot step into the same river twice—both the man and the river have changed. Obviously, the *context* makes all the difference.[90]

Accordingly, even by the early 1970s—only a very few years after the explosive events of 1968—most of our students at West Virginia University were no longer much interested in whether we did or did not have ROTC in the curriculum, whether recruiters from the DOW chemical company or the CIA came to our campus, or whether students or their representatives should be totally involved and consulted in university administration. On the contrary, even in 1972, most of our students at WVU and at most other major comprehensive universities for that matter were already considering a more self-interested ideology. Somehow, they seemed to believe that their altogether too brief sojourn with us had much more to do with their future opportunities for attaining the *good life* than with social or political activism. Their politics had moved from the left more toward the center, and the appeal that was beginning to emerge in those times by Republican (i.e., Party) interests which emphasized individual economic concerns rather than the selfless socio-economics of the past twenty years had great appeal for this new generation of college students.[91] Needless perhaps to say, almost suddenly, the more popular majors were in Business Administration or some other of our Business School's fields, and not a few of our more promising undergraduates targeted law school as their

---

[90] The full quotation: "No man ever steps into the same river twice, for it's not the same river and he's not the same man," from the *Fragments*.

[91] Obviously, as a member of that generation who started college in 1971, I think my father is exaggerating the selfishness of students in the early 70s. I think his observations would be more accurate for students in the 80s, but this is his book and not mine!

primary graduate school aims. I'd guess, in those early 70s, that our WVU law school had a real problem in trying to decide how to determine who and who not to admit.

At the same time, in my own area, the College of Education, we saw a significant decline in the number of applications for teacher education. We'd been caught up in those times in a kind of double whammy: significant national criticism about the quality and preparation of neophyte teachers on the one hand and teachers' incomes that had lagged far behind inflationary trends on the other. Accordingly, between 1970 and 1980, teacher salaries, despite much unionized activity, had simply not kept pace with other fields. Too, more popular opportunities in areas such as business and the opening up of traditionally restricted fields for women such as engineering and the sciences detracted from fields like teacher education, social work, and nursing which had been traditionally female-dominated.

Thus, between 1975 and 1985—that ten-year period—our own education fields and some others that had been traditionally female-dominated, suffered. Curiously (or maybe not so curiously in retrospect) advanced fields such as educational administration and administrative opportunities in higher education became quite popular. Most of this surge was due, again, to the opening up of more advancement opportunities for both minorities and women. In that period, though without data to support it otherwise, I'd still guess that our enrollment in HRE's various higher education program areas at the graduate level increased dramatically.[92] I do know that during some of those years, I regularly taught two particularly different required courses: one, the introductory course in public school administration that enrolled only about fifteen students; the other, a course in higher educational administration (I don't remember its designation) that enrolled about thirty students!

---

[92] "HRE": College of Human Resources and Education, West Virginia University, of which my father was dean from 1972 to 1982. It has since been renamed the College of Education and Human Services.

The Onslaught of the "Yuppies": A Heritage Unrecognized

Our undergraduate student in the 70s (and probably to a greater extent than I'd presumed, many graduate students as well) were an early cohort of the more pure strain of the so-called "baby boomers" and were intent, even if perhaps not clearly aware of it, on becoming what came to be known in the 80s as "yuppies."[93] Still, the institutions they entered in 1972 and subsequently exited several years later were much changed, and I have often wondered whether many of them understood even dimly that the radicalization of higher education during the late sixties had earned for them a recognition of rights and institutional obligations that they could take for granted only because that recognition had come at great cost.

At Western Kentucky State in the late 40s

Certainly, too, the institutions my cohort entered in 1948 were different, and so were we. As I think about it, I'm convinced that one of the greatest possible differences between college students of my generation and those of today has simply to do with the idea of obligation. There have never been successive American generations, except perhaps for a few brief years in the late 20s, that have confronted less genuine civic obligations than those that have come along since about 1975. These young adults have confronted no military conscription. They have enjoyed respectively, a long period of general tranquility and remarkable prosperity in the main, and they have inherited a legacy of egalitarianism that insures their rights to equal opportunity and protection of due process to a greater extent than any previous generations. (And, *most* curiously, some aspects of the last-mentioned of these most hard-earned achievements are now increasingly discounted as being too much the consequence of the "liberal" establishment! *Weird*!)

---

[93] "Young Upwardly Mobile Professionals"

Perhaps the lesson in that is that if you want to make a contemporary conservative Republican out of a traditionally liberal Democrat, provide him or her the means of earning enough money to become a property-owning, stock-and-bonds-trading, all-consuming Capitalist. And interesting as well, many of these "new" politically and economically well-off "conservatives" are young professionals—women and men alike—who could never have had the opportunity to have become well-informed critics of the so-called "welfare state" without the opportunities that federal regulatory agencies made for them. Curious indeed! So, despite what some conservative culture watchers today argue—to the effect that contemporary younger adults are self-interested because they have had their behavior shaped by existentialist and phenomenological philosophy—the easer truth may be that they have simply been able to give greater consideration to their own enlightened self-interest because there have been so few real external anxieties to otherwise occupy their energies.

Back in the Good 'Ol Days?

That was certainly not the case when my generation entered into the college milieu. First of all, a large proportion of us had either been in the thick of World War II or had come perilously close to it. I was one of the more fortunate latter ones. I had entered military service in 1946, almost a year after the war ended, but I spent almost my entire period of service, short though it was, in the contingent that occupied Japan. And, incidentally, based on that experience, had anyone told me that Japan would have become the prosperous and economically powerful nation that it is today, I'd have thought them out of their heads! It was a devastated, depressed, impoverished, defeated, and primitive country in 1946-47 during my time there. Interesting.

The advantage, as I have previously discussed, was that we were the beneficiaries of the G.I. Bill of Rights, which entitled us to a specified length of time in college subsidized by the government and based on a formula related to our lengths of service. Mine came to twenty-seven months, and I managed, by registering for the maximum permitted loads in most terms, to complete a baccalaureate degree right on the button. In addition to tuition, books, and reasonable supplies, as I recall, we were paid a stipend of $90 per month if single, and $120 if married. Through whatever arrangements were imaginatively managed by the institution, we were also provided housing. Most of it was little more than basic shelter, but one should remember that, after several years in the military, it didn't look so bad to us.

It had been Jane's and my plan to enter the University of Kentucky in Lexington, but there were a couple of problems with that. First, we would have had to take our turn on a long waiting list for housing, and our circumstances were such that we required university housing immediately, since we could not afford anything else. Secondly, my high school record did not include some courses required by the university, and I would have had to make those up before I could be regularly enrolled for credit in any degree program. This was most disheartening at first.

My intent had been to enroll in the School of Journalism, for I had it in my fancy to pursue a career in "newspapering." So, somewhat dejected, we returned to my home in Bowling Green, where Western Kentucky State Teachers College was located, and we decided that I would enroll there, even if only temporarily. It was Western State Teachers College at that time, and, subsequently, as it grew and prospered, it evolved first by dropping the "Teachers College" label and becoming Western Kentucky State College, and is now known as Western Kentucky University. Our contingency plan was that I would enroll at Western, pursue courses that were appropriate, and then, when housing became available in Lexington, we would transfer. In this way, we could live temporarily with my folks, difficult though that would be, and was, for everyone. But, as is often the case, our situation at Western turned out to be very satisfying, and when the time came to carry through with the plan, we decided not to do so. And not more than three or four months after enrolling, we were provided housing at Western.

I liked Western. At that time, its entire enrollment was only about 1,500 students, and I probably knew almost all of them. I had originally intended to enroll in "pre"-Journalism, but although the college offered a complement of courses in Journalism, there was no such major. I had always enjoyed Geography, and had just spent a couple of years of my life learning an awful lot of it first-hand, so I decided on that. No other of a variety of available options captured my interests, and that too seemed as good a reason as any. I guess, in truth, the question of a "major" didn't seem all that vital in any case. After all, I endured a genuine lack of confidence that I really had any business in college in the first place, and beneath the surface of consciousness, there was this little nagging notion that I'd probably flunk out anyway.

One needs to understand that, for me, the idea of college was still much enmeshed in a naïve but well-developed intuition about social structure. "People like me" didn't ordinarily to go to college, and curiously, that feeling must have been deep-seated because even in the last stages of my doctoral study, that mood was always there: that surely something would happen even at the final hour that would clearly prove I'd been right all along not to expect so much.

As a college student in 1948

Accordingly, for me, even when the work was in an easier course or with an uninspired instructor, I never felt as though my success was all that authentic. Years afterward, when, as a college teacher or administrator myself, I confronted students who seemed to exhibit a similar lack of self-esteem, I tried to make them see that such a view is not necessarily fatal. But even if I had known how to completely dispel that sense, I never would have tried because for some—as it has always been for me—that sense of impending doom, so long as it doesn't become pathological, is a source of productive motivation. Rather, I merely advised such students on more than a few occasions that for people "like us," it must be taken one piece at a time and with a little more seriousness than for others who enjoy more confidence. But given that, we would prevail. I still believe that. Much later in life, I ran onto something Whitehead said that I liked and have often repeated. He said that he was profoundly suspicious of the "A man,

> (who) can say back what you want to hear in an examination.... But the ability to give you back what is expected argues a certain shallowness and superficiality. Your 'B' man may be a bit muddle-headed, but muddle-headedness is a condition to independent thought and may be independent creative thought in its first stages."[94]

I like to think that I have always been a "B" man. In truth, though, I think that, in my case, I had a well-developed sense of something akin to what later became commonly known as "street smarts." I don't know what the arcane relationship is, exactly, between wits and intelligence, but I know that I survived more often than not in virtue of my wits.

---

[94] The quote comes from one of my father's favorite books by his favorite philosopher: Alfred North Whitehead (with Lucien Price), *Dialogues of Alfred North Whitehead as Recorded by Lucien Price* (Boston: Little, Brown, and Company, 1954), 46.

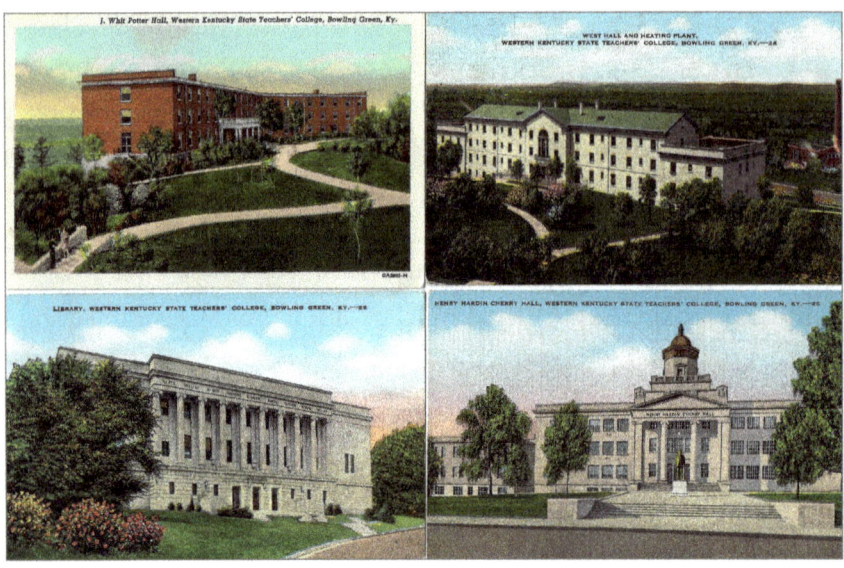

Series of old postcards showing views of Western Kentucky State College in the early 1950s when my father attended

In any case, I really had little idea of what to expect of college or of myself in the process. I didn't even know what a "college hour" was when I began the process of registering. From the briefest kinds of conversations with officials, I understood that courses were measured in such units, but how they came to be known as "hours" rather than as "units" (as in high school) remained a mystery for years. Also, there were few explicitly required courses, except for "Chapel." Otherwise, courses could be elected from larger groupings, a practice not all that different from the kind of "core" requirements that are common today. Consequently, one was expected to accumulate a required number of such courses from the various groupings: Social Science, Natural and Physical Science and Mathematics, English, Humanities, and so forth.

The requirement that all Freshmen attend "Chapel" is remarkable when I think about it. (Prior to my graduation, it was changed to "Freshman Lecture," but for all intents and purposes, it was still "Chapel.") This practice was a carry-over from the pre-war years when most public education institutions in the South were really sort of like Protestant parochial schools. At Western, in these once-weekly scheduled "Chapel" sessions, lasting usually the better part of an hour, it was common practice for one to have to endure some visiting preacher. Attendance was compulsory, and to make escape difficult, a proctor of some sort checked off one's name. Amazing!

Interestingly, I don't recall any objection to this procedure on either philosophical or legal bases, even though many of us at the time were more mature than the average college-aged students. There was much objection to the general quality of such "lectures," and much more to the policy of required attendance. Again, that had nothing to do with our first amendment rights. Rather, it was merely an imposition on our leisure. Our concerns for freedom were much more a matter of time than of ideology. By the time I had become a senior, the practice had been discontinued entirely. Again, I don't think objections by students regarding their religious attitudes had anything to do with that, though that certainly may have been the case so far as the college administration was concerned. But, like many other practices, I'd guess it was more likely that its passing was a recognition of the diversity of a student body that included a large number of veterans and spelled the beginnings of the end of the doctrine of "in loco parentis" ["in the place of a parent" (ed.)]. Many such practices just no longer seemed very reasonable.

Another advantage offered by Western over the university at Lexington was a simple matter of timing. I had been discharged from the Army the day after Christmas in 1947. Because Western was, at that time, on the Quarter System, I was able to enroll in March. Otherwise, at UK, I would have had to wait at least until the summer of '48. In retrospect, that made it possible for me to complete all of my work much more quickly. Though the academic calendar was changed while I was in college, by enrolling for the maximum load every time they opened the doors including summers, I completed all of the work for my BS by the end of the first semester in 1950. But also, in retrospect, I found that it is not propitious to finish college in mid-year. The job market doesn't function that way, and jobs, especially in teaching, were almost impossible to come by.

I did well at Western, all things considered, though I had few genuine pre-collegiate skills. My high school experiences had been chaotic and undistinguished. I had transferred across both local high schools a couple of times, mostly to participate in athletics, and had subsequently just completely dropped out in the eleventh grade and went off to join the Merchant Marine. After a short stint in that much maligned service, in which I served first as a Saloon Steward in the officer's mess aboard a Liberty ship and afterwards as an Ordinary Seaman, I returned home, got married, and returned to high school to complete my senior year.[95]

Being a merchant seaman did not exempt one from regular military service, nor did it "count" in any fashion. One worked for some shipping company rather than for the US Navy, and each time one left any ship, he was "discharged" from that one and made arrangements through the Maritime Union to hire on in another. In my case, our ship came steaming into the Sacramento River at San Francisco with a load of raw sugar from Hawaii on the night the war with Japan ended, so, of course, *nobody* on that ship intended to remain with it, though its captain tried valiantly to ensure that. He anchored the ship out in the middle of the river up near Stockton where the sugar refinery was located with the intention to buy enough time to "freeze" us through some bureaucratic maneuver.

But several of us, with the resolve of unthinking youth and a great sense of homesickness, would have no part of that! With the complicity of a sympathetic ship's officer, we bundled our belongings together in water-tight compactness, put on our swim suits, and bailed over the side into the darkest, coldest water I ever experienced. But we knew where the docks were, and they were dimly lighted, so after a very cold swim of about 150 meters, we made it without a hitch. With only a few dollars in my pockets, I enjoyed the wildest night of my life in Market Square in San Francisco, and the following day, wired home to my father for enough money to catch a bus home.

It was obvious that I would have to fulfill my service obligation, so Jane and I planned accordingly. We married two months after I quit the ship, on October 18, 1945. I secured an exemption to complete high school, and did so in June of 1946. Then, rather than be drafted

---

[95] Here, interestingly, my father offers a summary of his jobs in the Merchant Marine that is more accurate than the one he gives in the chapter *on* that service! He then follows with a few paragraphs re-summarizing his wartime service. One assumes that there was a time gap in the writing of the two chapters.

for some indeterminant amount of time, I enlisted in the army under a special eighteen-month plan. We calculated it about right. That would entitle me to about three full years of college. I guess in truth, this was more Jane's plan than my own. She always had a clear head for that sort of longer-range thinking even at the tender age of nineteen. For me, it seemed as good a plan as any, and as I've indicated, I never really gave its realization much of a serious chance.

It seems incredible perhaps that I did not even know that when one was in college, he only had to attend classes at the times and days listed in the schedule. Isn't that remarkable? That suggests another difference between then and now. Though, in general, most of us in those times had very good basic skills—in other words, we could write reasonably literate sentences, and we could read with more than adequate comprehension—we were not nearly as familiar with so-called "retrieval" skills as today's college students, and I think that is the case regardless of the size or type of institution.

My high school had an enrollment of only about 200 students, and our library was not much larger than the average classroom. It was typical practice for such facilities to be utilized as "study halls" almost every period of the day, so most of the reading that occurred there was either merely to pass the time—which meant that the magazines got heavy use—or a few people read the more appealing new novels that were acquired. But the kind of serious library usage and fundamental study-skills that every student comes to the university with now were rare. (Unfortunately, too many of them don't write half as well as even the poorest of us did then.)[96]

In any case, as a consequence, many of us didn't use the college library all that much except when we had some compelling quick need to flesh out a superficial assignment. Our instructors therefore also did not require much of that sort of work from us. I can recall only one course in all of my undergraduate work that included an outside reading list. That was a course in the Novel, and we were required to read about eight of them—largely, dreary kinds of things that I never

---

[96] And based on my own experience, I can testify that they don't necessarily arrive with great study skills either!

really enjoyed. (To this day, I still can't get through *Moby Dick*, which was one of those required, though, as I recall it, I rather liked *Moll Flanders* and *Tom Jones* even though I didn't understand all that much of those either. Most of them were wasted on me at the time.) I never had a course that had a reserve reading list until I entered graduate school to work on my MA at George Peabody College for Teachers in Nashville. Needless to say, I learned very quickly that I needed to use the library there! But those skills were self-taught, and I think I've always suffered somewhat as a consequence.

As I look back on it from my present more experienced perspective, there were other reasons for the lack of library usage. Not least of those was that libraries are expensive tools, and their inadequacy is often a target of criticism whenever accreditation teams visit. That is still the case today, and it is certainly true at West Virginia University, which, for an institution of its size and prestige, has terribly inadequate library holdings. But, more to the point, most of our instructors at Western in those days did not hold doctoral degrees. If as much as ten percent of the total faculty held such terminal degrees, I'd be surprised. Like many small state colleges today, Western was a *teaching* institution.

Though he does not mention it in his memoir, my father served as president of the Geography Club in his senior year (front row, third from left)

Accordingly, most of the faculty held Masters degrees. As a matter of fact, the MA was the standard teaching credential for college teachers in places like Western, and even many state universities had fewer than thirty percent of faculties with doctorates as late as 1955.

Nevertheless, with remarkably few exceptions, the instruction was quite good. Teachers were diligent, gave us much personal attention, knew who we were, and were wise to our tricks and deceptions. The Geography department was combined with Geology, but not much of the latter was very scientifically rigorous or comprehensive. Accordingly, the Geography piece had the most emphasis, and it was quite comprehensive. I elected a strong History minor and a second minor in English. The presumption among just about all students was that we were being prepared as teachers. Thus, almost without giving it more than a passing thought, one also followed a Teacher Education "track." That being the case, with secondary school curricula already beginning to undergo some reconstruction, so-called "Social Studies" was beginning to be more common, and the dual pattern would enable me to have two sets of teaching fields in that area plus English as a kind of "fall-back" field. But actually, it was *never* my presumption that I would become a school teacher. As a matter of fact, it was merely a curricular choice that was easily available, and I merely elected it as a kind of occupational insurance. My plan still was to become a newspaper man or a writer of some kind.

The Social Life

The social life at Western was thoroughly enjoyable. The returning force of veterans added much zest to that. When I entered Western it was college policy (and fairly well enforced) that one didn't even smoke on campus, but by the time I graduated, there were even some classes in which smoking was allowed. How quickly custom expires. Of course, smoking was as normal as breathing in those days (no pun intended). There were many married students, and the college had already begun to establish its version of married student housing for veterans with the assistance of the federal government and its surplus property functions. In the summer of 1948, Jane and I were authorized for such a unit.

The college had set aside about twenty-five acres of land it owned adjacent to the college farm and had secured several dozen trailers (now known as mobile homes). There were two sizes of these, and the idea was to take what one could get and then graduate up to something better as such became available. The first one we were assigned was a sight to behold. It was no more than twenty feet long, and as we've joked about it so many times, we could lie in the makeshift bed and open the refrigerator! It is almost literally true that if you went in the small outside door head first, you had to back out. Fortunately, we only had to endure that thing for about three weeks when we became eligible for another, larger and better outfitted one. That unit had an almost private bedroom which employed a little sliding door to separate it from the kitchen area, and it also had a small living area which included a built-in couch and room for a couple of small chairs.

View of the "Veterans Village" at Western Kentucky State Teachers College after the war showing the trailers. The bathing facilities are presumably the larger structures in the center[97]

The unit was heated—as were all of them—by small oil heaters, and the kerosene was provided as part of the rent. Each of us had a five gallon can, and we went daily to tanks suspended on racks and filled them. Also,

---

[97] Photo from Lynne E. Niedermeier, "Veterans' Village" (2007). *WKU History.* Paper 1. https://digitalcommons.wku.edu/dlsc_ua_wku_hist/1. Consulted 6 November 2020.

there were not bathing facilities in any of the units. Only cold water was piped in for cooking and drinking. There was a fairly substantial, centrally located facility with toilets and showers, and this was what we used. Jane and I have often marveled at the fact that we trudged to that place every morning to bathe, every season, frequently in the bitter cold of winter with snow on the ground and never had a head cold.

Always at the end of the month when we were paid, there was an impromptu party. Someone would instigate it, we'd kick in a share to buy a case of beer, and life would be reasonably prosperous for a few days. But we were all badly "strapped," and we saved our returnable cola and milk bottles with a passion. Toward the end of the month, not a single returnable bottle could be found anywhere. We also played a lot of bridge—it cost nothing and was thoroughly enjoyable. It was a genuine community there in the "Vet Village," and some of those friendships have survived across all the years since. Also, I'd guess that more young adults learned to play bridge in those days than ever have before or ever will again. Even between classes at the ubiquitous college hangout (at Western it was "The Goal Post"), there was always a bridge game in progress. When one person had to leave to attend a class, someone else just took that place.

The "Goal Post" in Bowling Green, Kentucky[98]

---

[98] Photo from the Western Kentucky University archives: https://digitalcommons.wku.edu/wku_timeline/119/ (consulted 15 January 2021).

In those times, there were several big college dances each year, and these were the highlights of the college social calendar. It was rare that we were able to bring in some well-known "name" orchestra for these dances, so usually, our own sort of "franchised" college dance band performed. Our band was "the Red and Grey," and it was franchised to the extent that whoever led the group owned the music and the stands, and when he graduated, someone else would buy it. Even when I had been in high school, I had been a vocalist with several different itinerant regional orchestras, so when I got to Western, I became the vocalist with the Red and Grey, too.[99]

Pictured far right (beside a bass he didn't play!) with the Red and Grey Orchestra

As I think about that, it occurs to me how much technology influences musical patterns. In those days, we purchased "stock" arrangements which we sort of revised to our own needs and capacities, but all of these were based on the pattern then characteristic of 78 RPM records. That is, such an arrangement consisted of going

---

[99] Actually, according to a letter from his oldest brother to the family in 1944, he had sung with the Red and Grey band while in high school. See Appendix B.

through an entire ballad, for example, and then returning to the "bridge" and repeating just the chorus and the final verse. That's the way everything was written and performed because that was the limit of what a 78 RPM record could "hold." Moreover, there was not electronic music at all, thus no guitars or electric basses. We used drums, piano, and string bass for our rhythm complement. Typical too was a reed section of maybe five pieces and usually three trumpets and two trombones for the brass. But we did make *very* good music. The vocalists—there were usually two of us, male and female—were the lowest paid members, and in addition to singing, my job was also to set up the stands, the sound system, such as it was, and arrange the stage. Generally, for a three-hour dance, I was paid about ten dollars.

These big dances were regularly scheduled as part of the college tradition, and each one marked a particular event in the academic year. Thus, we always had a Military Ball when those of us in ROTC (almost all veterans were in ROTC because we received a small compensation for that) wore our uniforms, and at all dances, we crowned some kind of Queen, which was a big deal for the co-eds. Another big dance at Western in those days was the Talisman Ball, so named as celebration of the publication of the college yearbook whose title was *The Talisman*.

These were very formal dances, and although men didn't wear tuxedos, they were required to wear suits or coats and ties. The girls always wore formal dresses, and it was assumed that one's date (whether wife or girlfriend) would be provided a corsage of gardenias or carnations or an orchid. Also, these dances had "programs" which meant that when one entered and presented his tickets, one received this little program which the girl kept. It included and listed a series of about five or six pre-determined "no-breaks" which the girls scheduled by writing in the name of a man when approached and properly asked, and if she was so inclined. This meant that during these special numbers, she would be obligated to dance the entire song only with the man whose name was penciled in for that number. It needs to be understood that not all of the young men would have dates for these dances and were thus admitted (at a lesser charge) as "stags." So, it was common and accepted practice for men to "cut in" on a dancing couple, and if the man acquiesced, he would relinquish the lady to the person "cutting in." The idea of a female "stag" simply would not have occurred to anyone in those days. The "no-breaks" insured that for at least some songs, no one could "cut in." And these were always slow dances rather than "jump tunes." Very romantic.

Talisman Ball, 1950

Dancing was a completely different activity then. Probably, dancing is as good a manifestation of generation and era and period as any of our youthful rituals. In those days, however, dancing was a more precise and performed kind of ritual than the bouncing-by-yourself kind of solo carrying-on that characterizes the modern time. It was an activity that had to be learned, and it was carried through with a series of meaningful and precise maneuvers that were pleasant to do or to watch. Not everyone was good at it, to be sure, but most were, and it was great fun. There were small stalls at each end of the college gymnasium where these dances were held where one could get soft drinks. Alcohol was strictly forbidden, which not only chafed the sensibilities of some of us older veterans, it also provided a great challenge. And although few people ever got out of hand, booze was always surreptitiously smuggled in and very carefully consumed. There were always assigned "chaperones" from the long-suffering faculty, and they were content that their presence alone and our clear understanding of the consequences were sufficient to keep things orderly. And that did work. Anyone who drank too much was generally handled by other students with dispatch, for otherwise, it would have spoiled the affair for everybody else. After these dances—they usually ended by midnight—groups of celebrants would gather at some local late-night eatery to relive the evening and finish it off with bacon and eggs. It was all most enjoyable, and each dance was something to look forward to and plan for many weeks in advance.

I can still so clearly remember that one of the more popular establishments prior to a big college dance was the local pressing-and-shoe-shine-parlor—all of our so-called dress-up clothes in those days were dry-clean-only fabrics. We wanted to be sure that our pants were pressed smartly and our shoes brightly shined. "Gus's Shoe-Shine Parlor" on Main Street next to the Capitol Theatre in downtown Bowling Green was always a bee-hive of activity on any dance day. We'd retire to one of his several little dressing rooms, pass out our pants, and wait patiently while they were pressed to a sharp set of creases that would almost cut your finger! All during the late afternoons there would be a steady stream of customers, and the conversations were ripe with anticipation and excitement.

The "13ers"

Fraternities and Sororities were not authorized at Western in those days, but we had something roughly equivalent to them in the form of "Clubs." Needless to say, these were not sanctioned by the College but were tolerated since, for all intents and purposes, they were organized and sustained by students themselves apart from any official recognition. In many ways, these clubs imitated Fraternities and Sororities, and much of what we did in them was often foolish and raunchy. But in other ways, they provided a special social group and activities that contributed to our life as students.

Pledging the Thirteeners (bottom right) from a yearbook page unofficially devoted to the Club

In my period there were two dominant male clubs, the "Barons" and the "13ers." I was invited to join the "13ers" since many of our friends were members of that club. There were a couple of similar kinds of clubs for females, but I can't remember what those were called. We had officers and regular meetings and looked after the management of our very meager resources, which included a "cabin" out in the countryside on the river, and which was always in a state of pristine "becoming." The cabin was a fairly large, dilapidated facility, and we spent many Saturdays working on it, and that was a marvelous excuse for partying as well. (We didn't need much of an excuse.)

As was typical of collegiate "secret societies," there was a ritual one had to endure as a pledge, and sometimes the hazing involved did get a bit out of hand. As the institution matured and evolved across the years, it is my understanding that these old clubs evolved into full-fledged social fraternities within the established national framework.[100] In those

---

[100] The Thirteeners eventually became the Epsilon Xi chapter of the Delta Tau Delta fraternity on the Western Kentucky University campus.

days, it was sufficient that we had a group of our own with our own special affairs. Among the latter was a spring banquet and dance usually held at some private country club in the area at which everybody got very drunk. Yet, those clubs provided lifelong friendships, and even still today, Jane and I enjoy visiting with some of those men and women that we came to know well through the "13ers."

Robert "Bob" Proctor, senior class photo

And the membership was mixed between some of us who were married and others who weren't. Among some of those lasting friendships were Bob and "Pete" Proctor, and J. H. Cowles, whom we still see at least once or twice a year. Bob worked during his collegiate years in a "do-everything" role at the local radio station and hosted an afternoon "DJ" program that was very popular with the college crowd. Collegiate radio was unheard of in most places in those days, and Bob's station was the only local one. His wife, "Pete" (I don't think anyone ever called her by her "real" name, Opal) had also grown up in Bowling Green where her father had managed a riverside city water works facility, and, taking advantage of a naturally agreeable location, established a very popular swimming facility there.[101] It was managed by "Pete's" mother Goldie, who had a great sense of humor and often acted as surrogate mother to dozens of unruly "river rats" who spent most of many summer days at that Barren River "beach."

There were no municipal pools, although Western had a spacious one which it opened to the public on a very restricted basis. (One had to use college-owned swimming suits, outrageously ugly cotton things that, whatever color they might have been, had all become a bilious shade of green due to long use in heavily chlorinated water—most of us preferred the river!) Needless to say, "Pete" was a superb swimmer. Had she come along in these times, with "natatoria" and good coaching commonly available, she might well have been a champion.

Joseph "J. H." Cowles, senior class photo

J. H. Cowles is another whose friendship has remained continuous across those years. Always somewhat conservative in both style and opin-

---

[101] Because Opal "Pete" Proctor was not a student, there is unhappily no class photograph of her.

ion, "Jay" had a taciturn kind of dry wit—still does—and was always good company. He completed the ROTC program at Western and went on to a quite distinguished career in the U.S. Army, retiring at a field grade rank.[102]

When I attended Peabody College some years later, I reconnected with several other former "13ers," and during my first summer there, in 1953, several of us shared an apartment. One of those I particularly remember was Bill Myles, but during our undergraduate days, he was not really known to most of us as "Bill."[103] (In retrospect, I'm not sure I even knew his given name in those days.) In those days, for us "13ers," he was affectionately known as "Pig" Myles. It's curious as to why he ever might have been so called, and I never knew why. He was certainly not "piggish" in any sense of that idea—tall, handsome, and smart as a whip. By the same token, that nickname was never used by any of us who knew him with anything other than affection and had no more meaning than is attached to any pet name. Some of us were often called by far worse. But, from conversations with others since then, I've come to realize that he didn't like the name much. I wish he'd told us so.

Another former Western "13er" who shared our Nashville apartment was a chap named Al Simpson.[104] He went on to a distinguished career as a school administrator in Kentucky but suffered an untimely death from cancer. Al was just about the most "up" person I've ever known. Almost *nothing* ever got the best of him, and I remember how agonized I was about some upcoming test that I confronted, and Al said to me, "have you studied for it?" And I said, "yes, I studied a lot." And he said, "well, forget it, you'll do ok!" And I did. Al sort of "rode herd" on us during that summer. He made sure that we did our work and took care of our obligations. He was very good for us although he was wilder than a march hare when the pressure was off. But, back to Western.

---

[102] Joseph H. Cowles fought in Vietnam and reached the rank of Lieutenant-Colonel, according to his obituary in 2001.

[103] Unfortunately, there is no sign of Bill Myles (under any spelling) in either of the two surviving Western Kentucky yearbooks from my father's time there.

[104] Again, there is no sign of an Al Simpson in either of the two yearbooks, meaning that he had probably already graduated before my father attended.

Married Student Life

Being a married college student was a new development for both the colleges and for us as students, yet the institution managed that remarkably well in retrospect. Colleges found that married students were rather solid citizens who were fairly serious about their work and who presented very few problems as students. For our part, those of us who were married had a fairly difficult time making proverbial "ends" meet. Jane had previously finished a year-long course at Bowling Green Business University, which was, incidentally, then nationally recognized in its fields, and consequently, she had some marketable skills in stenography and office management. She secured a job rather quickly with a small loan firm. She never enjoyed that because she saw so many people whom she was always convinced were being taken advantage of by the very high interest rates, and who had to mortgage their belongings to get loans. She worked five and a half days per week, and as I recall, earned about $22.50. A few years later, she secured a much better job with the state highway department, but for most of our college years, she worked at the loan company. I also worked when and where I could, mostly as a clerk in department stores on Saturdays. I would work from eight in the morning until nine at night on for fifty cents an hour, and usually, we used my $4.50 to have a sandwich and go to a movie on Saturday night (and still had a couple of dollars left over). Jane was a good manager, and we survived reasonably well, all things considered. Sometimes, too, we would join a group of other couples and go dancing at a particularly popular "road house" known as the Dixie Belle, or in the summer months, to another popular spot on the river known as "McFarland's Beach" with an intimate open-air dance floor suspended on the side of the bluff. But one of our most favorite watering holes was the Moose Club.

Kentucky did not permit liquor by the drink, so there were no cocktail lounges or taverns except for beer. Liquor was sold in "package stores," and when one went to a roadhouse, one ordered "setups" and concocted mixed drinks surreptitiously and carefully from the hidden bottle on the floor. But, apparently, the law allowed for liquor by the drink at private fraternal clubs such as the Elks and the

Moose. Because the Moose Club was located conveniently in the heart of town, did not cost much to join, and provided a most economical opportunity for an evening of pleasant conversation without much need for a lot of imbibing, it was the club of choice for our crowd. It also usually employed a small music combo from among our acquaintances in the "Red and Grey" orchestra, which added to its merits. Its bartender was not exactly an accomplished virtuoso, so whatever one ordered with gin in it except for a martini came out exactly the same as any other, but the price was right—about fifty cents, and beer was available at fifteen cents a bottle. The ritual of induction was all male and like something right out of Jackie Gleason's "Honeymooners," but on those occasions, there was also a grand spread of food and drink, and we almost never missed one.

Closer to the campus, we also frequented a popular barbecue place that served beer and excellent hickory-fired barbecue sandwiches and dinners. The place was named after its proprietor, "Bill Hardin's," and though occupying a kind of ramshackle, rough wooden building that had grown like "Topsy," it was a favorite place to gather and unwind, especially after exams.[105]

---

[105] The term "growed like Topsy," describing something that grew or increased by itself, without apparent design, originates with a character in Harriet Beecher Stowe's *Uncle Tom's Cabin*. Asked who had made her, the character Topsy answered "I spect I grow'd. Don't think nobody ever made me." This is the kind of cultural reference that someone raised in the South in the 30s might be expected to know!

Our Succession of Used Cars

Even though we had little money, it was increasingly obvious that we needed some kind of transportation. There was no public transportation of any kind locally, and when we occasionally wanted to visit Jane's folks in the western part of the state, we had to take the bus. Otherwise, and around town and campus, we just walked. During my time in service, we had managed to save almost a thousand dollars, and in about 1949, I talked Jane into spending a big hunk of it for a used car. We laugh a lot about that now, but in those days, our experiences with used cars weren't so entertaining. It really never occurred to us to try and buy a new car because we simply could not have made payments, so we bought a used Chrysler and paid cash for it.

One must remember that we were just coming out of the war, and cars were very precious. Our first purchase was a 1938 Chrysler coach, a two-door sedan. The guy we bought most of our cars from in Bowling Green surely must have seen us coming, for we bought several cars from him, each time trading up a year or so. We subsequently traded the Chrysler for a 1939 Plymouth four-door and that one for a 1941 Dodge. The Dodge was a fairly good car, but all of them were little more than jalopies. We didn't buy a new car until 1956, when I accepted a job with the Kentucky State Department of Education, but among the best used cars we ever owned was a 1951 Kaiser which we bought when I was teaching and coaching in Marion, Kentucky. It was a splendid automobile, and long after we had traded it in on the new Ford Station Wagon in 1956, I used to see it all around the streets of Marion.

Greg in the front seat of the 1951 Kaiser, ca 1955

A 1951 Kaiser

But those early used cars were mostly worn out by the time we got them, although we paid more for each than any of them had cost when new. That's how inflation and scarcity had driven up the price of cars during the war. Still, they provided us adequate transportation, and we were able to drive to Marion without more than an occasional mechanical problem. Gasoline was only about twenty cents a gallon, and most of those cars used as much oil as gas. Jane still says that we were real suckers for buying most of those rattle traps, but, in truth, almost everybody else was in about the same boat, and they did fill the bill for us. But I can still remember when Bob Proctor bought a very fancy Hudson, either new or almost new, and we all thought it about the sleekest, most comfortable vehicle possible.[106]

The End of an Era

I finished my B.S. at the end of the first semester in 1950-51, and my degree was conferred the following June. I wasn't able to attend that commencement since, by that time, I was working for the Southern States Cooperative as a Management Trainee. But *that* is another, though non-distinctive story. I wasn't very good at it, to say the least, and we parted company by very mutual agreement.[107] In the fall of 1952, I began my career in the field of Education, not having the remotest idea that I would devote a lifetime to it.

My time as an undergraduate student certainly changed my life and my life chances much more than I could have ever possibly imagined at the time. It was an altogether pleasant and satisfying set of experiences, and Western Kentucky State Teachers College (no matter that it has since grown up and evolved into a first-rate state university) was, and remains, very special to my success such as it has been. More so, Western is special in my memory for having captured me in a time

---

[106] Despite a love of cars that lasted his entire life, my father did not take photos of his cars until 1968, when he bought a beautiful 1963 Austin Healey 3000 sports car. Until then, photos of family cars were incidental to those of family members. Thus, the only surviving photo of our Kaiser exists because I was sitting in it.

[107] According to a few surviving letters to my mother, he really hated the job, not least because traveling for it took him away from her for long periods. Having suffered a "distance relationship" while in the army, he was disinclined to do it again.

and a circumstance that was probably just about right for me then. I'm convinced that it marked one of the several most significant turning points in my life, and I don't think any of what has happened to me since could probably have happened otherwise. There is a "motto" at the base of a statue of Western's most revered president, Henry Hardin

The statue of Cherry still stands at Western Kentucky University

Cherry, that stands on a promenade near the front of "Cherry Hall"—the building that bears his name—and this statue occupies the most prominent point at the "top of the hill," which accounts for Western's collegiate name: "The Hilltoppers." The motto, etched into a granite base of the statue, is scripted in a kind of awkward scrawl, and it reads: "The Spirit Makes the Master." And you know, as far as I am concerned, it turns out to be just about right. Moreover, in all of the several really great universities with which it has been our privilege to have been associated, that "motto" is applicable to all of them.

"Spirit" is a curiously elusive notion, but nowhere is it more apparent than in colleges and universities. In every university that Jane and I have enjoyed, whether as students or faculty, the idea of "spirit" has been vital. We fought with Western's "Hilltoppers," rejoined or died with Michigan State's "Spartans," enjoyed sustained pride with Oklahoma's "Sooners," wept, died, and were reborn with Iowa's "Hawkeyes," and learned about the heights and the depths of emotions with the mighty "Mountaineers" at West Virginia University. Yet, in each place, the "spirit" echoed so much more than the successes or failures of our athletic teams, for these are merely important symbols of institutional culture, and withal, there was always the special feeling of accomplishment that characterized these institutions as manifestations of the triumphs of the collegiate spirit—of young people setting off to become something more and of faculties and staffs and alumni all enjoying the satisfactions of sharing in quite significant achievements as being part of the very special idea of belonging to *something* that is larger than each of us. In truth, that is what makes colleges and universities unique. It has been a particular satisfaction to have known and to have participated for so many years in that very special kind of institutional existence.

Who could possibly have enjoyed a better or a more spirited life? Indeed, though most of us fall considerably short of becoming "masters" in any sense of that idea, the "spirit" that we are infected with in our collegiate lives does imbue even the least of us with an indelible sense of the idea of community, a togetherness of purpose and contemplation and activism that truly means that if indeed the "spirit" doesn't *make* the master, it most surely molds the potential.

Senior class photo

Western Kentucky State College diploma

CHAPTER IV

On Becoming an Educator

Until I accepted an appointment as Dean of the College of Human Resources and Education at West Virginia University in 1972, my experiences with collegiate teacher education had been miniscule.[108] Almost all of my experiences in the professoriate had been exclusively at the graduate level. I was involved in some undergraduate teaching during five years that I was on the faculty at the University of Oklahoma, and though at that time, I taught courses in the teacher education program, I was still quite aloof from any of the genuine issues, problems, and curricular concerns involved in the processes by which young people pursue programs leading to licensure as novice teachers. I mention that only to emphasize that once I became a dean at a university school of education, I quickly realized how little I really knew about that significant piece of such enterprises. Of course, I also learned that there is a great deal that I didn't know about many things in those early days of "deaning," and in truth, throughout a long career in the academy, I have come to be particularly impressed by a remarkable increase in *many* things that I know nothing about!

But I mention it as well to introduce the idea that, regardless of what an army of critics have had to say across those critical years between about 1975 and 1985 about the inadequacies of teacher training, what our students at WVU learned in the early 70s in pursuit of a variety of teacher education options was a literal quantum leap in preparation and sophistication compared to my own program

---

[108] The name of the College was changed in 2012 to the College of Education and Human Services.

at Western Kentucky State at the end of the 40s. And I should add that what our teacher education students at WVU in the 90s have the opportunity to learn as they are prepared to teach is still another remarkable leap over what those in the early 70s experienced. What that suggests is that the program I pursued at Western Kentucky State was little more than an orientation to school teaching. Whatever I might have done reasonably well in actual practice was therefore a simple matter of muddling through. As I look back on it, my program was based on the "deep water model." You throw people in, and they either learn to swim or they drown. That's a dramatically instructive model to be sure, but one does tend to lose a disproportionate number of learners in the process. Now, to be sure, our *theoretical* preparation was fairly good—we learned a lot about curriculum issues—but when it came to actually conducting classes with kids who'd have preferred to be anyplace other than in school, we didn't learn all that much.

In my teacher preparation, such as it was, Western utilized its own Training School for what was felicitously known as student teaching. Most teachers' colleges and many quite good state universities in those times had such schools attached, and they were called by several names: Demonstration schools, Laboratory schools, or Training schools. But their general function was the same: practicing at teaching and observing fulltime professional teachers *doing* it. Additionally, for some of the more renowned of such institutions, as for example, the University of Iowa's nationally recognized Training School and George Peabody College's Demonstration School, much educational research was conducted, and across a whole variety of pedagogical concerns. Accordingly, there were only a few such schools in those times that were particularly renowned for their research work, and most of these collegiate "attached" Training Schools were recognized for their superb instruction. (Of course, one must realize that even the worst of such schools still enrolled kids who were quite selectively admitted and thus were already pre-conditioned to academic expectations.)

Accordingly, these collegiate training schools were particularly good for several reasons: First of all, they employed the best instructors, since typically, teachers in such schools not only earned comparatively better salaries but also enjoyed status (and often academic rank) in the university faculty itself, and that brought a variety of other advantages. Secondly, these teachers enjoyed a more motivated and docile student body since, all too often, these schools enrolled predominantly faculty children who'd already been conditioned to understand the value and function of education. Finally, instructors in these kinds of college-attached institutions were often more intimately familiar with well-known university faculty in their various specialties, which gave them a whole variety of opportunities for cutting-edge kinds of teaching advantages.

But all such university schools are increasingly rare today. They have passed out of existence for several reasons, not least of which is that the numbers of undergraduate education majors seeking to teach have outgrown the capacities of such collegiate training schools to accommodate them, and colleges of education, beginning in around 1960 or so, have had to seek cooperative arrangements with the public schools in their regions for that purpose. Also, such schools were not considered worth their costs to university administrators in the face of competing and presumably more direct functions that ranked higher in institutional priorities. Finally, in not a few cases, such schools were too frequently captured by special interest groups and became sort of "special interest" prep schools for faculty children. Thus, almost any research performed was too biased by higher than average achieving student bodies for it to be generalizable. Accordingly, by the end of the 1960s, many such schools had simply disappeared.

In My Own Case

In my college years as a teacher-education student, one registered for the practice teaching courses over at the Training School no differently than any other college course, and one went over to the Training School at the scheduled hour, did what was required, and after that period of time—maybe two clock hours—returned to other pursuits. It was common for one to have additionally scheduled regular college classes during the same term that the student teaching course was pursued. It wasn't until much later that the practice developed whereby the student teacher spent all or the larger portion of an entire semester in real school classrooms, full time, and that alone has made an enormous difference in the quality of training. One can then imagine how truly unprepared most of those of us were who endured the older pattern. It was little more than a passing glance at what is really involved in the teaching-learning process.

Finding a Job in 1951

When I finished my college degree in January 1951, it was the middle of winter, and I made no effort to find a teaching post, since I presumed that what I was told—that mid-year appointments were simply not to be had—was true. But I had no compelling desire to teach school anyway, and instead began to look about for something "more worthy" to occupy my skills. Of course, truth be known, I really didn't have any genuinely marketable skills, for at that time, there was no great outcry for novice Geographers. I finally found work as a "management trainee" with the Southern States Cooperative, a relatively new and struggling farmer-owned operation that was valiantly trying to engage farmers in the pattern of Granges and Farm Bureau "Co-ops" that had proved quite successful in the upper Midwest. This was a kind of new thing for many Kentucky farmers, and although the organization had done well in the mideast, particularly in Virginia and Maryland (its home offices were in Richmond), the beachhead it wanted to establish in Western Kentucky was often agonizing. The piece of the organization with which I became associated was aimed at providing farmers with petroleum products—gasoline, oils, compressed gases for heating, and so forth—and was separate from its more established and somewhat more successful feed-seed-and-fertilizer operations.

After a rather brief period of training that took me to Maryland and Delaware, I was appointed as the Manager of one of the Company's new facilities in Franklin, Kentucky.[109] Incidentally, one of the nicer things

---

[109] There is still a Southern States Cooperative operation in Franklin, Kentucky as of this writing.

about that entire experience was a visit from Jane during my training period in Delaware. She came all the way up there on the "B&O" railroad, and I met her in Baltimore, and we were able to spend a week together while I worked in Delaware. At that time, we stayed in an older couple's home in a small town near Dover, and since the man whose home we lived in there also owned a local appliance store, we enjoyed evenings watching TV down in his store—and one must remember that TV was altogether rather new in those days. In truth, there wasn't much else to do. That Jane came all that way on the train was itself quite adventurous. She had only a chair seat, and the trip must have taken fifteen hours or so, and it cost us more than we could otherwise afford.[110]

In any case, my experience with Southern States was dreary work to say the least, not only physically taxing since it often required us to dig huge holes into which we submerged gasoline storage tanks of various sizes, but, as well, we had to deliver fuel with vehicles and equipment that were almost constantly in disrepair. I also quickly learned that a "manager" was required to do just about as much work as even the lowliest of our employees. It was equally dreary in the frustrating effort to try to convince farmers that the organization was in their best interests. The parent company required us to maintain elaborate inventories of *everything* (which just never seemed to "check out" correctly), and each evening at the end of a work day, it was my sole responsibility to climb up a precarious ladder attached to one of several large storage tanks to measure the levels of gasoline or fuel oil therein. This required "chalking" a steel measuring tape and running it down into the tank, and this had to be done every day in all seasons. There were times in the dead of winter when, even at that adventurous age of twenty-five or so when little else was daunting, I still felt just a little insecure to be fifty feet up, wind blowing a gale, and ice covering the small cat-walks at the top of those huge tanks as I tried to measure the capacity of those tanks. The whole idea, of course, was to reconcile the amount of fuel we had delivered with the amount remaining in our supply. Needless perhaps to say, it seldom worked out with much precision.

---

[110] Several letters from my father survive from this period, including a fair number of discussions of early television sets!

Among the more painfully implicit things I learned from my experiences with Southern States is that farmers have to be among the most obdurate and suspicious class of people I have ever known! Based on that experience, at least, I concluded that they are indeed their own worst enemies. Some of them thought we were socialists or worse, and would stubbornly remain with some existing firm that provided inferior equipment at higher cost. Strange! In any case, it soon became obvious that this was not a right career choice for me. In late summer, Southern States and I reached a parting of the ways.

Teaching Certificate

An "Accidental Tourist" Finds a Job

Jane's father had been a member of the school board in Marion, Kentucky, a small far-west Kentucky town where she grew up, and at that time, there was a vacancy for a high school social studies teacher and assistant athletic coach. He genuinely thought that I might make a passably effective teacher, and since I enjoyed having graduated with a teaching credential that was still valid, with his influence, I was able to secure that post in the Marion, Kentucky school system.

The Marion Kentucky School Board in 1952.
My mother's father, Clarence Newcom, is at far right

I began my work there in the Fall of 1952. After my experiences with "agricultural socialism," I was much less negative about teaching school but still was not ready to think of it as anything approaching a life's work. Certainly, I had some other reservations about this turn of events. I would be living close to Jane's parents, for the town was quite small—about 2,500 counting cats and dogs—and Jane's father's considerable reputation in the community put added pressure on me. Also, I had real anxieties about the work, for as soon as I fully realized that I would very soon confront classes of real kids in a real school, I also began to realize how little prepared for it I was. But I liked my wife's parents, and they liked me. My father-in-law was a first-class person, and he and I had always gotten along very well. My own father had died in 1949 when I was still hardly an adult, and Jane's dad treated me more like a son than is often the case with in-laws. Thus, much of that part of the discomfort was not of great consequence.

Learning to Teach

As I have previously indicated, I really learned to teach while doing it.[111] To some extent that is always the case for everyone who teaches, but I would have been so much better at it had I known more about the nature of the "pedagogical encounter." Consequently, I now realize that I developed many bad habits and practice only perfected them. But the great difference between then and now was that public school students were themselves so different. They came from a different world of parental attitudes and a different set of values regarding what their role as a student amounted to and how they should accept it. In that small town in those times, "teacher" was still a title of considerable respect, and those of us who did it were held in remarkable esteem. That any student might have openly defied the authority of teachers or schools or engaged in the kinds of deviant behaviors that are now common, nor when any parent confronted a problem with a student severe enough to have required that their attention be called to it by the school and who might thereby not accept

---

[111] And here, I don't think he gives himself enough credit. As his letters written while he was in the army in Japan indicate (see Appendix A), he had already learned some rudiments of teaching at that time and developed something of an aptitude for it.

that school as being almost automatically in the "right"—any of that was simply unthinkable. Needless to say, that context made teaching a much easier set of tasks than is the case today. So, for the most part, pupils in those times came to the schools with no chips on their shoulders and were conditioned by the nature of their circumstances and attitudes to expect to learn and to be taught. Contrarily, too many in the contemporary world come with sullenness or boredom or the cavalier arrogance of an already all-knowing sophistication. Accordingly, the work of the teacher in the present time is much more stressful and exhausting. Since one of my own sons is now a public school teacher, I am made even more aware of the facts of the matter.

The salary when I began there was $2,500 for the year, and that included about $300 that I received additionally for the coaching work. But there was no tax on that, so it was all "take-home." Needless to say, Jane had also to find some work in order for us to do at all well, and she subsequently secured a position as a secretary at a nearby military base [Camp Breckinridge (ed.)]. Unfortunately, this required her to carpool for about an eighty-mile round-trip commute every day, and that was very trying, especially so, when soon thereafter, she became pregnant with our first child.

"Old" Marion High School building

I began the work of teaching with considerable apprehension, having little knowledge of the "tricks-of-trade" in how to handle disciplinary problems, or how best to work up lesson plans, manage the all-important "attendance register," construct and administer appropriate tests, and apply the proper methods for assigning marks, and all the other things that I had no idea teachers were expected to do. But I learned quickly, and while I tended too much to teach as I had been taught—by lecturing and talking too much—I also learned that when one is heavily loaded through the entire day, one has to find other ways to do the job. Thus, I also learned how to question and to probe and to engage the students in often exciting dialogue. And I began to like it and was beginning to be acknowledged as rather good at it.

My father, far left, as part of the three-man coaching staff at Marion High School

It was the conventional assumption that the only way one advanced in the profession—and that is still the case—was by further advancing credentials, and the only way to do that was to endure additional schooling. There was little so-called in-service education as that term is currently employed, and the common practice was to enroll in some college somewhere during the summer to gain additional training. Jane and I talked a lot about that, and when it became reasonably accepted that teaching would be something that would occupy us for more than just the foreseeable future, we began to consider our alternatives in that regard.

A number of my colleagues in the school—most of them, as a matter of fact—typically attended Murray State Teachers College, which was not too far away and therefore more accessible than Western. Since Murray had always been *the* great rival of Western, my still immature heart simply couldn't abide the prospect of attending Murray! More importantly, neither of those more accessible state institutions offered the MA degree teaching fields, and I wanted to begin work somewhere that would allow me to pursue a continuing program that would lead to a degree without having to worry about transferring credit and all that sort of thing. Jane and I decided on George Peabody College for Teachers in Nashville, Tennessee.

Peabody College was not all that far away and enjoyed an acknowledged and deserved reputation as the best of its kind in the South and among the half dozen best of its kind anywhere. I must admit, however, that at the time, I knew almost nothing of it other than its reputation. We did know, however, that it was a private institution and was expensive. Nevertheless, we began to check into Peabody as a real possibility, and since it looked very good, all other things considered, we began to save some money with Peabody in mind. During the first summer in Marion, I worked for the School Board. Together with several other male teachers, including our entire coaching staff (three of us!), we did maintenance chores—repaired bleachers at the football field, painted buildings, and other similar odd jobs. But finally, by the summer of 1953, Jane and I had saved enough to give Peabody a try.

Graduate School

I secured catalogues, applied for and was authorized admission, followed procedure, investigated accommodations, and all the other things that one must do when planning such a venture; and then showed up at the appointed time for matriculation. I was assigned a dormitory room on the Vanderbilt University campus, met with my major advisor, completed the appropriate registration processes, paid my substantial fees, and purchased my several (also expensive) textbooks, and by about 5 o'clock of a long and tiring day, found my way to my room. And that was most depressing. It was about what one would expect to be provided to a Trappist Monk! A small, unventilated room; a bed not unlike what the Army had provided me, and a desk little larger than a bed tray. There was a free-standing wardrobe of sorts that would hold a few belongings and two or three ancient and rusting metal coat hangers. To say that the room was Spartan is something of an overstatement. There was no plumbing in the room, and the bath was a "gang-john" half a mile down the corridor. And it was hot!

No one can imagine what Nashville is like in the heat of summer who has not experienced it firsthand. I had no sheets nor mattress cover since I was not aware that I would have to provide those myself. The mattress, suffering from long use, was rolled over on the small cot, and the whole place smelled of stale non-use, not unclean of course, only unused. I had seen no familiar faces at this place, knew no one, nor had I found my conversations with my new advisor particularly encouraging. Now, though married for a number of years by this time, I was still only in my mid-twenties and terribly naïve. Needless to say, I found the entire situation to be lonely and disheartening.

J. Russell Whitaker

I had indicated a "Social Science" area as my preferred major, but this meant that I needed to choose from about equal portions of content from two sub-fields. Since my previous work had been in Geography and History, those were my choices, and with Geography as the leading focus, I had been directed to that Department for academic guidance. My "advisor" turned out to be a Dr. J. Russell Whitaker, (full) professor, who had written widely in the field of Conservation.

With several books to his credit, he was apparently a grand scholar in Geography, and I felt that he suffered my assignment to him lightly, to say the least. He asked me only a few pointed questions, examined my transcripts equally briefly and without enthusiasm, and then quickly penciled off the ubiquitous yellow pad, several courses that he decided would be appropriate for me. The entire interview lasted perhaps ten minutes, and he ended it by directing me to the History Department where, he indicated, I would be similarly advised regarding that work.

*Old postcard showing the main buildings of
George Peabody College for Teachers in the early 1950s*

By the time that afternoon was over, I had a complete listing of all the work that I needed to complete my Masters Degree, and, in retrospect, the system worked remarkably well. But, reflecting on that impressive listing of work to be done and in the confines of that small, severely institutional dormitory room, my melancholy mood might be understandable. I remember briefly examining my set of brand new (expensive) and altogether intimidating textbooks, and they seemed to exude a kind of newly-printed smell of foreboding difficulty. So, needless to say, my first night there, quite totally alone and completely aware of my insecurities, was discomforting and dispiriting. I was very close to loading up the car and driving home.

Things Looked Up

The following day, however, my humor brightened. I met several former "Westerners" of my acquaintance, and before the day was done, we had agreed that our separate dismal circumstances could be greatly improved were we to pool our resources and share quarters together. Accordingly, we were able to rent and share a nearby, fairly spacious apartment with a most adequate kitchen where we could prepare our own meals. In the bargain, I was able to withdraw from my dormitory commitment and recover my costs. Pooling our rather meager assets in this fashion promised a more pleasant summer, and such it turned out to be. Thus, I began to look with more favor on this new experience.

Painting the Streets

I think at this point, I must admit to an unsavory practice we engaged in for a short time that summer, though at the time it seemed an altogether enterprising innovation. Since we were always in need of funds, the idea occurred to us to purchase some numerical stencils and white paint and go about the nearby areas where we lived in the fashionable west Nashville neighborhoods near to Peabody and Vanderbilt, painting street addresses on the curbs and then seeking some voluntary contribution from the home owner for that generous gesture. However, we also hit on what we thought was a sure-fire wrinkle to this work. We would have printed up some small cards which stated something like: *WE ARE HEARING-IMPAIRED AND HAVE JUST PAINTED YOUR ADDRESS ON THE CURB. DONATIONS APPRECIATED.* Now, to carry this off required studied discipline, for one can easily see how the scheme could come to disaster by involuntary response to any spoken word, and especially so were one's back to be turned. Nevertheless, we tried it out with great success, and after a daily effort of only about two hours, would meet at a neighborhood tavern over a couple of pitchers of beer to divide our substantial earnings. We did very well in this endeavor, but after only a few days of quite successful efforts, we got cold feet, and our sense of guilt got the better of us, so we retired the stencils and brushes. Isn't that an awful thing to have done?

Work and Study

Wirth's well-used textbook

The work at Peabody was much more disciplined than anything I'd known as an undergraduate. It was one of the few institutions, however, where one could complete the MA by attending only in summers and was thus tailored to the needs of full-time professional teachers. I learned much and enjoyed my teachers. Professor Whitaker even turned out to be not quite so intimidating as I'd previously presumed, though he was, all in all, not a particularly warm or pleasant personality. He expected much of his students, and I always had the private notion that if one ever impressed him unfavorably for almost any reason, one might never fully recover. My other "major" professor was equally renowned: Dr. Fremont P. Wirth in American History. He was very famous to me since I had used his high school American History textbook in my own classes at Marion.

He graciously autographed a copy of it for me, which I treasured for many years but have misplaced somehow across many years of moves across the country. He was an animated instructor, though never in a dramatic fashion, and his anecdotes and asides made the subject alive and compelling. All of my Peabody teachers required much use of the Library, and I and my apartment mates spent much free time in "JUL"—the Joint University Library—which served that Nashville academic community.[112]

This was really an academic community in the middle of an urban place. Situated in the west end of Nashville, Vanderbilt and Peabody were adjacent to each other—across the street—but there were also a couple of other, less well-known institutions that shared the general area. These included Scarritt College, Belmont, and David Lipscomb College. Accordingly, the entire area was pervaded by an academic culture. In those days, too, Peabody had a very distinguished faculty, much more so even than those of us who were there at the time were clearly aware.

Old postcard showing the original Joint University Library in the early 1950s

In Education, there were such people as Harold Benjamin, who had written the famous satire, *The Saber-Toothed Curriculum*, and Willard Goslin, who had gained national attention for his heroic stand against radical "right-wing" interests when he had been superintendent of schools in Pasadena, California, and who had been elected to the Presidency of the American Association of School Administrators.[113] There was Dr. Clifton Hall in Social Foundations of Education;

---

[112] In fact, the library was shared between Peabody and Vanderbilt, thus its name. The two institutions were across the street from each other.

[113] Harold R. W. Benjamin, writing under the pseudonym, J. Abner Peddiwell, *The Sabre-Tooth Curriculum* (New York: McGraw-Hill, 1939).

Drs. Whitaker and Jewell Phelps in Geography; and Wirth and Dr. Jack Anderson in History; and Dr. Brierley in Sociology of Education. I well remember the latter telling us that when someone ever asked him where he had taken his Doctorate, he never replied, at North Carolina University, but rather, merely, that had done his "work" with Odum! That reference was to Howard W. Odum, a prolific contributor to sociological knowledge about Southern culture and society, and who, for many years, edited the prestigious *Journal of Social Forces* out of Chapel Hill.[114]

It was a rich atmosphere in the early fifties and spelled the end of an era, though we had no notion of that at the time. Soon after those years, Peabody began to decline as the greatest of Southern educational institutions. Some have said that it was because its faculty became *too* notable and thereby spent too much of their time jaunting about the entire world on one or another kind of generous grant. Others have said that it was merely an inevitable mark in the progress of time as the larger, comprehensive state universities in the South began to eclipse Peabody because of their more competitive advantages. Whatever the reasons, Peabody suffered increasing constraints beginning in the 60s and finally merged with its richer neighbor across the street to become Vanderbilt University's nominal School of Education. Probably, that has been beneficial to both institutions.[115]

Still, the *idea* of Peabody, which was the last and only remaining single-purpose comprehensive Teachers College when it became part of Vanderbilt and was a shining light in the education of literally thousands of teachers, school administrators, and faculty members in collegiate schools of education throughout the nation—such an "idea" has passed with sadness and regret. Vanderbilt, indeed! It couldn't ever begin to live up to the Peabody mystique in the minds and hearts of so many who knew both well.

---

[114] To clarify: The University of North Carolina at Chapel Hill, flagship university of that state.

[115] My father's good friend and colleague, Franklin Parker, wrote a fine biography of the college's founder: *George Peabody: A Biography* (Nashville: Vanderbilt University Press, 1971, rev. ed., 1995).

On to the Bureaucracy

I completed my work at Peabody in the summer of 1955 and still can easily recall the trepidation all of us endured who stood in its commencement line that hot August day as a "Marshall" in full academic regalia strode down the line with a sheet of paper in hand, pulling out those who had failed their comprehensive examinations. Timing was the key involved: From the date of completion of "comps" until graduation was little more than a long weekend. Thus no one knew for certain that they had passed until that Marshall passed them in the line without incident. I held my breath as all others did and was so relieved that I remember nothing else, not who spoke to us or what was said.

Incidentally, in those days, one had to complete a quite comprehensive written and oral examination to qualify for the MA degree. In my own case, my two fields, Geography and American History, were combined, and I had to "sit" for the Orals with professors from both fields at the same session. To help us prepare for these examinations (particularly in History), Professor Wirth suggested that we "sit in" on similar examinations over at Fisk University (also in Nashville) which was, at that time, probably the foremost primarily Black university in the South. So, about four or five of us trekked over to Fisk, gained permission to sit in the "gallery" and observed Oral Examinations in that institution's History Department. The examining room was a fairly spacious place that—we were told—had once served as an Operating Room when, at some previous time, this particular facility at Fisk had served for medical education. Thus, there was this sort of primitive observational area overlooking the examining room where we could sit and watch without being a disturbing distraction.

We were flabbergasted when the chief inquisitor, a white-haired professor wearing full academic regalia, asked the candidate, who was a young woman, maybe around twenty-five or so: "Let us begin with a survey question to just get us started. Hitting only the high points, would you please trace the foreign policy of the U.S. from George

Washington through Eisenhower?" We nearly collapsed! Was this what we might have to endure? Were it so, we were all just totally unprepared! This young woman just clicked it off like you wouldn't believe, and we were stunned. It was only later that we learned that he *always* began his examinations with this question, so candidates were ready for it, but for us, it was a most sobering shock! Needless to say, observing those Orals, we went back to our books and notes with a vengeance.

Receiving his degree at Peabody, 1955

Fortunately, my written and oral examinations went, apparently, reasonably well. I *was* awarded my degree. Then, Jane and I (for she had joined me in Nashville for the second two summers) loaded up our car and returned to Marion and were so flatly broke that we had not eaten that day, and in Clarksville, Tennessee, en route, stopped at a super market to buy a package of cookies with what money we had left. How we have laughed about *that*! Though it was not at all so funny then, for though I had carefully calculated the cost of the cookies, I had neglected to remember that Tennessee assessed a sales tax, and, embarrassed beyond words, I had to return the package and select a slightly less costly item.

Peabody Diploma

I now had the MA degree and had begun to give serious thought to seeking a better paying position. I had examined Peabody's "placement files" and had applied to a couple of Junior Colleges, for I wanted badly to try higher education, and I knew that without a doctorate, my chances were not at all that good. But none of those efforts were fruitful. In the 1955-56 school year, we remained in Marion, but began seriously to consider the possibility of prospects elsewhere.

A Journalistic Interlude

That was also a year in which I became something approaching a world-class "Assistant." Still the assistant football coach, I was also appointed as an Assistant Principal, and had begun another "moonlighting" activity in the previous year with a newly established weekly newspaper as an "Assistant Editor." After all those years of having thought about Journalism, here was a real opportunity to give it something of a try. That title was really rather meaningless since there were only three of us who ran the paper.[116]

*Issue of the Marion Reporter.
Note the subscription price of $1 per year!*

There was an editor, a genuine professional who looked after most of the real details of getting the paper out. I ended up writing a large part of the paper (with much early and useful instruction from the editor) or edited the "correspondents news" from this and that corner of the county, and we employed a young woman who looked after the office. We had no printing facilities and contracted with a firm in another town to print it. This meant that we had to have all of our "copy" and our ads—everything—provided to them on Wednesdays, and then had to go and pick up the papers late Thursday evening for delivery on Friday.

It was a hectic enterprise, and the editor was a kind of professional itinerant who, though most competent and entertaining, nevertheless occasionally enjoyed more than an appropriate

---

[116] He never names the paper, but he kept a copy of *The Marion Reporter*, pictured. Sources show it was published from 1954 to 1955, which would match his account here, and this copy includes an article penned by him!

amount of bourbon whiskey and was thus not always as dependable as such a fragile operation necessitated. Consequently, we truly never knew whether the damned thing was going to see the light of a Friday morning or not. Somehow, it always did! The paper was the brainchild of a local and fairly wealthy townsman known for his idiosyncratic and single-minded definitions of the ways of progress, and because he had become involved in a philosophical feud with the much more well established and profitable existing weekly newspaper (I no longer recall the nature of the dispute), he had decided to start his own newspaper in order that contrary opinions might enjoy equal exposure. Given those circumstances, it was properly assumed that the venture would certainly be short-lived.

Nonetheless, we enjoyed a brief and heady existence and managed to add enough fuel to heighten some controversial fires and generated a few of our own. After about a year, having accomplished what he set out to do, the publisher "sold" the paper to the existing and established newspaper firm as part of some kind of package when that latter enterprise itself passed into new ownership. Of course, all that he really "sold" was his willingness to stop trying to compete, but some sort of deal was struck all the same, and a part of that arrangement was that I would join the older Weekly in a part-time function. When I returned from my final summer at Peabody, I also returned to the other newspaper and placed myself at the disposal of its new publisher.[117]

That year was a very pleasant one for me. There was little of the anxiety that we had endured with getting out the other paper, since we enjoyed our own printing equipment, and I had more opportunity to learn about aspects of the enterprise than previously had been the case. The new owner-publisher was a young, well-trained professional, and he took it upon himself to tutor me in the ways of such work.

---

[117] The established newspaper was *The Crittenden Press* (named for the county in which Marion was located). As of this writing (2021), it is still published in print and online: http://crittendenpress.blogspot.com/.

The Coincidences of Good Fortune

Early on in some of these personal remembrances, I commented about the extent to which "chance" plays such an important function in human lives. This experience with small town newspapering is an important course of that belief for me. One of the issues that we decided to push in that year was our conviction that the local, "independent" public school system needed to be merged with the county system. In Kentucky, the county is the constitutionally established system for the conduct of schooling, but over the years, the legal pattern, not unlike that in many southern states, had allowed and encouraged "independent" or "city" districts to be established within, but independently of, the counties. These city districts had their own Boards of Education, their own established attendance boundaries, buildings, and so forth. This pattern had developed because the quality of schooling as managed by the counties had been almost universally inadequate, and persons living in the towns and cities had been unwilling to suffer that quality of education and were willing to tax themselves to provide something better. After the war, demographics began to change that. People began to be able to elevate the quality of their lifestyles. They built houses and for the most part prospered such that expansion inevitably pushed the service areas further and further into the countryside. As this began to happen, the laws being as they were, these newly prosperous emerging middle class people had no choice but to utilize the county schools, and they soon became unhappy with their quality.

All across America, there was similar restiveness occurring, and in the middle fifties, continuing on into the mid-60s, there was a great flurry of school consolidations and school district mergers. It had become obvious that new patterns of efficiency and effectiveness required larger-sized schools capable of providing greater enrichment opportunities for children whose parents now wanted something much better than had previously been provided. A part of that mood also had to do with interscholastic athletics, truth be known. To an increasing extent, the advantages that had previously been enjoyed by the city school teams had begun to dissipate, and county high schools with new-found resources and greater numbers of kids had begun to turn that tide. Even as many school districts considered merging with others, the older pattern of small, isolated county high schools had changed too. Increasingly, counties began to consolidate small schools into larger, well-planned, new plants with good equipment, better salaries for personnel, and effective systems of school transportation.

These events were not lost on us at Marion. A couple of years previously, the local Marion Board of Education, upon the retirement of the man who had held the position for many years, had appointed a progressive young superintendent of schools with whom I had worked closely and had come to much admire. Soon, it became equally apparent to him that merger with the county system was the only rational solution to our growing educational problems. Clearly, a small county like ours could not continue to support two separate school systems and expect either to be as effective as a single system could be. So, with combined effort from many right-thinking people, the work of merger was begun in 1955-56, and a year later was realized.

Such school system rearrangements were exceedingly difficult, and our efforts in that regard were a long and drawn-out affair. There is great sentiment attached to existing schools, to teachers, and to the "we feelings" that capture the hearts of so many people who have themselves been a part of the traditions of established schools. We learned much about the intensity of that mood and of what "institutionalization" really means. It was not without much pain and sometimes hard feelings that the effort was realized. It meant that one school system was, in effect, willing to just practically give away its buildings and its operations. Almost of equal importance, it also required giving up, or certainly compromising, many traditions, rituals, even the colors and mottoes and emblems that had identified a unique history. And these concerns arose from both parties, since compromises were required on the part of both. Nevertheless, with many meetings and much discussion, consultation with state agencies, responsible reporting and editorial policy by our newspaper, the support of important and energetic people, and especially with the leadership of that young superintendent of schools who was willing to sacrifice his own position in the process, we pulled it off. The Class of 1957 was the last to graduate from Marion High School. That young superintendent's name was Richard L. (Lee) Gentry, and after the business was finalized, he accepted a position as an official in the State Department of Education in Frankfort, Kentucky, a circumstance that was also subsequently to have an important influence on my own career.

Richard Lee Gentry, pictured in late career as a professor at Eastern Kentucky University

Brief Tenure as a "Supervising Teacher"

I think that it was in the early summer of 1956, quite surprisingly, that I was contacted by Murray State College inquiring if I would be interested in an American History position as a "Critic Teacher" in its Laboratory School (we now refer to such people as "Supervising Teachers") and indicating that it might also involve some teaching to lower division college students in introductory Sociology, a field in which I had begun to have considerable interest as a consequence of my work at Peabody. I later learned that a local bank president in Marion, Mr. Hollis Franklin, who was prominent in regional affairs and a member of Murray's Board of Trustees, with whom I had become rather closely acquainted, was instrumental in influencing the offer.

At that time, my salary at Marion had risen to a little over $3000.00 annually, and the Murray offer was for $3,600.00. My status in the newly consolidated pattern had not been established at that time, but there was no reason to presume that I would not be retained. But salary questions were moot, and the Murray offer was substantial. Due to the incidental generosity of Jane's parents, my work at the newspaper, and basketball officiating in season, our standard of living would not necessarily improve much (if at all), but after considerable discussion, Jane and I both saw it as an opportunity, and I accepted. I knew next to nothing about the vicissitudes of a "supervising teacher," needless to say, but I was willing to learn.

As it turned out, my "tenure" in the Murray situation surely is among the shortest on anyone's record. Chance again intervened. We moved to Murray and rented a most agreeable and rather new house only a short walk from the campus. My father-in-law had presented me with a handsome leather briefcase in recognition of my graduation at Peabody, and the three of us—our oldest son Greg was then three years old—quickly became an accepted part of the Murray community.[118] I would add that, at that time too, Jane was pregnant with our second child. One of my most pleasant memories is walking over to the college from our house near the edge of the campus on sunny September days with my handsome leather briefcase and thinking that life wasn't all that bad at all.[119] I taught four classes daily at Murray's Training School and had about five college student teachers under my supervision. My students were enterprising, and my colleagues were solicitous and very professional. It was an altogether most promising circumstance.

Then, one otherwise ordinary day in mid-September, the school secretary came to my room and informed me that I was wanted on the telephone by someone in the office of the State Superintendent of Schools. Since I was in the middle of teaching, and she did not indicate any urgency, I told her to take the number, and I'd return the call, which I did soon thereafter. The conversation was with the "man" himself—the State Superintendent of Schools—and, as I recall it, did not particularly suggest the possibility of a position. He said that he had something in which I might have an interest, that it could be a contribution to efforts to improve education in the state as was his plan, and that perhaps I might be able to come into Frankfort at

---

[118] And thus, I make my very first appearance by name in this memoir—as a parenthetical addition. I gave my father a hard time about that!

[119] My brother Joe would be born the following February 21st in Frankfort, Kentucky.

my early convenience to discuss it further. I was very complimented to be talking in such a way with the chief state school officer, and I presumed that he wanted me to serve on some state study committee or some such similar kind of responsibility. I advised him that since it would be difficult for me to get away during the week, I could come to Frankfort on the following Saturday. He found that acceptable, but suggested that I come to his house, preferably before noon, and then provided me rather obscure directions to find it.

I brought this news home to Jane with a considerable feeling of self-importance, for I assumed that it certainly meant that I was being recognized as an up-and-coming young professional. Always more incisive than I, she found it rather curious that I would be beckoned more than half way across the whole state just to be considered for some kind of professional committee work. That set us both to wondering, and she was much exasperated with me for not being better informed. In any case, I gassed up the old Kaiser and arose very early on Saturday morning—about three am—to begin this curious journey. From Murray to Frankfort is a very long trip even by today's standards. In 1956, it was forever![120] But I arrived without mishap about 9 o'clock or thereabouts and did find my way to his home. What I found there was much confusion and activity.

At that time, Kentucky was in the midst of very tense events associated with efforts to racially desegregate many of its schools, and, as it happened, serious difficulties had arisen only two days previously in Sturgis, Kentucky—a system in the western part of the state—and which required the possibility of calling out the National Guard.[121] I arrived in the middle of this serious crisis, and though I had followed the events in the newspapers and on the radio, I really did not appreciate the possibility that the School Chief's residence would have taken on

---

[120] It is useful to remember that there were no interstate highways in 1956, the year the act authorizing them was passed. The route was entirely by two-lane highway through towns.

[121] Kentucky was a border state, but it was heavily segregated, an issue I will deal with briefly in my own memoir. Brown Vs Board of Education, ordering school desegregation, had only been decided by the Supreme Court two years previously, in 1954.

the character of a command post. The state police director was there, as was the Attorney General and several high-ranking officials of the State Department of Education and who-knows-who else. Nevertheless, having made myself known, I was introduced to the Chief, invited to have a cup of coffee, and told that he would be with me presently. His wife took me in tow, provided me with the coffee, which I most appreciated, and as I was able then to be unobtrusive for a little while, I had a chance to reflect on exactly what the heck I was doing there!

The Superintendent was Dr. Robert R. Martin, whom I had only seen once previously when he had made a speech at a regional education meeting at Murray a year previously. He had been elected to his office by bipartisan popular vote, and had won rather handily, as I remembered. I also knew that he was the first truly qualified state school chief ever elected to that office. He had an earned doctorate from Teacher's College, Columbia University, where he had majored in school finance with the great Paul Mort. Of course, such details I only learned somewhat later, but I did know that he was widely acknowledged as able, and was well thought of in professional and political circles.

Dr. Martin was a big man physically and projected a striking image of competence and authority.[122] Then, and for most of the years that I knew him well, he struggled to control his weight, for he loved nothing more than yielding to a ravenous appetite. Yet, for the most part, he carried the weight reasonably well on a large frame. Well over six feet, he reminded me in countenance of the actor Charles Laughton. On that morning, he certainly was not at his best. Clearly not having slept much, he was still in bathrobe and slippers, and I don't think I ever again saw him when he was anyway other than dressed very smartly in suit and tie.

After perhaps an hour and whatever issues were at hand had been resolved, the crowd dispersed, and he and I began our discussion. It was relatively brief, and, typical of his style as I was to learn, to the point. He indicated that he had been advised that I had some experience working for newspapers, that he intended to initiate efforts to more effectively

---

[122] See photograph in the next chapter.

publicize some of the things that were and would be happening at the state level, and that in order to do that, he needed someone who knew something about that kind of writing and who also knew something about capital "E" Education. He said that what he had in mind was a position as an Administrative Assistant (to him) to carry out a variety of special assignments, and wondered whether I would have an interest in such a position. I was flabbergasted! I don't even remember if I asked him any useful, much less proper questions, but the idea of it seemed immediately impressive. After a few brief comments and questions, however, by which I gained some little clarification of what the role involved, I asked him the really important questions: How much would such a position pay? When would he like to have it begin?

He didn't hesitate. The job would pay $5,250.00 per year, and he would like me to begin October 1. That was little more than three weeks away. I think I must have gulped. That was more money than I could dream of, almost twice what I was presently contracted for. I pointed out that the only problem I had with it was that I had only quite recently accepted an appointment at Murray State, and I was a bit concerned about the propriety of leaving it under those circumstances, to which he responded that in his position, he also served as ex officio chairman of the boards of trustees of all state collegiate institutions including Murray's, and that was therefore a problem with which I need not be concerned. I said, "I'll take it!"

One needs to remember that these were the days before affirmative action, nor the kinds of required "searches" that are the pattern now. In those days, people in positions of influence and authority made such decisions unilaterally and finally. The source of my good fortune in this instance turned out to be my former superintendent friend Lee Gentry, who apparently had been privy to some incidental discussion about this new job, and when someone had wondered who might be qualified to fill it, had obviously suggested me based on our experiences together at Marion.[123] Such is the nature of luck and chance and acquaintanceship.

---

[123] Martin later became President of Eastern Kentucky University and brought Lee Gentry on as a professor, so the two were apparently fairly close.

I was *very* excited. All the way on the long drive home, I was bursting to share the news with Jane, but it would never have occurred to me, or her, that I might call long distance to tell her. That would have seemed, even then, a frivolous expense. But when I finally did get home and relate our miraculous good fortune, she was not at all that equally elated. Always more rational than I, she had begun to consider the consequences—having to move, the costs of doing so, finding suitable housing in Frankfort, and then finally, she reminded me that this would be a "political" appointment. Where, she wanted to know, would I be in four years when Dr. Martin's term ended. (Constitutional Officers could not succeed themselves in office in Kentucky.) Well, I hadn't given that any thought at all, so I said that I would call him immediately and put that question to him, which I did. He said, in response, something to the effect of "Where will you be *there* in another four years?" And, giving that sage counsel about thirty seconds of profound consideration, I said, "I'll take it!"

A Turning Point

That was another significant turning point in our life, maybe the most important, for it introduced us to a wider world not only so far as professional education was concerned, but in terms of a kind of exit from what, for us, had been a rather parochial way of life in many other ways (although we didn't really know that was the case). In a way, it was akin to what Barbara Ward meant, when she used that marvelous phrase, "the hinges of history." The move to Frankfort was our "hinge of history,"[124] for it put into motion the events that determined the inevitable direction of our lives and fortunes ever after.

---

[124] From Barbara Ward and René Dubos, *Only One Earth: The Care and Maintenance of a Small Planet* (New York: W. W. Norton, 1972), p. 12: "the two worlds of man—the biosphere of his inheritance, the technosphere of his creation—are out of balance, indeed potentially in deep conflict. And man is in the middle. This is the hinge of history at which we stand, the door of the future opening on a crisis more sudden, more global, more inescapable and more bewildering than any ever encountered by the human species and one which will take decisive shape within the lifespan of children who are already born."

CHAPTER V

The Bureaucratic Interlude (1956-1958)

In one of his essays, Emerson observes that "every end is a beginning," and in the same passage, he also says that "Our life is an apprenticeship to the truth."[125] With the first of those ideas, I am in complete agreement, and my career is its prime proof, since, for the most part of the first twenty years of my professional life, Jane and I seemed almost always to be a cycle of ends-and-beginnings. Of the second notion, I am more skeptical, though dependent on what Emerson might have meant by "truth." In that regard, I have always favored Whitehead's view that the only real truths are half-truths.[126] Thus, especially in the modern world, I'd think it more accurate to suggest that our lives are apprenticed to half-truths, and the trick, all glorious, is to be very careful *not* to accept what is only half-true for what is all true.

That couldn't have occurred to me at the time, since in those days, I gave little thought to any such philosophical concerns. Life in a state agency bureaucracy was then and is still a veritable cauldron of half-truths. Foremost among them is that these large organizations are professional systems. They are, and they are not, because, though genuinely trying to function as professional and technocratic systems, these big state organizations were then and still everywhere are, nevertheless, primarily *political* organizations. The complex processes through which such competing cultural values like technocracy and

---

[125] From Emerson's *Essays, First Series*: Chapter 10: "Circles," first paragraph.

[126] My father is here recalling another passage from one his favorite books, *Dialogues of Alfred North Whitehead*, previously cited: "There are no whole truths; all truths are half-truths. It is trying to treat them as whole truths that plays the devil." (p. 16)

politics are melded into productive effort and even occasionally quite remarkable accomplishment is thus almost entirely a matter of very skillful and effective leadership. More about that later.

Another New Beginning

Suffice to say that back there in 1956 when I was appointed to a position in the Kentucky State Department of Education, that time of such a heady new *beginning* for me, it was enough merely to know that I was to be part of a great, exciting, and altogether noble enterprise. One of the first things that Jane and I did after accepting the Frankfort position was to trade in our old 1951 Kaiser sedan for a brand new 1956 Ford "Ranch Wagon." That old Kaiser had been a faithful and reliable machine. (And, interestingly, the 1951 Kaiser model was far ahead of its time, and even today, many automobiles still reflect similarities to its design.) But the "Ranch Wagon" was the first *new* automobile we ever bought.

*A 1956 Ford Ranch Wagon like ours,
save that ours was white rather than blue*

In those days, before banks discovered how much money they could *really* make on "small loans" (automobile loans or otherwise), our small-town, "user-friendly" banker, a delightful man named Neil Guess, who was President of Marion, Kentucky's People's Bank, merely extended to us a 90-day renewable Note. At the end of 90 days, the Note was renewed for a smaller balance. Amazing! Moreover, a couple of years later, that marvelous man gave me a *blank* note already signed that I could use if the circumstance arose. Fortunately, the need never did arise, but I carried it folded three ways in my billfold until it wore away, as such treasured papers will do when carried that way. Alas, indeed, how our world changes!

In our new white two-door Ford Ranch Wagon with the vinyl upholstery the color of an almost ripe watermelon, Jane and I traveled to Frankfort (in style!) to find a place to live and were fortunate to rent a pleasant and relatively new house in a small development across the road a ways from the big Stag Whiskey Distillery. I remember that well since, whenever there was a damp and humid kind of day, the aroma of sour mash was so heavy hanging in the air that the birds behaved quite erratically.

Greg on his new tricycle in front of the first house in Frankfurt. The new Ford is barely visible in the carport

But it was a very nice place with an attached portico—carports as they came to be known—and among about a dozen similar ones that lined both sides of a dead-end street. There were sidewalks for the kids to ride their tricycles, and most of the other residents were in about the same circumstances as were we. Frankfort, Kentucky was a jewel of a town, and, I'd guess though much larger and more congested now, still is. It is situated at a lovely spot on the Kentucky River not far between

Louisville and Lexington though close to the latter, and Lexington became our "city" for weekend excursions and for shopping.

On our shopping excursions, we purchased little but looked a lot, so it has always been a recreational activity for us. Jane was trained in those ways by her mother, a real champion at it, and I have often said that were there an Olympic event in shopping, Jane would be a gold medalist! Lexington is also the home of the University of Kentucky, and that provided additional enrichment for us, though we weren't able to take as much advantage of that as we'd have liked. In any case, this move was a great adventure for us, and we entered it with much enthusiasm. At that time, Jane was already pregnant with our second son, and I had just turned 29, so as we look back on it, and considering that we were very unsophisticated people in every imaginable way, that willingness to move to Frankfort and to a job, the nature of which I had only dim notions, was almost revolutionary for us. In truth, we (and especially me) were too naïve not to have enormous confidence. Hell's bells! I figured we could do anything we set our minds to do.

Joining the Staff

When I reported for work, I had no idea of what to expect. I was "processed" through all of the rigmarole that one had to endure to get on a state payroll and was assigned to a temporary work place. I was presumably given most of that first morning to settle in, so to speak. I was given a new, very impressive blue-gray desk and an executive swivel chair, and a generous supply of the ubiquitous yellow legal pads. It was like falling into the proverbial lap of luxury. In all of my previous experience in teaching, I'd survived entirely on government surplus stuff, olive drab and rickety. The boss's own secretary took me around and introduced me to many of my coworkers. For the time being, my space was adjacent to her own, just outside the Superintendent's large office where we, she on one side and me on the opposite wall, occupied space that was cordoned off by a waist high railing with a little swinging gate. It was too cramped for two work stations and was therefore only temporary. But it was briefly instructive, since, without needing to be told, it was clear to me that this was a traffic area of some importance. Anyone who came or went had to pass by us. Before the first week was over, I had absorbed a lot of "lore" about that place, and though I knew nothing at all about organizational culture then, my sociological common sense was fairly acute.

It obviously wasn't a good arrangement, and after about ten days, I was moved to more permanent space down the hall about fifty paces and into an entry room outside the Deputy Superintendent's office. This was a much larger space and less public, though it, too, employed the rail and gate. The room housed the Deputy's personal secretary in addition to me, and, as soon as it could be expedited, my own secretary. (I hadn't the remotest idea as to how one went about properly utilizing a secretary!) These offices were separated from the Chief's by a large and ornate Conference Room, and both ours and his enjoyed separate access to it. Thus, when either the Deputy or I had to see him, or (more often the case) he us, we were not required to go out and down the hallway. Within about three weeks' time, I had a secretary, had already accumulated a number of assignments, had been issued the precious parking permit, and had begun to really know my way around the "shop." The assignments solved the problem of how to utilize the secretary, and I picked up the dictation techniques with little difficulty. I had begun to get to know some of the staff, and I found them all to be accommodating and helpful. Some of them are still among my good friends, and we remain in touch.

In essence, my primary tasks as Administrative Assistant to the Chief State School Officer were primarily public relations and public information kinds of things, though we didn't call it by those names much. The first major chore was to put together a monthly *Newsletter* that would go out to all of Kentucky's district superintendents, to develop a routine for writing, editing, and disseminating press releases, to attend every meeting of any importance, and to learn how to use, in that regard, a handsome, unwieldy, and very expensive Speed-Graphic Press Camera. In addition to these familiar kinds of activities, I was also expected to try my hand at speech-writing. As it turned out, I began to do more and more of that, and by the time I left the Department, I was writing almost every word that the Superintendent formally uttered from any kind of platform. Speech-writing is a uniquely enlightening craft. Unquestionably, it is the best kind of education that anyone can get in a political organization, and, bureaucracy or not, that's what state agencies really are. And writing speeches simply ensures that whoever does it gets to know more about an organization and what it's about than anyone else.

I think that one has to have something of a talent for speech-writing and not so much with reference to the writing itself, but rather to the nature and content of the speech itself, and being able to fit the speech to the style and personality of the speaker. Oh sure, it is seldom that any speech isn't touched up, changed, and adjusted by the person who's going to deliver it, but the more one does it, and if one has a flair for it, the less the speaker seems to have to do much of that. Also, it is often the case that several different people are involved in drafting pieces of a particularly important speech, and in that circumstance, the task is for one person to then go through it and make it flow so that it doesn't come out sounding exactly like what it is, a statement prepared by a committee. I guess there's another thing about speech writers. Most of them probably are convinced they could deliver it better than the guy they wrote it for. But I didn't really have that problem. I think that the speeches I wrote for Dr. Bob Martin were more *his* than *mine*. Had I been delivering them, I'd probably have written the speech differently. In any case, I enjoyed that part of the job as much or more than anything else. It gave me a chance to talk to a lot of staff people in various areas of responsibility, and in a lot of cases, especially in the first year, they'd have to spend almost as much time teaching me about the technicalities of their fields of expertise as whatever tidbit of information I needed to know to incorporate into a speech.

For example, I didn't know beans from first base about school finance—about equalization formulas and "assessed evaluation per pupil" and flat grants and capital outlay and God knows what else! But when I joined the Kentucky State Department of Education way back there in 1956, school finance was *the* major initiative we were involved with. Under the leadership of the State Superintendent, Dr. Robert Martin, the entire system of financing schools in the state had undergone revolutionary change. It was called the "Foundation Program," and in theory, it was fairly simple: Make it possible for every system in the state to provide a basic and adequate "level" (foundation) of educational quality for every child, and if any local school system wanted to do more than that, they were free to try to do so based on local initiative and effort. But putting that theory into practical, operational procedures was enormously complex. So, the Chief did a lot of public speaking about that, and I got a quick and dirty apprenticeship in school finance. The man who was our technical expert in that whole area, and who, in most ways, was the primary author of our legislative program was my "tutor," a guy named Stanley Hecker.

Stan Hecker had a Ph.D. from the University of Kentucky and had served a short tenure as a school superintendent in a small school district midway between Frankfort and Lexington. Stan, as it turned out, not only provided me the essentials of practicable instruction in our newly inaugurated "School Foundation Program," but was significantly instrumental in my later career. A little more about that presently. Mostly, in those days, the entire system of Education in Kentucky, at least in the K-12 sector, was being reformed. We gave that big effort a catchy slogan, "Advancing Education in Kentucky," and invented an attractive logo with "AEK" as the central motif, and we spent a lot of time taking that message out in the state.[127] But it became very clear to me very quickly that ours was a phenotypic political bureaucracy. The Chief School Officer was the only Constitutional Officer elected on a nonpartisan ballot, but he was nevertheless elected by popular vote all the same. Moreover, by constitutional provision, all elected state office holders in Kentucky, including the Governor, were limited to a single four-year term (that remains the case still), and thus, could not succeed themselves.[128] One could run again after missing a term, and that was fairly common. But it didn't require great sophistication to soon realize that a very important byproduct of

---

[127] Articles with this title appeared in various newspapers around the state, showing Dr. Martin as author, but presumably drafted by my father. See for example: "Advancing Education in Kentucky: Music Has Important Place in Modern School Curriculum; Is Gaining in Popularity" in the Moorhead College newspaper *The Trail Blazer*, March 11, 1958, p. 4, https://scholarworks.moreheadstate.edu/cgi/viewcontent.cgi?article=1571&context=trail_blazer (consulted 18 January 2021).

[128] Actually, my father was mistaken here. Starting in 1992, elected officials in Kentucky could be reelected to a second four-year term.

what I was expected to do was to ensure that the Chief enjoyed his fair share of reflected glory from all of our initiatives. It would be inaccurate, however, not to emphasize the fact that the Chief fairly deserved considerable credit for most of the good things that were in the works.

Robert Martin

The important thing about the work I tried to do there—and writing speeches is the appropriate referent in which to frame it—was the experience and opportunity to watch and be quite close to a very effective administrator, and, with remarkably few exceptions, a generally effective staff. He was a most able man and remains among a few of the genuinely effective administrators that I've known intimately across the years. Some comment about this man: Robert R. Martin, a native Kentuckian, was the first truly professional and qualified State Superintendent we'd ever had up until that time, though there have been several since. But, like most states at that time, and many still, there were no statutory qualifications for holding statewide public office, even as the chief education official, other than being a citizen and at least twenty-one years old. That's not to imply that there had not been some very able men who'd held the office and some with considerable distinction. But the office itself had not enjoyed much need for distinction, since, by and large, the State Department of Education until about the time Dr. Martin came in, had been largely a data-gathering and supervisory agency, and like many other similar state agencies, particularly throughout the South, was often looked upon as a kind of refuge for aging public school administrators who had reached the end of their careers. So, it isn't much of an exaggeration to suggest that historically, not much was expected of it nor probably wanted, if truth be told.

Dr. Martin really changed all of that. He had earned a doctorate from Teachers College, Columbia University, where he had studied with the great Paul Mort, among the half dozen most renowned authorities on school finance in the nation then and still! Interestingly, Dr. Martin had never held a public school superintendency, although he had served with impressive effectiveness as principal of a large consolidated high school. But he brought to his responsibilities as State Superintendent a keen sense of organizational competence, somehow knew the right kind of professionals to appoint to key jobs, and was a "quick study" kind of person. That is, he could take a paper or a document or an issue and could understand it with incredible accuracy in almost no time at all. I always marveled at that, and I've noticed a similar skill in a number of other effective leaders and administrators with whom I've been closely associated over the years.

He was a big man, well over six feet, with a kind of intimidating appearance and manner, and in the face, always reminded me a lot of the actor Charles Laughton. Always struggling to try to keep his weight under at least reasonable control, he tended, where food was concerned, to ultimately accept the idea that the only way to avoid temptation was to yield to it, and then he would go on a brief fasting spree and be very hard to endure. Partly because he was a sizable man, he was not really comfortable driving an automobile, but actually, that was a good thing, because he also wasn't very good at it. Riding with him when he was doing the driving was always a perilous adventure. Consequently, when anyone accompanied him on official business, and someone almost always did, that person, by mutual appreciation for survival, did the driving. I drove him around about as much or more than anybody else, and that, too, was fortunate, because we engaged in some really lively dialogue, and I could "pick" his knowledge. He was a well-read man, as we used to say, and had a marvelous grasp of issues, and he enjoyed these automobile seminars about as much as I did.

The Organization

The Kentucky State Office Building, constructed in the 1930s, where the Department of Education was presumably located in the mid 1950s. It was thought to be haunted because it was built on a space formerly occupied by a penitentiary

The general structure of the agency was fairly typical of the time—matter of fact, fairly typical of *all* times. There were five major "bureaus." Instruction was the principal one, since, after all, that was any state's educational "raison d'être." In addition, there was a Bureau of Finance which had the enormous responsibility of monitoring and managing the emerging initiatives in addition to a number of other services ranging from free textbooks, school lunch, library services, and so forth, to purchasing and accounting, and "internal affairs." Then, there was a Bureau of Teacher Education and Certification which looked after the always complicated issues regarding who and under what circumstances professionals were licensed in a variety of areas. There was a Bureau of Vocational Rehabilitation, which had sort of been assigned to the Education Department because it was difficult probably to know of any place else to house it, and a Bureau of Vocational Education, which had responsibility for dealing with that enormous can of worms. Finally, there was a fairly recently established Bureau of Guidance and Counseling, though I'm reasonably sure it wasn't called exactly that in those days.

Of course, there were many concerns that didn't quite "fit" this structure. The Deputy Superintendent was primarily responsible for dealing with the concerns and problems of local school superintendents, and he was also our designated "sea lawyer."[129] This meant that most questions relating to legal affairs, and statutory considerations explicitly (or implicitly) related to our ever-growing School Codes and legislative matters fell into his domain. And there were others: external concerns with other state agencies and the governor's offices, issues concerning school mergers and consolidation, State Board of Education agendas, and the ubiquitous questions that they, as a Board or as individuals, raised, and routine kinds of crises that always emerged that might be handled by almost anybody. Still, it was a quite coherent organizational pattern all things considered and functioned with quite remarkable efficiency.

---

[129] The term refers to a seaman who talked about the law as if he knew something about it but in fact knew nothing—not a particularly complimentary reference! It seems more likely that the Deputy Superintendent did, in fact, know something of the law but simply lacked the law degree.

As I have indicated previously, we enjoyed the luxury of those days of not having to worry too much about latter day inventions like Affirmative Action and Equal Employment Opportunity, and since, as mentioned, we were indeed a *political* bureaucracy, those in higher echelons of executive roles (and not a few much further down the hierarchy) held their position mostly at the "will and pleasure" of whoever hired them. That's just another way of saying that a particular kind of patronage was routinely accepted as a risk of upward mobility, and one who obligated himself on behalf of a new regime could anticipate at least some possibility that the debt would be repaid and, usually, with a position. Accordingly, although all of the bureau heads were competent and appropriately "credentialed," they generally recognized that their jobs were most likely limited to the four years that the Superintendent held office. Just below the bureau heads, however, were a variety of *directors*, and most of these were career professional bureaucrats who held their positions *outside* patronage consideration, and it was fairly common for these persons to survive in their functions regardless of who the next elected Chief School Officer happened to be. Still, when Dr. Martin came into office, a number of these persons were replaced, and almost without exception, by much more able professionals.

Regardless of its obvious weaknesses, however, this system had significant advantages as well. I can't think of a single case in which any person was appointed to any position for which he or she was not qualified. Dr. Martin was always straightforward about that. Moreover, this pattern enabled an executive to move expeditiously when a position needed to be filled, and although there was, indeed, a particular version of a "search," the question of who would or would not be appointed to a position was very much a matter of picking up the telephone and making the offer. Certainly, there *was* a civil service process, and the great majority of the staff and support personnel had secure civil service status, but at higher levels of the bureaucracy, a cabinet officer had great flexibility in personnel matters. To the extent that the system was dominated by white males and there were no provisions nor statutory constraints in favor of anything like the contemporary notion of equal employment opportunity, there were still some visibly responsible minority persons and women in positions of some consequence, but not many. This was a time prior to any required consideration of circumstance.[130]

Accordingly, politics being what it is, one could be assured that the executive staff would be quite loyal at the outset, and those persons were appointed on the basis of their commitment to the agenda that was being promoted on the one hand, and their competence to help carry it out on the other. On the whole, considering the context of the times, I think of it in retrospect as a cohesive and dynamic organizational pattern when managed with competence, which, during my brief tenure with it, was indeed the case. Its disadvantages are perhaps equally apparent: It was sometimes difficult to know whether one agreed with you because he thought your ideas were sound or that he didn't want to tell you something you didn't want to hear.

To some extent, of course, that is a problem even in the most autonomous and occupationally secure organizations, for there is always some competition for favor and affection. (It was, in fact, a problem I often encountered as dean, even in an organizational culture where there is a long-established tradition of tolerable curmudgeon antipathy to established authority!) But, in a state bureaucracy, too, with popularly-elected heads—like the situation in Kentucky—there is, as well, the vexing problem of continuity of initiatives over time and the inevitable, nervous maneuvering for advantage and the "looking about" of the senior (political) people when the four years begin to approach their end.

In point of fact, the temporary nature of professional life in those days was its worst feature. Since the Chief could only fill the position for four years, the last of those was too often preoccupied with his, and his highest level directors' concerns for where they would be *next*

---

[130] In other words, it was the fifties, and the Civil Rights Movement as well as the movement for Women's rights, was either barely nascent or yet to occur. Kentucky may have been a "border" state, but it was still segregated. The tone of these remarks might imply that my father was insensitive to these issues, but that is not the case. He was a life-long Liberal Democrat, deeply devoted to the various movements for equal rights that mostly grew up in the 1960s.

year. It created a circumstance in which it was almost impossible to plan very effectively far beyond about four or five years, since the next guy would surely come into the place with a new set of goals and plans. As an aside, I've thought about this state of affairs a lot across the past thirty years, and I've not resolved it to any satisfaction. I still come down only in the middle of the dilemma: Is it better to be able to make plans for the longer range in a bureaucracy? Certainly, it is vital in many cases to be able to provide for continuity of leadership and to believe, with Max Weber, the original guru of bureaucracy, to the effect that "appointed officials always function more exactly than elected ones."[131] But there is also a lot to be said on behalf of the benefits of a new cycle. (Emerson's notion about "endings" and "beginnings" comes to mind.[132]) The obvious difference has to do with whether those "incoming" do, in fact, have a thoughtful set of goals and the ability to animate them. Dr. Martin had that vision, but I don't think the majority of elected officials do—then or now.

It has occurred to me that even at the level of the United States presidency where there is at least a better than even chance for at least eight years of leadership, the enormous problems associated with continuity of agendas has merely created as a by-product, immensely growing size and power within what is felicitously referred to as the "Executive Branch." I'd guess that it isn't particularly arguable that the executive branch has grown out of all proportion to the other branches of government on no basis other than the fundamental idea of continuity of agenda. Certainly, that is clearly the case with foreign policy and not to too much less an extent with economic policy. Unfortunately, the conditions that can ensure continuity also tend to foster sluggish performance and tend thereby both to protect

---

[131] Max Weber, *Economy and Society*, ed., Guenther Roth and Claus Wittich. (New York: Bedminister Press, 1968), vol. 3, p. 961.

[132] "Our life is an apprenticeship to the truth that around every circle another can be drawn; that there is no end in nature, but every end is a beginning; that there is always another dawn risen on mid-noon, and under every deep a lower deep opens." Ralph Waldo Emerson, *Essays, First Series*, Chapter 10: Circles, p. 149 [http://www.literaturepage.com/read.php?titleid=emersonessays1&abspage=149&bookmark=1] Consulted 30 March 2018.

and to disguise a secure mediocrity. Even good people are dulled by routine, and in that regard, I recall Robert Ulam's observation to the effect that "those who advocate change risk danger for they take safety away from the little minds."[133]

Even in those positions of administrative leadership where, most things being magnanimous, there is a fairly reasonable presumption of lifetime tenure—in deanships and university presidencies, for example—it is my considered judgement that one shouldn't stay too long. About seven or eight years is the extent of effectiveness as a general rule. And if one stays beyond five years, one should most certainly *not* consider signing on for an additional "hitch" without a careful assessment of what has been accomplished on the one hand, and a well-developed new set of goals to pursue for the next period of time on the other.[134]

Another of those half-truths that I began to understand is that organizational process is not a function of organizational purpose. It is the other way around: Organizational purpose is a byproduct of process and activity. And almost in the nature of things, it is the activity that is more rewarding and more exciting. Much later, in my more contemplative academic life, I realized that this is a part of what Whitehead meant when he insisted that it is the process itself that is the reality.[135] This is a particular characteristic of state bureaucracy and, I think, of most any other kind. We are not very good at purpose definition in any case in the American scheme of things. Ours is not a goal-oriented

---

[133] The source of this quotation eludes me. I can find no mention of the author for this exact quotation anywhere, neither in Google nor even in Worldcat, the largest publication index on earth.

[134] My father stayed ten years in the deanship at WVU, but, as will become clear later in this memoir, he came to wish that he had left earlier.

[135] Here again, my father paraphrases a passage in the *Dialogues*, p. 213: "The process is itself the actuality." The relationship between process and reality was important to Whitehead's philosophy. He delivered a collection of lectures on the subject that were published as *Process and Reality: An Essay in Cosomology (Gifford Lectures Delivered in the University of Edinburgh during the Session 1927-28)*, corrected edition, ed., David Ray Griffin and Donald W. Sherburne (New York: Free Press, 1978).

society. We are much more enamored of means than ends. And we are particularly bad at purpose definition in state agencies or any other kind of organization whose organizational life is reasonably assured. There is the presumption that purposes are sort of given and then only shaped (if sometimes largely) by policy makers—legislators, boards, and commissions. Thus, I have come to the conclusion that the bulk of policy and so-called "strategic planning" and "task force" initiation and all the other assumptions about planned change are ultimately aimed at trying to do unchanging things a little better. Thus, much of it is tinkering and fine tuning and all that.

What was exciting during most of my brief tenure in the State Department of Education in the late 1950s was that we *were* engaged, and if not entirely in new kinds of purposes, then some very active attempts to initiate more effective ways to pursue well-established older ones. For example, the idea that every child ought to have equal opportunity for, and access to, the best possible education has long been accepted, but it was a half-truth when put to the test of effectiveness. As a matter of fact, the pattern of financing schools until about World War II and especially in most of the southern and border states had the almost opposite result. Since funds were allocated to local school districts based primarily on "school census" data and a per capita allotment, it was not unusual at all for some school districts to be provided state financial aid to keep youngsters *out* of school.

It worked like this: There is a certain amount of dollars in the state school fund. There are "x" number of children between certain ages (according to law) who are eligible to go to school. Thus, the number of children was divided into the amount of dollars, and then that average was multiplied by the census data for each district, and that total amount of money was forwarded. In the parlance of school finance, this pattern is referred to as "flat grants." Obviously, no matter how many children are counted as being eligible, the less of them that actually showed up, the more money there was to spend on only those who did! During my first couple of years as a high school teacher in Kentucky, for example, a couple of days were set aside in the spring when all teachers in all school systems actually went out in the district with forms and pencils and literally *counted* all children in every household between the ages of six and sixteen. That was our *census*, and it was the basis upon which our state eligible funds were allocated. It was serious business, and there were all manner of safeguards to prevent any district from "padding" its data. Somehow, these procedures were tied into the State Constitution itself, so the first order of business in developing a more equitable and effective model was to eliminate the old provisions. Under Dr. Martin's leadership, we were able to do this by getting a constitutional amendment on a statewide ballot that struck out that part of the Constitution. This was marvelous politics, since once that set of articles was eliminated, we found ourselves in the envious position of having *no* provisions at all for the financing of schools. Accordingly, almost anything we came up with would surely be approved, and that did, indeed, turn out to be the case.

According to Dr. Martin's plan, we moved away from census data as the primary method for allocating funds and went instead to "average daily attendance" (ADA). In effect, this simply meant that now schools would receive funds only for those children who actually came to school. Neat. Well, it was all considerably more complicated than that, but that's the gist of it. Of course, what this now required was much more scrupulous attention to attendance, and each teacher was issued a *Register* which was like gold and dynamite simultaneously. Moreover, as is typically the case with regulatory agencies, there is a necessity to ensure that even well-intentioned people don't get tempted to make their situations better than they really are (cheat!). Therefore, a whole new set of activities and personnel came into being in the Agency—auditors! But these auditors did not audit receipts and expenditures; they audited "teacher registers."

There were other similar kinds of initiatives. We were able to utilize the newly developed procedures of "state central purchasing" to help school districts get much better prices on a variety of materials and equipment. Among the most innovative was the mass purchasing of school buses. But it was like pulling teeth to get cooperation from local administrators and boards. The problem was that when purchases are made on the basis of bids, if one participated, one was obligated to take whatever product or brand might win the bidding. We learned anew that old habits and preferences die very hard. Many districts that participated in central bus purchases, for example, were miffed (or worse!) when it turned out that they would no longer be able to use Chevrolets or Fords or whatever they'd previously gotten used to. In addition, there was a good bit of political pressure and maneuvering, since this was a threat to existing business relationships between some school districts and local automobile (and truck) dealers. (As a matter of fact—as I remember it—there was a hint of collusion among bus body manufacturers, since, quite extraordinarily, the several major national firms involved all seemed to bid the same price! We rather quickly resolved *that* problem.) Many of the things we tried to do in those days were as difficult to sell as they were reasonable to do. But good common sense hasn't always triumphed over entrenched habits and entrepreneurial advantage.

Although my experiences with state education agencies in recent years have been less intimate, I have nevertheless had numbers of occasions to deal with them, particularly in the ten years that I served as a university dean. If there is a major difference between state education agencies in contemporary times and my experiences in those days, it is that they now provide far less of that kind of genuine help and seem much more preoccupied with regulatory mandates, exaggerated oversight to ensure compliance with an incredible variety of policies, an obsession with legal procedure, and, generally, a kind of insatiable appetite for just merely knowing what local districts are involved with. It's almost as if they don't really care all that much whether what's going on is necessarily good or not so good but merely have to *know* about it.

And, of course, it requires many score more people merely to track everything. Such agencies are therefore much more immense in size and scope, with layers and layers of structure. In addition, since their pay scales are quite generous, they are able to hire many newly minted Ph.D.'s who, though they may not be quite up to the standards required for competitive scholarship in universities, are nevertheless bright and energetic. Needless to say, when any bureaucracy hires smart people and expects them to spend eight hours a day doing *something*, they can make a lot of trouble for all the rest of us. I'm convinced that the Kentucky Department at the time I was a part of it was one of those happy exceptions that occasionally come along. We had a mission, good leadership, and an able and committed staff. It's happened before in all kinds of organizations, and it will happen again, but it is just a little unusual. So, it was all terribly engrossing in those days.

Politics Again

Dr. Martin was elected in 1954 and assumed office in 1955. By 1958, he had begun to give serious thought to what he was going to do next, since, as I've indicated, he was prohibited by constitutional provision from succeeding himself in office. Incidentally, we had tried in about 1957 to change the Constitution to provide for an appointed State Superintendent, but I think we miscalculated on that. We had written the provision such that both the Superintendent and the State Board of Education would be appointed, and we lost, rather decisively as I recall. I think had we provided for the State Board to be elected, one from each of the state's congressional districts, we might have pulled it off. But, alas, and despite the prevailing tendency across the country for chief state school officers to be appointed, Kentucky's system remains the same to this day.[136]

In late winter 1958, a meeting was scheduled down in Louisville where a number of prominent "politicos" were to gather in the ubiquitous smoke-filled room, a decidedly *un*official convention, and to which Dr. Martin asked me to accompany him. My seeming primary responsibility was to act as a sort of drink pourer during a protracted poker session. While the idea was certainly to engage in some serious card playing, the *real* purpose was to discuss politics and prospects. To make a long story short, Dr. Martin felt, with considerable justification, that he had a good inside-track on the nomination for Lieutenant Governor, and this big strategy session was really aimed

---

[136] That changed after my father wrote this work. While I cannot find a date for the change, the Kentucky State "Commissioner" of Schools is now appointed by the eleven-member State Board of Education, which is itself appointed by the governor.

at trying to settle who would run for what. Of course, when one has been involved in any successful statewide political race and he or she literally occupies an office, it is altogether likely that it—the office itself—will happen to have something of a view of the governor's mansion out of some lofty office window. I'd suppose, in an occasionally quiet moment of contemplation and fantasy, all such persons must surely ask themselves why not me? Consequently, when decisions are made and however they are made, all such persons certainly feel that they deserve to be considered.

After two days of heavy debate (and whereby I managed to win about fifty dollars!), it was finally decided that my man was simply not well enough known at county political levels for the party to slate him as its candidate for the second spot. Instead, the idea was that since he had superb organizational abilities, he would manage the gubernatorial campaign of an obscure judge from the eastern part of Kentucky, and, if that went reasonably well, it would be his turn next time around. Obviously, his work on behalf of the slated candidate would make him much more familiar to county politicians. Now, in those days in Kentucky, there were really three parties: the Republicans (who didn't amount to much) and *two* factions of Democrats. The incumbent Democratic Party was tightly controlled by the then governor, A. B. "Happy" Chandler, with whom Dr. Martin and most of the others at that meeting had increasingly little status. "We" were the *other* Democrats!

On the ride back to Frankfort, I shared none of the enthusiasm that was beginning to animate my boss. After all, I too had learned something of the nature of things. Beating Governor Chandler's hand-picked successor, the then Lieutenant Governor Harry Lee Waterfield, simply seemed hopeless to me, and, I might add, to almost anyone else at the time who knew very much at all about Kentucky politics! The candidate they had decided on in Louisville was almost unheard of. His name was Bert Coombs, and though he'd enjoyed an excellent record as judge, was bright, and of an unspoiled reputation, he was a *nobody*! And then Dr. Martin advised me that he wanted me to be significantly involved in the upcoming campaign's press relations. He'd loan me to the re-election committee, raise my salary considerably, and my job would be to help this guy get well-known as the election campaign got underway. Needless to say, I was pretty low when I got home and reluctantly related this turn of events to Jane.

In the first place, I knew almost nothing of the technicalities of managing press relations for a major political race. Although I had gotten to know many people in the media, most of those were as obscure in their organizations as I was in my own. In the second place, I was not totally ignorant of political reality, and I'd never even heard of this judge! Any incumbent governor in that state at that time enjoyed significant power and influence, and "Happy" Chandler was a popular if obviously somewhat controversial politician.

Albert "Happy" Chandler

If his machine (and that was indeed an appropriate metaphor) had slated Waterfield as the candidate, I, like most other people at the time, clearly knew that odds in favor of success for him were at least in the vicinity of about 8 to 5! Just about the same odds that a major league batter would foul off a 3-2 pitch![137]

I have never been much of a poker player, but this much at least I knew: When one is looking at a player with three aces showing in a five-card stud game, you don't call a big bet trying to draw to an inside straight unless you either have a lot of money on the table or you're just a little stupid. In this case, I qualified on neither condition! Moreover, I knew that when I talked about this with Jane, she would remind me of her earlier concerns about the political implications of this job in the first place. I also knew full well what the implications were of Dr. Martin taking on any such commitment as this: It meant sixteen-hour days, full speed ahead, and no consideration of anything other than the task at hand. I could see myself spending long days in Louisville at the headquarters, calling home late and saying I wouldn't be able to get home, and enduring probably additional disharmony at home about that—and properly so. After all, at that time, we were a young family with a four-year-old and another barely more than eighteen months. Although I would be rather handsomely paid for my work, I didn't know much about what I would be expected to do, and there was always the nagging conviction that it was a futile endeavor.

Michigan State and The Luck of the Irish

And then, that old Irish luck came through for me again, or at least, that's the way it looked at the time. Maybe no more than ten days after the Louisville meeting, I received a phone call one morning from Stan Hecker. Stan had left his position as Director of School Finance in the Department of Education mid-year to accept an Assistant Professorship at Michigan State University. It was, again, one of those circumstances in which someone knew somebody and that someone knew somebody else. When Stan had done his graduate work at the University of Ken-

---

[137] This was one of my father's favorite sayings. Whenever we would watch a baseball game, and the count would go to 3-2, he would wink at me and say, "do you know the odds that he'll foul it off? 8 to 5!" I don't think a single baseball game ever passed that he didn't say it.

tucky, he'd become acquainted with a chap named Robert (Bob) Hopper. Dr. Hopper had "sat" briefly as Director of UK's Bureau of Educational Research and then had subsequently accepted an appointment at New York University in Educational Administration. He'd admired Stan's work, had kept track of him, and upon moving to Michigan State University as Chairman of its newly reorganized Department of Educational Administration, had hired Stan when an opening occurred for a specialist in school finance. I had gotten to know Stan very well, had come to have genuine respect and affection for him as a professional and a friend. He'd learned that Dr. Bill Roe, a professor and colleague of his at MSU, was looking about for someone to do some research work concerning the ways schools were reflected in newspapers, and Stan had mentioned my work and background. Consequently, he (Hecker) suggested that I might want to look into it, since, all things considered, it might lead to a doctoral dissertation and advanced degree.[138]

Stan and Mary Hecker later in life

---

[138] My father remained close to Stan Hecker for the rest of the latter's life. They exchanged emails—mostly in the form of bad jokes!—until Hecker's death in 2007. This photo was kindly sent to me by his son, also named Stan, who also enjoyed a distinguished career at Michigan State.

In truth, I had *never* considered the remote possibility of additional graduate work, much less in the field of school administration. Still, it sounded at least worth exploring, and considering my state of mind, I thought it worth considering, so when I got home that evening, Jane and I talked about it. Now, Jane has always had more confidence in me than I have. She thought I ought to go up there and talk with Professor Roe and see what was possible, so the next day, I called Stan Hecker back and asked him what was involved. "Well," he said, "you'll have to come up here and talk to these people. If things seem reasonably ok, then you'll have to go through the qualification procedures." I asked what that involved. He said I'd have to take some university standardized tests, some kinds of reading and writing examinations specifically designed for advanced graduate applicants and something called the "Miller Analogy Test." I then asked whether or not, all these things considered, I could look forward to any kind of support. "Oh sure," he said. "Dr. Roe has some kind of grant from the Midwest Administration Center at the University of Chicago to pursue this study." He indicated that he had no idea how much of a stipend was involved, but graduate assistantships (which was what was involved) paid around $1,800 a year, and he also advised that Jane could probably find some part-time work, and if there was an occasional contract with any of the many Michigan school districts for "surveys" or consultation, I could probably make an extra few dollars, and these were, at that time, routinely common. He also advised that if there was even the remote possibility that I might be interested in going on for the Ph.D., this was a good prospect.

So, I advised my superiors in Kentucky that I needed to take a couple of days of Leave, and the following Monday, I gassed up the Ranch Wagon and took off for East Lansing, Michigan, having absolutely no idea what awaited me. I remember so clearly that one of the things that most impressed me as I approached East Lansing is that I accidentally tuned the car radio to the Michigan State University radio station. The idea that a university had its own radio station just somehow struck me as terribly important. And it also began to dawn on me that Michigan State was a very "big deal" as universities go. But that was only the beginning of my impressions.

By the time I arrived, I was almost overwhelmed. One must remember that this was 1958. In those days, Michigan State already enrolled something like 25,000 students. It was the biggest place I'd ever seen! It was bigger than the town where I grew up in Kentucky, and that city, Bowling Green, was about the fourth or fifth largest city in the whole darned state. But here was this grand land grant university, sprawled across hundreds of acres, a *humongous* football stadium, and as a former jock and ex-football coach, I was clearly aware of the MSU Spartans' prowess in football with their great coach [Clarence] "Biggie" Munn. They'd just come off a near national championship in football and had only rather recently become a member of the Big Ten Conference. So that monstrous stadium was all the more impressive. And there were new buildings up or under construction just *everywhere*. There was this marvelous new Kellogg center, which was, for all practical purposes, no more nor less than an on-campus Hotel with big conference rooms and restaurants (and, as I later learned, the practicum site for its Hotel and Restaurant Management School), and as I wandered (lost) through its campus, I simply marveled at the scope and complexity of this marvelous university. Needless to say, as I began to fantasize about being part of whatever Michigan State was, the whole idea of it was intoxicating.

Stan and his lovely wife Mary were temporarily occupying space in "Married Housing" while their own home was being constructed, and I stayed with them. I don't remember how Mary managed that since it was a tiny apartment, but I do remember that I accompanied Stan on an extension class way off somewhere in the state so that we could talk, and I could bring him up to date on the departmental gossip. We hurried back in order to get to a liquor store and stock up on beer and spent most of the rest of the night, and into the wee hours of the morning, reminiscing and enjoying each other's company. Unfortunately, neither of us gave proper consideration to the fact that I had to report to Morrill Hall, an old building on campus that then housed the College of Education while a new and thoroughly modern facility for the college was nearing completion across the Red Cedar River in a newer area of campus. Incidentally, one of Stan's tasks that year was to manage all of the equipment and furniture acquisitions being readied for the new building, so he was deluged with vendors and samples.

In any case, when I reported early the next morning for my battery of tests, I wasn't in the best of shape! I'd only had about three of those bottles of beer, but we'd talked deep into the morning, and I hadn't slept more than a few hours, so, needless to say, I was very groggy. Still, youth is its own cure, and I faced the tasks with (apparently) remarkable vigor. That must have been the case. A few days after I'd returned home, Professor Roe called to advise that I'd scored at the 90th percentile on the MAT. (I've often wondered how I'd have done had I gotten a good night's sleep and been thoroughly refreshed!) Anyway, on the basis of my performance, they'd decided to offer me not a GA but a part-time Instructorship which paid $2,600!

Professor Bill Roe

In the meantime, with Stan Hecker squiring me about and having spent time visiting with various staff in Educational Administration including the chairman, Dr. Hopper, and being particularly impressed by Dr. Bill Roe with whom I spent a couple of engaging hours, I came home from East Lansing just very excited about the whole business. Jane and I talked about it a lot prior to the phone call, and we were well aware that it would involve a lot of scrimping and a lot of sacrifice. Still, I'd been able, while I was there, to check with the people in university housing, and, at that time, the University was constructing brand new married housing which was most attractive and very affordable, and I was assured that, were I to be accepted, we would be accommodated in the new Spartan Village married student apartments. So, when Dr. Roe called me to advise that I was acceptable and they had an appointment for me should I decide to accept, we had already decided to do it.

WHEN I WENT TO SEE DR. MARTIN, I WAS VERY NERVOUS. IN MANY ways, I felt almost disloyal that I had decided not to be a part of his new political adventure. Because I wasn't at all sure as to how things would go at East Lansing, I wanted to know whether I might be able to get a leave of absence. I realized that such a request was perhaps an imposition since I had decided to leave in any case, and at the beginning of the new effort. But he was typically generous and encouraging. We talked for the better part of an hour. I mentioned my lack of confidence about the political campaign, mostly my own concerns about my competencies. He pooh-poohed that but pointed out that advanced graduate school was *always* a good option and that it had certainly been a good decision in his own case. He further assured me that he would address a memo to the file that would assure a place for me in the Department were I to exercise that option, which was most generous (and as I now know, a difficult commitment for him to make). And then, he said something to me that I have never forgotten. He said that he would make sure that my leave would be honored, but, and with almost a little twinkle in his eye, said, "But I think you will never come back here. When you get your doctorate—and I don't think you will have any real problem with that—there will be new and different things you'll want to do and new and different places you'll want to go."

And, of course, he was right about all of that.

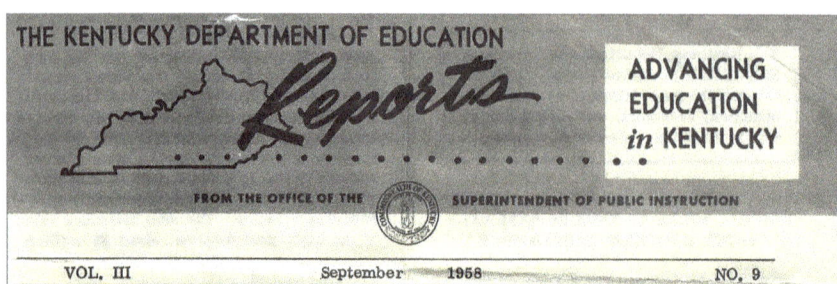

THE KENTUCKY DEPARTMENT OF EDUCATION

ADVANCING EDUCATION in KENTUCKY

FROM THE OFFICE OF THE SUPERINTENDENT OF PUBLIC INSTRUCTION

VOL. III   September 1958   NO. 9

EDITOR OF "REPORTS" GRANTED LEAVE TO STUDY FOR DOCTORATE AT MICHIGAN STATE UNIVERSITY

Mr. William G. Monahan, Editor of the REPORTS and for two years Administrative Assistant to the Superintendent of Public Instruction, has been granted leave to accept a teaching fellowship at Michigan State University. Mr. Monahan will study for his doctorate with the Michigan Communications Study and will do specialized research in education coverage through newspaper media in Michigan schools. The objective of this study will be to determine the extent to which newspapers contribute to public knowledge of education matters and to draw implications from the study which have a contribution for public school administrators.

During Mr. Monahan's service as Administrative Assistant in the Department of Education, he was also responsible for Department publications and for a public relations program with press, radio and television. He did special research for the Superintendent, set up arrangements and managed major conferences sponsored by the Department and prepared special informational research materials for distribution to the public.

Prior to joining the Department of Education Staff, Mr. Monahan had a broad and varied experience, both as a professional educator and in other areas. He has served as both high school and college teacher, high school football coach and editor of a weekly newspaper. He also had brief careers as a professional singer and as a merchant seaman. At the time of his appointment to the Department, Mr. Monahan was on the faculty of Murray State College as an instructor and critic teacher at Murray Training School.

Mr. Monahan received a Bachelor of Science Degree at Western in 1951 and a Master's Degree from George Peabody College in 1955. Mrs. Monahan and their two boys will accompany him to Michigan for the period of his leave.

The members of the Department of Education Staff bid Bill an informal farewell at a luncheon in his honor on Wednesday, September 10th. His many friends both in the Department and over the State extend sincere congratulations for the honor which he has received in his appointment to Michigan State University. Such honor reflects not only upon the level of the professional staff of

Newsletter announcing my father's departure from the Kentucky Department of Education

But, as I look back on it, and though I didn't know it much at that time, and I doubt he really gave it much thought either, he was, in retrospect, a most significant influence in my life and in my career. As the years have moved along, more and more I have learned to respect that man and how much he helped a raw, unsophisticated, young, naïve man to have become something much, much more than that.

AND, SPEAK OF SURPRISES? YOU KNOW, THEY *WON* THAT ELECTION! Dr. Martin and Bert Coombs did beat Harry Lee Waterfield, and Judge Coombs became one of the better governors that melancholy old state of the "dark and bloody ground" ever had.[139]

Bert Coombs

And all of those who were significantly involved in the effort did ok. Dr. Martin, for example, was subsequently named as President of Eastern Kentucky State University in Richmond and is acknowledged as one of its great men. His successful management of the political activity at the time certainly was instrumental in his being named to that high office, but his record as its president speaks for itself. And what it says is this: this man knew where he wanted this place to go, he knew how he wanted it to get there, and he knew how to appoint the kind of people who would help him to lead it there. And after he retired from Eastern, he still wasn't through. He then successfully

---

[139] I'm not sure where my father got the idea that "Kentucky" was an Indian term for "dark and bloody ground," but modern references indicate it derives from an Iroquois word, "ken-tah-ten," meaning "Land of Tomorrow," a considerably more optimistic etymology!

From Cabbage to Cauliflower

ran for election to the Kentucky State Senate and served with notable distinction in that body for a number of years.

I've lost track of him in the past few years, but I do remember one day in Boca Raton, Florida, in about 1980, at a meeting of the Southern Regional Education Board when I was still a university dean and serving at that time on a rather prestigious SREB committee, Dr. Martin and his wife, Ann—that elegant lady who made a very young and naïve school teacher feel a bit more comfortable on that Saturday long before when he first offered me a job—were in attendance, and I was able to seek him out and pay my respects. He looked pretty much the same, but I'd guess he'd have long forgotten much of this stuff. Anyway, for what it was worth, I said hello and thanks. And I'd guess, though I rather awkwardly tried to convey my gratitude, it would never have occurred to him that he was so significantly influential in influencing the career of a young man who very much admired him and owing to his example hasn't turned out all that badly in his own right.

CHAPTER VI

The Professorial Years: Michigan State University and Oklahoma University (1958-1965)

One of the most pleasant and satisfying events of my career in higher education occurred in 1975 when I was invited back to Michigan State University's College of Education to deliver a "round-up" speech. The round-up was a kind of alumni and friends get together at State that was originated by the late Dr. Clyde Campbell, a former professor of Educational Administration who was widely respected (and deservedly so) throughout Michigan and the upper Midwest. The round-up's emphasis was on the Department of Educational Administration at MSU and its many graduates in fields of educational administration across the years.

That occasion is also one of my more rueful remembrances because at that time, feeling terribly full of my status as sitting dean, my speech was ill-conceived. In truth, there were important things that I had to say, and did say, but it is probably more likely remembered for some rather deliberate profanities that I included trying to illustrate the nature of changing times in higher education at that time. I fear that the point I wanted to convey was never quite carried off, and I'm sure, even to this day, those remarks are remembered with some chagrin. At least, *I* certainly remember that speech that way. More importantly, at a regularly planned banquet in the evening on that day, I was surprised by being presented with the College of Education's Distinguished Alumnus Award! I was just flabbergasted! Michigan State was very good for me.

My experiences there significantly influenced my entire career in higher education, and not the least because I learned there that graduate students (all students, for that matter) should be treated by their professors with equal good will. It was a lesson that I never forgot.

Our small two-bedroom apartment on the ground floor in MSU's Spartan Village

WE WENT UP TO MICHIGAN STATE UNIVERSITY IN THE FALL OF 1958 with considerable trepidation. At least, I certainly felt that way. Janie, on the other hand, never really indicated any lack of confidence, though she was never all that comfortable with my rather *political* situation in the Kentucky State Department of Education in Frankfort and would probably have been willing for us to try almost anything otherwise. As I have noted previously, my own sense of academic confidence was not all that secure. After all, I had stood for some kind of qualification examination for advanced graduate potential in Geography which had been my major area of concentration at George Peabody College toward the end of my MA program, and, in truth, I don't remember what kind of examination it was. I had apparently not done all that well. At least, Professor Russell Whitaker, my program chairman at Peabody (and at that time, an internationally recognized authority in conservational aspects of Geography) had apparently examined the results, and in a rather uncomfortable interview toward the end of the summer of 1955, had discouraged me from any further presumptions about advanced graduate work in that field or at Peabody (or anywhere else for that matter!).[140]

Dr. Whitaker had an imposing and autocratic style. He was an intimidating and imperious kind of man and almost automatically put any student on the defensive, and, after all, one (like me) who was so easily impressed by anyone who'd written several books and was acknowledged as a giant in the field, was all the more easily put off by his judgement. I'd guess that I spent no more than twenty minutes in his office that very hot July day in 1955, and I left with the clear conviction that I'd pretty well reached the edge of the end so far as any further graduate work was concerned. Consequently, I'd made reasonable peace with any ambitions I might have had otherwise about further graduate study of any kind.

Still, I am and have always been an incurable optimist, and, all things considered, I felt pretty good. After all, I'd completed an M.A. degree in one of America's most prestigious Teacher Education institutions, and I'd done so with more than just an adequate record. My work in Geography was well above a "B" average, and my work in History (my minor) and in all of my Education ("corollary courses") was straight "A." Moreover, I'd enjoyed my work in History with the (late) great Fremont P. Wirth. Perhaps more importantly, Professor Wirth had indicated to me personally that he thought I was pretty good, and that had reinforced a most needed sense of consolation. So, all things considered, a year later, when Jane and I had moved to Frankfort, and I had assumed this new and rather important position, I felt particularly fortunate and excited. Two years later when that whole idea about further study sort of reemerged, we were realistic about its promises and its risks.

Graduate Study

We matriculated for advanced graduate work at Michigan State University at just about the best time possible, and maybe, the best time

---

[140] For a photograph of Whitaker, see Chapter Four.

in all of the history of higher education in America! You have to know what the world was like in 1958. *Everything* was just literally booming! Enrollments in higher education were mushrooming, and all institutions from the smallest to the largest were constructing buildings, expanding curricula, adding staff, departments, new courses, and equipment. Even entirely new colleges were being introduced in universities, and budgets were multiplying. There were grants and funding opportunities and new foundations, and much more demand than supply could accommodate. Colleges were building new dormitories as fast as self-liquidating bonds could be sold to finance them, and state legislatures were authorizing new capital outlays as fast as they could vote the measures. Enrollments doubled and tripled annually, and *everybody* wanted to get into colleges and universities. It was what is now looked back upon as the "golden age" in higher education, and nobody presumed that it would ever end! And it was smack dab in the middle of this unparalleled prosperity and optimism that I went up to Michigan State University to begin my advanced graduate work. It just couldn't have come at a better time for an ordinarily good though otherwise highly motivated student. Certainly, I was reasonably bright, if too naïve to know any better than to embark on such a perilous endeavor, but I had enjoyed good and appropriate experiences, and I was at just about the right age—I had just turned 31 when I registered for MSU's Fall Quarter in September, 1958.

Moreover, I was appropriately impressed by the opportunity, and I not only knew something about the reputations of the people with whom I would subsequently study and work, but I was awed by their stature. Some of those were internationally renowned, and at the time, they were among the best in their fields. Consider: Ernest Melby, formerly president of the University of Montana and just retired from the education deanship at NYU when he came to MSU; and George Counts, also retired from NYU, who was a literal "giant" in the field of Education Philosophy and Comparative Education (and who had been persuaded to join the MSU faculty by Melby). And outside the College of Education, there were the Useems (he and she) in cultural anthropology, Archie Haller, Leo Haak, and Paul Miller, all in Sociology (the latter was subsequently appointed President of West Virginia

University). And in General Communication Arts, the field of my minor concentration, there were some really rising stars: Malcolm MacLean, my advisor, and Paul Deutschmann, Hideya Kumata, and David Berlo. (I'll have a bit more to say about some of these people a little further on.)

In addition, the MSU College of Education staff was distinguished, and in my own area of educational administration, there were people like Bill Roe (my committee chairman), Karl Hereford, Clyde Campbell, and Bob Hopper in addition to Melby and, later, Counts. These may not be names easily recognized outside that field or even yet remembered today, but in those times, these were *very* well known and nationally recognized scholars. Moreover, our full-time graduate students were all first rate. Regarding our status as graduate students, there was little of the ceremonial aloofness and status differentiation that I later confronted as a faculty member at the University of Oklahoma and, later still, at West Virginia University.

Interestingly, my professors in those days at "State" always referred to themselves as "Mr." rather than as "Dr." and treated those of us who were full time Graduate or Research Assistants or Assistant Instructors as if we were colleagues. I later realized that, to a large extent, this pattern of style was owing to the example and leadership of the AES (Administration and Education Services) department's chairman, Dr. Robert Hopper, and to the comfortable sense of security that the staff in that department enjoyed. After all, almost all of the professors from the newest probationary Assistant Professor to the most senior among the "Fulls" enjoyed considerable academic prestige and status. They didn't have to worry too much about whether or not they were accorded appropriate deference across the Big Ten and the nation itself.

It was into this rather heady milieu that I began my post-graduate work. I have thought about that a lot when I have remembered discussions with my older son regarding his own graduate experiences in the very prestigious Department of History at North Carolina University, Chapel Hill, where he completed his M.A. in European History. Most of his professors seemed to be prima donnas who wouldn't give even the best of their grad students the time of day. Even to this day, he looks back on his experiences there as distasteful and demeaning.[141]

The Work Itself

In the context of contemporary times, it is rather odd that anyone could have completed a doctoral degree in just less than two years, but those of us in those days who were full-time students did it almost routinely. As graduate students, we worked hard, but we did little else. We were a "cohort," although we didn't necessarily know that at the time. We officed together, worked together, studied together, suffered together, enjoyed each other's successes, and shared our frequent failures.

Old postcard showing then-new building of the College of Education at Michigan State University in East Lansing

We were officed together in a special area set aside on the fourth floor of the new College of Education building which we referred to as "the Bull Pen" in a structure (probably by deliberate intent) that encouraged argument and discussion of the difficulties of the times. Accordingly,

---

[141] Well, not all of them, but my father's sensitivity to the difference in our experiences may well have informed this section of his memoir. I should add that my experiences as a graduate student at West Virginia University later on were considerably more positive, something, again, I will explore in my own memoir.

we knew with certainty the solutions to our profession's problems and dilemmas and worried over "Type II" errors, chi squares, and the merits of "descriptive" vs "experimental" designs. We were a curious kind of community, and though we didn't even know that either, we *grew*!

A Dissertational Digression

In about March of 1960, it almost suddenly became rather obvious to me that I just *might* finish my doctoral work. My dissertation was concerned with the "content analysis" of the ways schools were treated in Michigan newspapers, and the work was *most* tedious. My sample included twenty-four weekly newspapers and four big Michigan dailies, and I had to meticulously measure *all* of the school content in each of them according to quite precise, pre-determined categories. Needless to say, one can easily get a bit behind in such chores, and I literally had newspapers coming out of my "kazoo"! My father-in-law had designed a kind of holding rack for all these papers, and my office in the College of Education building (which I now shared with another Graduate Instructor) had become a kind of departmental curiosity! There were papers just *everywhere*![142]

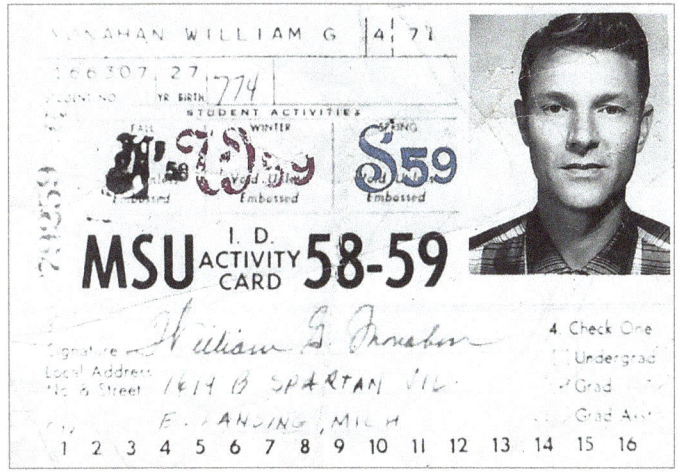

My father's first ID card at Michigan State

---

[142] Alas, it never occurred to my father to take a photo of his office or this "rack" designed by my grandfather.

One must realize that this was in a time before personal computers, and I had to literally measure every column inch of school news in each of a half a dozen categories in each of those newspapers. I had worked out a paper and pencil system, and each day, I would meticulously measure content.

Now, the doctoral dissertation is surely an invention of some kind of now nameless professorial sadistic devil. Whoever originally conceived of the idea that anyone seeking a Ph.D. degree should submit a formal proposal, get it approved (by those who've already endured something similar, and many of whom, by the way, think it always ought to be harder for anyone who comes thereafter!), then pursue its curious meanderings, and finally write it all up in a terribly terse, boring, and altogether antiseptic fashion, must surely have been a frustrated and pathological personality. Doctoral dissertations are painful work! And, for what it's worth, none are probably more painful than "content analysis"!

Content analysis is a laborious process, and having endured this most tiresome activity, I can assure anyone who might read these comments that I have *never* required *any* of the more than sixty doctoral students whose committees I have chaired as a graduate advisor in three different universities to utilize this methodology. Moreover, I have never repeated that process myself. Once, most surely, was enough! There are occasional experiences in our lives when a *single* episode has sufficed—it may have been a parachute jump or a heart attack or even a divorce—but that one time provided all the learning I have ever needed to know about the nature of trends in the daily and weekly Press.

The Doctoral Paper:
Basic Research or Learning Experience?

I've sort of come to the conviction across a great many years in the professorial business that the doctoral thesis is, indeed, a special kind of learning experience, and for whatever else I might have learned from it, that at least is what my content-analysis study convinced me of. There are still many fields, particularly in some areas of the Humanities and the Sciences, where there is a kind of presumption that doctoral research *ought* to plow "new ground," i.e., that such research *ought* to unearth knowledge that might, heretofore have been hidden or not known. I have genuine appreciation for that premise, and in some fields that certainly makes considerable sense, but in other fields, such a view is ridiculous! Better in such fields is the attitude (that I have adopted) that the doctoral paper and the research leading to its completion is primarily a unique learning experience. In my own case, that was true. It was very hard work, and I did learn from pursuing it. The methodology was exacting, the discipline was rewarding, and the ultimate result was satisfying. More, I could not otherwise expect from any graduate student under my subsequent supervision, and I think most of them have felt similarly.

In that regard, I'm reminded of an observation by a former decanal colleague at West Virginia University, Dr. Stanley Wearden, now enjoying his role as a semi-retired Professor of Statistics. Dr. Wearden was at that time our Graduate Dean at WVU. It is a position and/or office, by the way, that we no longer include in our overall organizational structure, since some time in recent years, in its infinite wisdom, our institution decided that a Graduate School was somewhat superfluous. (Record me here as "opposed"!)

Stan Wearden

In any case, the comment he made that I remember was in reference to a dissertation of a student in some field of the Sciences that apparently wasn't all that well received by his doctoral committee, and after a rather prolonged discussion of the merits and limitations of the particular thesis involved, Dean Wearden said, "I recommend that we vote to accept this paper. One should remember that Linus Pauling received three Nobel Prizes and not one of them for his dissertation." On that note, the Committee voted to pass the student!

The Finishing Touches

But I have digressed! Suffice to say that ever so slowly, my graduate work progressed, and by March 1960, the research itself was pretty well completed. All that remained was to write it all up and make some sense of it. In these times, graduate students have access to computers and word processing programs and computer attached printers which altogether completely redefine the whole process of writing, but in those days, we wrote either in longhand or composed on typewriters. My preference (mostly from newspapering days) was to compose on the typewriter, and, fortunately, the college provided me with a super-duper IBM electric machine.[143] I would write *long* passages, correct them, "x" out stuff, and rewrite all on the same page. But my long-suffering wife, who had the unenviable task of typing this paper for finished copy, had no access to such a machine and had to utilize our home-owned, manual, Smith-Corona portable. She nearly went *nuts* trying to figure out my hieroglyphics! After all, using only that small portable, it was *she* who had to finally type my thesis with the required *five* additional copies (on "onion skin"). It's amazing in retrospect that she could even have done it at all. That she did so with almost no errors and readable copies is even more amazing!

But *oh boy* did we ever argue a lot in the process! She had this uncontrollable urge to question so much of my prose: "Does this make sense?" she would ask. And, "How could you possibly say *that*?" and "Why would you use a double negative when all you want to say is…?" It almost caused us to come to blows! But somehow, the paper got done, and when I took it in for the Graduate Office to check it out, they complimented us on the quality of the preparation!

And, finally, and of at least some interest, I went into the final Oral Examination, and there was Professor George Counts, world famous and gloriously retired from Teachers College, Columbia University.

---

[143] My father was a "hunt and peck" typist, using only his index fingers, but he was fairly fast. My mother, of course, was much faster, having trained as a secretary.

George Counts

He had, by the way, joined our MSU faculty at the insistence of his former colleague Ernest Melby, who was an original member of my doctoral committee. Melby asked Counts to serve on the committee not alone owing to his acknowledged reputational stature but mostly from rather "soft" pressure from my chairman who knew of the affection between Melby and Counts, though in truth, Professor Counts didn't know beans about either the methodology or the topic. Moreover, Dr. Counts was surely among the absolutely *worst* teachers I've ever endured, but, anyway, to end this long explanation, Professor Counts said to me at the outset of the meeting: "Well, Mr. Monahan, the only problem with this thesis is that the front page and the back page are two hundred pages too far apart!" Needless to say, I was devastated, until, noticing a few smiles around the table, I began to realize that Professor Counts actually had a sense of humor! From that point on, things went rather well. I passed with the proverbial "flying colors."

Jane's Work: An Important Digression

During these almost two years, I had progressed from a part-time instructor to a full-time instructor, which, apart from the fact that the faculty had some confidence in my work, also meant that I had doubled my compensation (from a little over $2,500 annually to about $5,000). And my teaching responsibilities which always involved "off campus" courses had remained about the same, and the courses that I taught had not varied except that I had been permitted to offer an on-campus course for undergraduates in the "Foundations of Education" (a sort of History/Philosophy/Sociology of Education course) and which I truly enjoyed and did a rather good job at.

Since much of my graduate work in Mass Communications was significantly based in Sociology or in sociological kinds of research techniques and concerns, Sociology itself and/or "social" phenomena were important aspects of study. Accordingly, I was advised to enroll in several "pure" Sociology courses, and this brought me into contact with several Michigan State professors in those fields who made lasting impressions on my own scholarship. More importantly, during our years at State, Jane had accepted a part-time secretarial position in the Department of Sociology where she primarily worked with an outstanding Rural Sociologist named Archibald "Archie" Haller.

Archibald "Archie" Haller after his retirement

Haller had come to MSU from (I think) the University of Wisconsin, where he had already established a national reputation, and, at MSU, joined a strong core of faculty in Sociology who were in the process of establishing MSU as a first-rate leader in socio-metric and social psychological studies. Needless to say, I also profited from her association with the department since not only was she much respected by all of those in that faculty, but she became particularly familiar with much of the sociological terminology, which eased (at least a little) some of our dissertational arguments later on. Certainly, too, I profited in other ways. For example (when she and I were recalling those days) I remembered my first session in a seminar in the "Sociology of Mass Communications" with a terribly dull though otherwise renowned Sociology professor named Olmstead (one of the absolutely worst teachers I'd endured), and when he'd called my name off his enrollment sheet, he'd looked at me and asked "Are you related to Jane?" I think I'd have done ok in the class in any case, but his recognition of Jane surely didn't hurt! Jane worked in the Sociology Department most of the final year we were at State. She didn't earn all that much, but it was a godsend in those days, and it was a good experience for her in other ways.[144] It is difficult in any pattern of remembrances to put people and experiences in proper perspective. In remembering those days at MSU, perhaps this is as good a place as any to consider the importance and the contribution of Jane to everything that we are or have become.

Jane: The Early Years

Jane had always worked! Except for a brief period in the years we lived in Marion when I taught school and the two years we lived in Frankfurt, Jane had always worked![145] In truth, her record in a variety of jobs from the time we married in 1945 would itself make for a unique journal in its own right, and were she to tell it in her own words, it would be a story of perseverance and a remarkably single-minded vision of what she somehow curiously believed could be possible for our life together. Accordingly, though she never articulated that vision, early on, I came somehow to understand her hopes for us. Thus, she pushed, cajoled, nagged, motivated, encouraged, and planned. Somehow, it all worked out pretty much according to her ideas. In truth, I was no match for Jane! She was, and is, the most single-minded person I've ever known. Where I am languid, she is energetic. Where I put off, she is timely. I'd rather do nothing, she wants to do something! We are different in significant ways, but her drive has always pushed me to the limits of my capacities, and she is the soul of my achievements.

Almost immediately after we were married in 1945 and just having completed a program in Secretarial Science at the then best accredited "Business University" in the country at Bowling Green, Kentucky, and living with my folks in the Scott Street house in Bowling Green where

---

[144] Here, my father makes his only reference to our relative poverty while we lived at Michigan State. I will discuss that a bit more in my own memoir, sharing memories of living in a small two-bedroom married student apartment!

[145] Though he seldom, indeed, virtually never discusses the subject, her lack of work during these periods certainly resulted from her being the mother of a small baby—me!—in Marion, and of another small baby—my brother Joe—in Frankfort.

even the most affable of persons would have had much opportunity for conflict, she went to work at a small Dry Cleaning establishment, which lasted maybe a month! Not long afterward, she worked for a newly established Small Loan Company in Bowling Green, and a couple of years later, after I returned from military service, she resumed that employment.

Meantime, she'd persuaded me to go back to high school (I had dropped out to join the glorious effort to "win back democracy from the Axis Powers" by enlisting in the Merchant Marine.), and, while finishing high school through the rest of 1945 and until graduation in 1946, Jane endured a life totally unlike anything that she'd known before. We knew that my brief maritime service would not defer me from the military draft, and, because voluntary military service at that time provided fairly good incentives in the way of the GI Bill, we decided that enlistment was preferable to the draft. That way, at least, we'd know exactly how long I'd have to be in Service. By enlisting in the US Army for an eighteen-month "hitch," I would earn at least three full years of subsidized collegiate tuition, books, etc., so we decided that was what we would do.[146] I went off to the army in September 1946 after Jane had seen me though my high school graduation. (She subsequently saw me through three more of those Commencements, but we had no notion of that at that time!). She then returned home to Marion to live with her folks during my service where, again, she worked. She saved most of what she earned, and I sent along most of what I earned. This "nest egg" was aimed at providing additional support for our further plans. Now, all of this was by her designs. I'd like to take more space than might otherwise be worthy to remember my years in Japan as a soldier in the 19th Infantry Regiment of the 24th Infantry Division in Beppu, Kyushu, Japan from November 1946 until I returned home to Camp Stoneman, California to be discharged two days after Christmas in 1947, but that's probably a little irrelevant. Otherwise, suffice to say that my time in Japan was enlightening, and

---

[146] The fact that my father repeats these details that he already outlined in an earlier chapter would seem to indicate that the chapters were not written sequentially and often written some time apart from each other.

that, as a member of the 19th Infantry Glee Club, and, subsequently, its football team, I spent little time drilling and "pulling" guard duty. More importantly, I wasted a great opportunity to learn much firsthand about a unique culture and a marvelous people.[147]

My homecoming to Evansville, Indiana on a train from California where a wife I'd truly not really come to know all that well and her parents awaited me was nevertheless a glad occasion. Things had changed much during my absence, but Jane had everything figured out! First, she took me over to Evansville, Indiana and supervised the outfitting of new clothes. She'd already purchased some nice clothes for me including a marvelous velour corduroy sports coat what was at least one size too large (she must have imagined that I was more of a man that I actually was!). And she'd bought me a pair of gray flannel slacks to go with the coat. It was a handsome outfit, and even if just a bit too large, I thought I looked pretty good in it. Our shopping trip was productive: a soft gray, double-breasted pin-striped suit, shirts, ties (especially, a black knit one to wear with the jacket and slacks), and a very handsome gabardine topcoat which was subsequently stolen while we were attending a basketball game in Louisville a year or so later![148]

We moved back to Bowling Green, and in March of 1948, I entered Western Kentucky State as a Freshman. We then found a place to live in the "Veterans Village," and, again, Jane went to work! She worked for the same small loan company for about $30.00 a week, and what Jane learned working for that company held her in good stead for the rest of our productive lives. She learned what it really meant to have to borrow money at high rates of interest and how valuable a dollar is regardless of circumstances. She saw people who were really between the proverbial rock and hard place, and she learned that one is always better off to pay as you go if that is at all possible. Ever since, neither of us have ever been much seduced by so-called easy credit,

---

[147] As I have already noted, Appendix A has excerpts of his letters to my mother while serving in Japan.

[148] The remarkable detail here may owe more to my mother than my father. My mother would later make shopping something of an art form, and she had an amazing memory for clothes.

and we've always paid off our bills at the end of each month. The only long-term debt we've ever assumed was a mortgage for houses we've owned in Norman, Iowa City, and Morgantown. The last of those, in Morgantown, was paid off in 1993.[149]

But, suffice to say that Jane has always worked. Even in Morgantown when she didn't really need to do it, she took the Real Estate examination, passed it, and earned excellent money selling houses for a while. It's true that she took that on as much for something to do than as for a livelihood, but she was very good at that, too, and much of what she earned in that activity is a big part of our assets today. She was always very good at whatever she took on, except, maybe, the proper training of a husband who turned out to be an incurable academic and who dragged her through the trials and tribulations of one university after another. In retrospect, when we began our journey in Norman, Oklahoma all those years later, we couldn't have been much more satisfied with our lives than we were at Western in those beginning years of college in 1948.

The University of Oklahoma

In late March of 1960, it became apparent to everyone that I had to begin to think about something beyond graduate study. I had to seriously consider a *job*! My professorial colleagues (and friends) encouraged me to consider a superintendency. After all, that was my primary consideration, but I was a bit skittish about that. Still, I did look at a couple of such possibilities, but none of those ever reached the serious stage of interviews and negotiations. Now, one must remember that those kinds of positions paid very well in those times, much better by far than any typical probationary Assistant Professor's position even in the best of first-rate universities, so I did rather seriously consider such positions.

Then, curiously, in early April 1960, Dr. Robert Hopper, the chairman of our department, came into my office and advised that he had

---

[149] That would have been nine years early on a standard thirty-year mortgage.

talked with folks at the University of Oklahoma about a vacancy in their Education Administration faculty, and he had mentioned me as a good possibility. Our department had received a sizeable grant to do a study in a selected group of the North Central Association institutions of higher education (the NCA was a regional accrediting association), and among colleges that were planned to be visited were a couple of institutions in Arkansas and Oklahoma. Dr. Hopper further suggested that since the study required teams of two persons to visit assigned regions, that he would conduct the major activity of that study in that area, and that I could accompany him as the second team member. He took pains to point out that the "grant" would compensate me for all of my expenses and then suggested that it *just might* provide opportunity for me to spend a little time at the University of Oklahoma. (Incidentally, this gesture was characteristic of the "style" and accommodation of that remarkable program.)

So, I said "Fine!" I would be quickly trained in the methodology required of an "examiner," and it would give me a chance to meet with some of the Oklahoma people sort of informally, and both they and I could sort of feel each other out. Now, any reader must realize that this possibility was only that, and moreover, I had no burning itch to assume a faculty position at the University of Oklahoma or any other higher education institution for that matter. I hardly knew where OU was and felt no terribly critical urge at that time to be a candidate for a job anywhere in higher education. After all, I still held more than a little interest in a public school superintendency and knew well that such roles were most rewarding and challenging. On the other hand, I *did* need a job! I did enjoy the academic lifestyle, and I knew that I was a pretty good teacher and that, all things considered, I thought I could probably hold my own as a researcher and writer given a break here and there, so I thought, well, what the hell! Go and look and let the chips fall where they may.

Dr. Hopper and I administered the instruments at Harding College in Searcy, Arkansas (at that time a religiously affiliated institution with a flamboyant president who was a good bit further to the right than Attila the Hun) and at Panhandle A&M in Goodwell, Oklahoma (a four-year A&M institution still pleasantly mired in the nineteenth century). And in between those two sites, we spent a couple of days in Norman, Oklahoma with Dr. Claude Kelley and his wife Jean. Dr. Kelley was chairman of the program in Educational Administration at OU, and I liked him immediately.

Claude Kelley at West Virginia University[150]

That began another of those curious kinds of circumstances where chance redirects one's life, for Claude later joined our "boss" at OU (Dr. James G. Harlow, Dean of OU's College of Education) when Harlow assumed the presidency of West Virginia University in 1967, and both of them had much to do with my appointment at WVU as dean of its College of Huan Resources and Education in 1972.

Claude Kelley was a smallish man with a keen sense of humor and an always hurried kind of manner. He had grown up in Indiana where he had been a very successful high school basketball coach. He'd somehow found his way to North Texas State University where he completed his doctoral work and had then turned up at OU. What began at that early spring visit in 1960 lasted over many years, actually,

---

[150] Photo of Claude Kelley used with permission from the West Virginia Regional History Center.

until his and his wife's untimely deaths almost twelve years later in an automobile accident in Ireland. By that time (in late 1971), Claude had relinquished his important position as Vice-President at WVU, and he and Jean had embarked on a long-awaited trip to Ireland. Caught up in the confusion of left-handed driving, they'd apparently mis-perceived oncoming traffic and had been hit broadside. Jean apparently was killed almost instantly, but Claude seemed to be recovering. He'd finally been sent back to WVU's medical center, but complications developed, and a few weeks later, he also died. This all occurred just a little prior to my own active participation in the search for a dean at WVU, but there is little question that Claude Kelley had much to do with my being involved. It was a devastating loss not only to WVU, but certainly to me personally.

I really liked Claude Kelley. He was an avid football fan, a better than average golfer, an astute bridge player, and would play poker for any amount you could count and any game you could name at the drop of a hat. He was a most competent academic and had a genuine sense of compassion for students, and he had a marvelous kind of integrity that allowed for the intrusion of common sense. When Jane and I first went to Norman, Claude and Jean Kelley were our links to the academic community and remained our closest friends while we were there. I guess that those very early interactions with Dr. Kelley went reasonably well, since about a month or so later, I was invited to come down to Norman for a formal interview.

I remember very well coming home to our apartment in Spartan Village in East Lansing and telling Jane and our two young sons that I was going down to Norman, Oklahoma for a job interview. She said, "Who the hell ever went to the University of Oklahoma?" (Jane had become just a bit spoiled by the Big Ten "mystique.") And I remember saying something like "Well, Bud Wilkinson went there!" (In truth, all I knew about OU was its marvelous record in football, and Bud Wilkinson was the architect of that reputation.) I had not actually completed my dissertation when I went down to OU to interview for a job. But I really liked Norman. I interviewed quite well, and not least of the reasons was that I had used that textbook in our Foundations of Education course (which was the same book used in a similar course at OU), and that appealed to one of the important members of the Search Committee who later turned out to be another close friend of ours during our years in Norman. The upshot was that they offered me the job at $7,600 annually. It was, for us at the time, a more than reasonable proposition, and although Jane had some reservations about it, she, like me, was adventurous, and I called them back and accepted the offer. Perhaps the best thing about all that was the motivation for completing my doctoral paper. I wrote the final version of my dissertation in less than three weeks thereafter!

The Niceties of a New Job

1960 Oldsmobile similar to the one we owned

One of the first things we decided to do after having accepted the OU job was to shop around for a new car. Our old 1956 Ford "Ranch Wagon" had a zillion miles on it, and we had regularly replaced mufflers about every ten thousand miles. One of the marvelous things about living in East Lansing, Michigan was that just down the road in Lansing itself was the Oldsmobile factory. After checking about, we finally were able to purchase a brand new Oldsmobile "Dynamic 88" four-door sedan for even a little less than someone else might buy a Chevrolet. It *was* exhilarating!

Ah, but then! We had to rent a U-Haul trailer and try to stuff all of our belongings in it, and even though most of our regular furniture was still stored in Frankfort, Kentucky, getting all of our accumulated stuff in a haul-behind trailer was a chore. Moreover, new cars at that time did not have a bumper appropriate for pulling a trailer, so I had to go over to Sears and have them *bore* a hole in my brand new car to install a trailer hitch!

It required most of a full day and into the night for us to stuff that U-Haul full, and early the next day, we took off for Marion, Kentucky. We had almost to *crawl* through Indianapolis and on *race day* (would you believe?). And with very soft springs and shock absorbers on that new car, that trailer bumped every time we even *touched* a dip in the road. Let me tell you that there were a *million* dips in the roads in the old city of Indianapolis, and we were just about out of our minds with anxiety for the impact on our brand new automobile. There were long lines of motorists behind us honking (and cursing), and we just gave them the "bird" and went crawling toward Kentucky. Needless to say, when we got there, Jane's dad arranged for a local man to pull that U-Haul the rest of the way to Oklahoma, and from there on, we had an otherwise pleasant trip. Except, of course, that we somehow decided to drive all the way? But by the time we got to Springfield, Missouri, and then even a little "deep" into Oklahoma, both Jane and I were so sleepy we could hardly drive! When we finally arrived in Norman, we went directly to a very *cheap* motel and just buried ourselves for about ten hours.[151]

Living the Good Life

We loved Norman. Our beginnings were not all that great since I had to rent a house, and it was not without shortcomings. But after about a year (thanks again to the GI Bill), we were able to buy a house that was under construction. We were able to choose a lot of the essentials, and it was in a nice part of Norman. Our older son Greg was, at that time, just ready for the second grade. Joe was only barely four years old. We entered Greg in the OU Training School, which was nicely

---

[151] Even though I was only six years old, I still remember how inhumanely *hot* that drive was! My parents later had an after-market Frigiking air conditioner installed in that car that tended to overheat the engine fairly quickly—but it did feel nice in Oklahoma's hot summers! Likewise, when we would visit my grandparents in Kentucky from Oklahoma, they would always always drive the distance between Norman and Marion in one very long day, presumably so they wouldn't have to pay for a motel, and also because they wanted to maximize their vacation time in Kentucky. Those drives entailed getting up in the middle of the night for a 17-hour trip.

recommended, and I went about the work of trying to find out what I was expected to do.[152]

Rental house on Sherry Street, Norman Oklahoma, 1960

The same house on a trip to Norman in 2018, virtually unchanged

The Oakwood Drive house at the time we purchased it, ca 1961

The Oakwood Drive house in 2018, unchanged save for landscaping

We did very well in Oklahoma. My teaching went well, and I took on a number of really first-rate graduate students. My very first doctoral graduate was a young man from Wichita, Kansas named Keith Esch, who went on to become the Deputy Superintendent for Personnel in the Wichita Public Schools and has remained a good

---

[152] As my father noted in an earlier chapter, many universities operated "Laboratory" schools at this time, designed to train new teachers. My experiences in this school were definitely mixed, something I'll touch upon in my own memoir. Interestingly, this is the first mention by name of my brother Joe in this work. My father was a loving and caring father, but neither my brother nor I play a very large role in his autobiography until its later chapters.

friend across all the years.[153] Another student who turned out to be instrumental in my life was a young school superintendent in a small district in central Oklahoma who later, and while still my student, was selected as Superintendent of Schools in another district about halfway between Norman and Oklahoma City at Moore, Oklahoma. Now, at that time, Moore was a sleepy little town on the verge of becoming considerably more than that, and this chap, a man named Leslie Fisher, knew somehow that Moore was going to grow into something greater than most anybody would have guessed.[154]

While I was at MSU, I had participated in a number of what we referred to in those times as "school surveys." These were consulting studies whereby our MSU experts provided school districts information on enrollment projections, curriculum analyses, and other kinds of information to help boards and staff make reasonable future plans, and sometimes, these studies were provided with rather generous contracts. My role in a few of those studies had concerned enrollment projections, so when Mr. Fisher took over the Moore, Oklahoma schools, he was deeply concerned about the system's growth, and he asked me if I would like to consult regarding that. Being both naïve and impetuous (and *certainly* needing the money) I said, "Well sure, I could do that!" Well! Doing enrollment projections for any reasonably stable school system is easy. You just develop a nice linear projection—take birthrates and figure how many of those turn up in first grade, then calculate the so-called "survival rate" (linearly) from grade to grade, which provides a neat statistical pattern of *average* survival. Trouble is, with the Moore school system, there were no reliable "base" data for anchoring the projections. Families were moving in from *everywhere*, and what you had in the first grade last year simply made no sense for this year. What otherwise ought to be easy turned out to be totally unreliable.

And then, I hit on one of those remarkable inspirations that come along rarely in any researcher's experience. I found that in all of the

---

[153] For more on Keith Esch, including a photograph, see Chapter VIII.

[154] Moore is now part of the greater Oklahoma City/Norman metropolitan area and is the seventh largest city in the state, with more than 55,000 in population at this writing.

new subdivision open houses, prospective buyers filled out little cards which indicated how many children they had and what their ages were. Throughout the Moore school district, which was only about ten miles from Oklahoma City proper, there were about four or five new housing areas opening up. I went around to these open houses, and using these cards, developed a rough calculation of a census of these families. Then, I calculated the housing sales and double checked the percentage of sales based on a rough calculation of family pattern. I was then able to design a "mean" projection using the traditional formula. Accordingly, I then went before Dr. Fisher's board (he had subsequently earned his doctorate at OU) to provide my so-called "expert" opinion. Now, you have to know how insecure I really was, for at that time, the entire school population in the Moore school system was only about 1,200 students, but based on my projections, I was going before that board to tell them that in *only five years*, their total enrollments are going to be in the neighborhood of 11,000 students! Well, at first, they just sort of gasped. Then, a couple of them just laughed out loud, and I just sat there wondering how the hell did I ever take on this kind of stupid chore! But, I'd checked and double checked my data, and I told them that, to be totally candid, my projections were fairly conservative, that is, that the actual enrollments in ten years could be as high as 12,000!

But I have to give Fisher credit. He didn't bat an eyelash! He told the board, "look, maybe these projections are a little off since there's no way one can predict such patterns with certainty, but we'd be better safe than sorry." He told them that being so close to Oklahoma City, and with so much accessible money for relative low-cost housing available, and that with many people already moving into the district, "Well," he said, "Let's begin a building program to accommodate the number of kids that Dr. Monahan predicts because anyone with half an eye to see it knows that this area is growing like Topsy."[155] And that board did exactly that! With Fisher's guidance, they began the procedures for acquiring land, hired architects, and started building. Fortunately for me! When I left Oklahoma in 1965 to join the faculty at the University of Iowa,

---

[155] See note 105 on this idiom.

the Moore school system had an enrollment of 12,600 students, one year and 600 students ahead of my recommendations. Those who were members of that board then *still* think I'm a flat-out genius!

Apart from the nice fact that I earned a reputation for consulting expertise, perhaps the best thing about that was that the consulting money I made from Moore provided carpeting and new furniture for our new house on Oakwood Street in Norman, and Leslie Fisher went on to become State Superintendent of Schools in Oklahoma on an elected nonpartisan ballot and was returned to office again and again. The worst thing about all that was that this man who was such a good and loyal friend suffered from premature heart problems and died in 1985.[156] He is still remembered as one of the most competent state superintendents that state ever had even though he was sometimes almost *too* straightforward in his words and deeds. I loved the man. He helped me to become a better professor of educational administration because he helped to make it possible for me to be an active participant in the "field" of my interests.

As a result of my association with Dr. Fisher, I was accepted throughout Oklahoma and the southwestern regions as a professor who knew something more than theory and prescription. Many years after I left Oklahoma, I would still meet many of the superintendents from that state at conventions and meetings and was always acknowledged as "one of their own." They always felt that I was a true "Sooner" and that I had provided their organization and their work with competent advice and effective instruction. Even to this day, there are still men in Oklahoma who remember me even though my tenure at OU was a short five years.

Our Years in Norman

In retrospect, we could not have begun a career in any higher education faculty under better circumstances than at OU. Our College of Education there, in 1960, was relatively small as such institutions go.

---

[156] Leslie Fisher served as State Superintendent of Schools in Oklahoma from 1971 to 1984 and ran unsuccessfully for governor as a Democrat in 1986. He died at age 65. I was unable to locate a photograph, even though there is an elementary school in Moore today named for him.

OU College of Education building

We were a college of the whole. That is, there were no departments, although, of course, there were so-called "program areas" in which students, whether undergraduate or graduate student, were able to "major." Everyone was expected to teach both undergraduates and graduates, dependent, of course, on background qualifications and experience. And as I learned, those who'd been there the longest seemed to be able to avoid teaching the undergraduate courses. Our so-called teaching loads were fairly heavy at OU. In addition to my three graduate courses in educational administration, I was also assigned one undergraduate course, a course I'd also taught at Michigan State (we even used the same textbook). But my load of about a total of sixteen semester hours didn't really bother me. My undergraduate course, which *always* enrolled more than forty students, turned out to be a real back breaker! But I loved that class! Actually, in terms of sheer labor, the undergraduate course took more than half my time. But, since it was a kind of basic introduction to the whole idea of so-called "Foundations" of Capital "E" Education, I took the course very seriously, and I think I did a very good job of teaching it. And, as is usually the case, I learned far more than I taught.

My dean at OU was a man named James G. Harlow. Mr. Harlow (as we always addressed him and thought of him) was from an old Oklahoma family. The Harlows had been a publishing family in Oklahoma since about the time it became a state. He had always been something of an academic, and having completed work on his MA degree when he was barely twenty-two years old, had subsequently become much involved in science fields (His undergraduate major, as I recall, had been in Physics.). He'd served as Dean of Arts and Sciences at OU for a spell and then had gone up to the University of Chicago where he'd done his Ph.D. in Educational Administration. When he returned to Oklahoma, he'd taken on the responsibility for an organization known as the "Frontiers of Science" which, funded with significant money from various Oklahoma philanthropies, brought distinguished science scholars to Oklahoma schools to provide youngsters with first hand experiences and conversations with notable scientists. Sometime in the late fifties, the College of Education at OU found itself in need of a dean, and Mr. Harlow was appointed.

James G. Harlow

Now, needless to say, that also reflected the idea that "luck" or "chance" has much to do with one's life course. Dean Harlow became a genuine confidante for me, and in those days when higher education was literally booming, I had a number of opportunities to leave OU for other positions, and each time that I received such an offer, I always bounced it off Mr. Harlow. Several years later, after

I'd left OU for the University of Iowa, and he had been appointed as President of West Virginia University in Morgantown, West Virginia, he invited me to assume the Deanship of WVU's College of Human Resources and Education. But that will remain for some additional comment presently.

Our family really took to Oklahoma. While we were there, we bought our first house [already pictured above]. It was a modest three-bedroom place in the midst of much housing construction in west Norman only about a mile or so from the campus. We were in the company of many young faculty members in similar circumstances, and many of those have remained lifelong friends. During that time, too, Jane enrolled in and completed her own BA degree in elementary education at OU, and my own career seemed to prosper. I was fortunate to have several articles published and came to the attention of important people in my field, which made it possible for me to be able to attend a number of important national meetings and to be able to participate in some of those in somewhat significant ways.[157]

Jane's experiences in pursuing her own degree at OU were generally good, but we both still chuckle about a science-for-teachers course designed specifically for Teacher Education students. This course was taught by a marvelous "curmudgeon" kind of full professor in the Department of Biology, and it required field trips out into the boondocks which this chap conducted via his old, beat up international station wagon. Poor Jane endured these sojourns with a stiff upper lip even though on at least one or more occasions, they occurred in the midst of severe menstrual cramps and the deadly heat of Oklahoma summers. But goodness! She did learn a lot. Another undergraduate experience for her that we still marvel at was the requirement in those days at OU that no undergraduate would earn a degree without passing a relatively rigorous swimming course! Now, wouldn't you wonder? Here's a

---

[157] My father would later co-write and publish his first book with his good friend and colleague at Oklahoma, Robert Ohm, entitled *Educational Administration: Philosophy in Action* (Norman: University of Oklahoma Press, 1965).

state out in the great plains only twenty years removed from the dust bowl years, and you can't graduate unless you pass a course in *swimming*! But she did it![158]

My mother's OU diploma

But Sadness, Too

Although our five years in Norman were otherwise pleasant and rewarding, they were also touched with some regret. During our second year, in 1962, we learned that Jane was pregnant again. We hadn't planned on that, but as is typically the case, began to look forward to a new addition. Sadly, it didn't work out, and she miscarried

---

[158] My mother never used her degree to re-enter the teaching field (she taught stenography briefly in her home town of Marion, Kentucky while my father was serving in Japan in 1947), even though I think she would have made a fine teacher. Just getting the degree was enough for her!

only about three months into the pregnancy. We never knew what that child might have been nor wanted to know, but we still occasionally look back on it with understandable speculation.[159]

Luck and Circumstance, Again

At around that time, I came into contact with a man who was an executive editor with the Macmillan publishing company and who, throughout my life, became one of my best friends. Lloyd Chilton was a graduate of the University of Kentucky and was primarily responsible for screening manuscripts for Macmillan in a variety of scholarly fields.

My father and Lloyd Chilton looking over books published by WVU faculty, early 1970s

---

[159] The miscarriage led to a hysterectomy, thereby preventing further pregnancies. Alas, that last operation meant a lifetime of hormone medications and occasional headaches that would plague my mother for the rest of her life.

He'd originally contacted me about reviewing a manuscript that his firm was considering for a textbook, and he'd heard about me through one or another of my articles. He liked my critiques of the several manuscripts that he'd asked me to examine, and he and I sort of struck up an off-and-on kind of "chatty" correspondence. A little later on, after I moved to the University of Iowa, Lloyd and I developed a collaboration that resulted in four books that has lasted until the present.

Also at that time, my work at OU resulted in rather rapid promotion in rank, and in late 1965, I was recommended and approved for promotion to full professor, although the promotion had not been finalized or announced. Then, almost out of the blue, I received a phone call from a chap I had become acquainted with at the University of Iowa named Dr. Willard (Bill) Lane. Bill Lane was the Chairman of the Department of Educational Administration at Iowa, and he and I had talked several times at national meetings, particularly at meetings of the University Council for Educational Administration (UCEA), which was a remarkable kind of organization and provided many opportunities for young "Turks" like me to gain some national visibility at meetings here and there across the country.

The UCEA was a specially funded national (membership) consortium of major doctoral-granting universities which provided a lot of information and national symposia for scholars in our field to share ideas, present papers, and learn about new developments. It was a prestigious group and was particularly useful as a forum for younger professors to gain some visibility nationally, and I was particularly fortunate to have had the opportunity to participate actively in some of the UCEA's national meetings. It was in this manner that I had come to the attention of Bill Lane, and when an opening occurred in the educational administration staff at Iowa, he called me and asked whether I might be interested.

The situation there was promising. After all, Iowa was in what we referred to in those days as "the mainstream." It was a Big Ten institution, and I held my doctorate from a Big Ten university (Michigan State). The offer was for an Associate Professorship. (One should remember that I'd just been recommended for a fully tenured Full Professorship at OU, and though OU might have been just a rung below Big Ten institutions, it was still a major player in our field in every way.) I went immediately to Mr. Harlow for a little advice, and he was very candid. He told me that, given the compensation was adequately increased, I should probably consider it. "After all," he said, "Iowa is a first-rate institution with a marvelous reputation, and it would give you ample opportunity to make a national reputation." Having completed his own work at Chicago (which for all practical purposes was *still* a Big Ten institution) he knew of which he spoke.

The offer at Iowa was pretty good, all things considered, not *glorious* in any sense of the word, but not bad. They would give me a tenured associate professorship, pay me a little bit more than I was getting at OU, but for nine months (my appointment at OU was for twelve months). Plus, they would guarantee me summer employment for an additional 20% and an extension assignment for one course per term (it was limited to one course) for an additional 15% if I chose to elect that. So, all told, if I took advantage of everything available, my annual income at Iowa was going to be pretty good. But the issue which decided it for us was that Iowa would pay up to $1000.00 in moving expenses, and that *did* it![160] There was no affirmative action in those days. If someone wanted you, and you were willing, there was no need for interviews and this, that, or the other. You just said ok, I'll come, and that was it. That's the way we did it at Iowa. I never saw the place until I arrived there—no interviews, no campus visit, no nothing. They offered the job on the phone, I accepted it in a call back, and in August of 1965, Jane and I, our two boys, and a spirited little dog named "Sparty" took off for Iowa City.[161]

---

[160] It's useful to keep in mind that we were a single-earner family. My mother no longer worked outside the home and was then what was called a "home maker," and what is now more commonly called a "stay at home mom." Thus, salary and what extra money my father could make mattered very much.

[161] Sparty was a small "rat terrier" we acquired from the dog pound during our first year in Oklahoma. She was named, of course, for the Michigan State Spartans, the sports team of my father's doctoral alma mater.

Portrait of the family taken toward the end of our time in Oklahoma

CHAPTER VII

The Professorial Years: University of Iowa (1965-1972)

The University of Iowa was then, and still is, one of America's great universities. Iowa, as a state and a people, has somehow managed across its history to have inculcated a quite remarkable respect for education. Its system of public schools was then (and I presume, still is) among the best in the United States, and there were *many* school systems. Probably, this is owing to the fact that Iowa has always taken much pride in a kind of grassroots attitude about democracy and government, and people in even the smallest kinds of hamlets have insured that their schools serve their own. When I went out to Iowa back in 1965, there were more than 400 school districts in the state and *all* of them were well-supported, mostly from local taxation. In other words, the whole idea of a State Department of Education which kind of calls all the shots (as with West Virginia, for example) was not at all the case, and local control was a reality. But there was significant emphasis on basic education and kids learned! The Iowa Tests (which were administered, scored, and managed by the University of Iowa's Measurement Research Corporation) were almost universally used, and Iowa's public school students scored quite well on those. This same ideology carried over to the system of higher education. It should be noted that Iowa has *only* three public institutions of comprehensive higher education. There is the University of Iowa in Iowa City, Iowa State University in Ames, and the University of Northern Iowa in Cedar Falls. There is also a fairly elaborate system of Community Colleges, but so-called higher education is still managed within the framework of the three public universities.[162]

---

[162] That state also includes a fairly large number of private colleges, the most prestigious of which is probably Grinnell College, located in a town of the same name in the eastern part of the state.

Getting Settled

We had a difficult time getting a place to live in Iowa and only a few hours before our furniture arrived, we finally rented a house. In the following February [1966], we contracted for the construction of a new house in a very attractive section of Iowa City only a short walk from the university golf course and not far from the university's impressive medical facilities. Moreover, the new place was within walking distance to the football stadium and the Iowa Fieldhouse where, in those days, our basketball teams performed. It was a most pleasant place to live, and we still count many of our former neighbors among our closest friends.

Our rental house on Kimball Road in Iowa City

The new house on Mahaska Drive in Iowa City, 1966

We enrolled our kids in public schools, and in virtue of our neighborhood in our rental house had to enroll our older son Greg, who was to start seventh grade, in the Junior High School closest to us and which served the less well-off classes in Iowa City. It was a rather tough school, and though he endured some challenging circumstances, Greg was pretty resilient, and he managed ok. (In truth, he probably had a tougher time than either Jane or I could have known.)[163] I do remember one particular occasion when he received a poor grade in Physical Education, and it burned me up because I *knew* that he was being marked not on the basis of what he did or didn't do in the class, but on talent and skill (and he, not unlike his father, was somewhat lacking in adept muscular coordination activities). I objected appropriately, but I'm not sure it ever made any difference. On the other hand, because he was willing to try whatever was required of him, he earned considerable respect from some of his classmates.[164]

We entered Joseph in the third grade at another neighborhood school (I think it was known as "Horace Mann" [Ed. Note: it was]), but Joe had been the victim of unfortunate circumstances in Norman with a teacher who was absent most of the year. Consquently, he was far behind in reading and math, and his teachers in Iowa City decided that they would just work on his basics. And ultimately, that seemed to work out ok.[165]

Still, all things considered, and even though the move at that particular time required lots of "adjustments" for *all* of us, Iowa City turned out to be a good move for us, and my work in the College of Education and in my department went remarkably well. Moreover,

---

[163] He did, though more simply because it is always difficult to start in a new school than for class issues. Iowa City was a thoroughly middle-class town.

[164] My father overestimates my flexibility and inclinations. I was terrible at PE, was never motivated to do well in it, and my classmates were not charitable about my lack of ability at all. That said, that "D" grade invited the only direct intervention by him with one of my teachers in my memory. The poor man was pursuing a degree in teacher education at Iowa. My father summoned him to his office and chewed him out so fiercely that I don't think he ever got over it. I was completely unaware of this at the time, of course, and was mystified when that teacher suddenly took an interest in my progress—or woeful lack thereof—in PE class!

[165] My father returns to my brother's difficulties and eventual triumph over them later in this chapter.

the university itself was just great. In truth, in all of my experiences with several excellent universities including WVU, the University of Iowa stands out as the "best." There is or certainly was then a curious kind of milieu at "SUI" (State University of Iowa) that provided remarkable tolerance for ideas, and for a professorial genuine sense of responsibility. It was a truly great institution in those times, and I felt then and still do that it was a real stroke of fate that I was fortunate to have been a part of it.

The Productive Years

We were at Iowa from 1965 to 1972, and those seven years were probably my most productive and most satisfying as a university professor and among the most pleasant for our family. The house we built there (though the process of its construction nearly drove us mad!) was in a neighborhood that composed many university people, including a number of those in the medical faculty. Among the latter, some have remained our life-long friends.

Dr. Adrian Flatt, 1921-2017

Dr. Adrian Flatt, a genuinely world-renowned hand surgeon, lived across the street from us and has remained close to us across all these years. He subsequently left the university and became chairman of orthopedics at Baylor Medical Center in Texas. Interestingly, we called on Adrian for every kind of ailment that vexed us, and he always responded—albeit he often admitted that he knew nothing of what attacked us and was fond of saying "well, if it were your hands, I could help!" But, of course, that was overly modest. I remember one terrible time when I was beset with a kidney stone and was in unbearable pain and old Adrian came running over to see what he could do. He knew exactly what the problem was and had me in hospital in fifteen minutes. Another time, when

I suffered a knee injury playing volleyball (of all things!), he came over and, after a cursory examination, allowed as how I might have a bit more than a sprain (this did involve an area that was his field!). He got me to the hospital again and was right in his quick diagnosis. I had a hairline fracture. Adrian and his wife were wonderful neighbors, and they were fond of throwing elaborate parties. We enjoyed their hospitality on many occasions (not least of which sometimes resulted in bad hangovers!). I remember pleasantly a couple of occasions when we enjoyed impromptu martini sessions on our front lawns.

Over a couple of blocks from us were another medical family who became close life-long friends, Jack and Evalyn Filer. Jack was a pediatrician by training, but spent most of his time at Iowa in research. He held a distinguished chair as Mead-Johnson Professor which gave him access to M-J's facilities, including their Lear Jet, and required him to consult with that firm's officials in Evansville, Indiana.

On at least one or two occasions, he invited Jane to fly down there with him so that she could visit her parents in Marion, Kentucky. Jack was a gourmet cook and had a great catalogue of fine restaurants all over the world. Whenever we might have been going someplace, we'd always check with him for a good place to dine. In recent years, we haven't seen them, but a few years back, we did find ourselves together in Naples, Florida and enjoyed their company there.

Lloyd "Jack" Filer, 1919-1997

While we lived in Iowa City, our kids both attended newly constructed schools. Our older son Greg went to the new West High School not too far from our home, and Joseph attended a new Junior High School, though only for one year before we moved to West Virginia. Greg was fortunate to have received a marvelous education at West High even though some of his social experiences there left much to be desired. But he particularly enjoyed a very supportive English teacher and his band director.[166] He played the trombone, and as a result of early experiences with good instruction in Norman, did rather well.

---

[166] Dr. J. Brooke Workman was the English teacher, and Mr. John DeSalme the band director.

Jane and I still remember with the greatest pleasure one particular Jazz Band concert when, quite to our surprise, he played a solo on Tommy Dorsey's great theme, "I'm Gettin' Sentimental Over You," and dedicated it to his mother! We were flabbergasted, and he played it flawlessly. Now, it is a genuine measure of *any* sixteen-year-old's sense of self-assurance that he would dedicate such a performance to his mother under those circumstances. She will treasure it forever!

Joe's life as a kid was always made more difficult by our untimely moves. Moving from here and there is always difficult for children, and, as we look back on it, that was particularly the case for Joe. His unfortunate circumstances in his early grades in Norman unfairly penalized him, and in Iowa City, he found himself in a kind of constant catch-up mode. He was a fiercely independent kid in lots of ways and used to mount his bicycle and just take off for God-knows-where. He was a bit hyperactive and had never really developed very good study habits, and on top of everything else, had suffered for years with very bad tonsils which had caused lots of high fever sicknesses, and it wasn't until we were in Iowa that those problems were properly diagnosed and corrected.

I still remember so *many* nights in Norman when he was a very little guy, and he felt so bad with a fever that I would just hold him close on my abdomen while both of us tried to sleep. When we finally got those problems taken care of in Iowa City, he was at a distinct disadvantage academically, but to his credit, he not only survived all of that but went on to do very well ultimately. Of course, the move to West Virginia didn't help much either. We entered him in the Catholic School in Morgantown because we thought that would be best for him, but I'm not so sure in retrospect that it was. He surely did have a tough time of it, but he became an out and out, pure-blooded "Mountaineer" in every sense of the idea. In a sense, Joe really did grow up in West Virginia. He was a high school ninth grader when we came to WVU, and he literally cut his teeth on the Mountaineers and the culture of the hills.

When he was a student at WVU, he was selected for the marching band, which was quite an achievement, and I'd guess the idea of the WVU "Mountaineers" will always be a big piece of his ethos. Moreover, after a rather inauspicious Freshman year, he buckled down and graduated and subsequently earned his M.A. degree in Special Education with a perfect 4.0 GPA! His work as a Behavior Disorders teacher at Bridgeport (WV) Middle School for more than nine years has been notable, and despite a failed marriage (that left him more wounded than anybody might guess), he has done just *great*. Needless to say, his mother and I are immensely proud of him, and we are particularly impressed by his sensitive and genuine concern for our own welfare, for he is *always* thoughtful about our health and happiness. He may not remember birthdays or other occasions without subtle reminders because it just isn't in his nature to monitor such things (I'm not sure he ever knows exactly when his own birthday occurs.), but he's solicitous and good company. I'd guess we enjoy Joe now as much as we ever have, and his work and his successes have been a genuine source of pride to us.[167]

As we look back on it, things were not all that easy for Greg either. But he enjoyed a number of close friends, not least of whom was a chap with whom he shared a passion for "collecting." Greg collected comic books (his *Spiderman* collection is fairly complete and is probably worth quite a sum), and he and his close friend John also prowled through the Salvation Army store seeking old 78 rpm recordings. Some of these, too, are now probably fairly valuable, but importantly, his hobby brought him a particular appreciation for music, and his tastes remain remarkably eclectic. He likes *all* kinds of music and has been a collector ever since. He still enjoys a kind of exhibition of his collections by hosting a regular Sunday evening radio program at Eastern Oregon State College, and while he was a graduate student at the University of North Carolina [at Chapel Hill], also hosted a radio show on its

---

[167] He later moved from special education to history, becoming a fine high school teacher, and married a wonderful woman with two great kids. As of this writing, they still live in Bridgeport, WV.

station.¹⁶⁸ Iowa was also particularly significant for Greg because that's where he met his future wife. We had moved to West Virginia when Greg was still an undergraduate at Iowa. Rita [Rose Short] was a nursing student, and so far as we're concerned, he could not have made a better choice in a wife. She has always been a real partner in his life, and together they have provided us with two really prized grandchildren.¹⁶⁹

At that time—at the University of Iowa—our programs in Educational Administration and our "Center for Research in School Administration" (CRSA) had been recently housed in a downtown hotel in the heart of Iowa City that the university had acquired. It was just on the very edge of the university's campus. (One must know that the University of Iowa campus, somewhat like Harvard's, was almost indistinguishable from the city itself.) The university had managed to acquire this property as an alternative to its significant need for new construction which it could ill afford, though the entire university was badly in need of additional space. Thus, several of the College of Education's various programs that had been previously housed helter skelter, here and there, were consolidated in this six- or seven-story hotel. In our own case, we had been previously housed in the old EE building (Electrical Engineering) that was just across a parking lot from the (also) old but established College of Education building.

I particularly enjoyed my space in the old EE building. When I first joined the staff there, the entire educational administration operation had only recently moved into the old EE building, but for me, it was my first introduction to the university, and compared to the tiny office I'd occupied at OU, my office in this old building was spacious and comfortable.

---

[168] The friend my father mentions was and is John Bauserman whom I always visit on occasional trips back to Iowa. And while that collection of *Spiderman* is hardly complete, it does now possess some value!

[169] My wife would perish from colon cancer around three years after my father wrote this memoir, but that all lay in the future when he finished this work in 1996.

EE Building not long after its construction

After all, though the wooden floors creaked and always smelled of that special mix of floor wax and oil that they had to be treated with, and the place was a real fire trap, it was a warmly academic kind of atmosphere, and we largely had the upper floors of the building to ourselves. The lower floors, including the "below level first floor," had been significantly renovated to house a major Ford Foundation-funded operation that was known by the acronym "IEIC"—the "Iowa Education Information Center"—and which was probably the very first example of the application of computer-generated data-retrieval and information analysis activities aimed at charting and monitoring everything from grade reporting and curriculum scheduling for many public schools in the state of Iowa.

This is a rather significant digression in these comments, for were it not for the establishment of the IEIC, I would not have been invited to join the faculty of Iowa. The man who was chosen to head that operation was Robert Marker, who'd been selected for that job from his position as an Associate Professor in Educational Administration. It was his "slot" that I filled when I joined the faculty there. The IEIC and, for that matter, a whole variety of other significant innovations at the University of Iowa in the broad fields of testing, statistical systems, and technological developments, were all largely owing to the genius of a remarkable man named E. F. Lindquist. "Lind" is the only honest-to-God, genuine, one-hundred-percent genius that I have ever known personally.

E. F. Lindquist, 1901-1978

First of all, he authored or co-authored the best and most often used series of statistical textbooks that have been used in major colleges and universities throughout the United States and elsewhere. He pioneered a whole variety of statistical techniques but is perhaps still better known for having developed the famous *Iowa Tests of Educational Development* and the *Iowa Tests for Basic Skills*, and for establishing the ACT (*American College Testing*) program for assessing potential of high school students for college work, which has rivaled the SAT tests. These achievement tests are used throughout the entire world, and Lindquist not only developed the tests, he also invented a remarkable mass production hardware system for scoring and reporting the results. E. F. Lindquist thereby established the MRC (Measurement Research Corporation) at the University of Iowa—a quasi-public entity—for the purpose of administration and analysis of test data that made millions of dollars for both himself and the university. To his credit, he gave most of that money back to the university and, largely owing to his beneficence, the new College of Education facility at Iowa bears his name.[170]

My own special remembrances of "Lind," however, are much more mundane. Two examples suffice: On one occasion, "Lind," Dean Howard Jones, Bob Marker, and our Chairman of Ed Ad at Iowa at that time, Bill Lane, had occasion to be driving up to Des Moines to some kind of meeting, and they were all being transported in grand style in "Lind's"

---

[170] That facility was being built as my father left Iowa. It included the university's huge IBM 360-60 Computer in a temperature and humidity controlled room that was state-of-the-art in the 1970s.

marvelous big Cadillac when suddenly things went somewhat awry. "Something's wrong with this car," said Lindquist, and one of the others advised that it was rather likely that they had endured a flat tire. Lindquist brought the car to an abrupt stop and wondered what was the matter! "Well," said Dean Jones somewhat anxiously, "The first thing we need to do is to get this car to the side of the highway and off the fast lane!" (Lindquist had just stopped the thing right in the middle of the road.) While the occupants quickly got after the business of changing the tire, "Lind" began to read the owner's manual and unobtrusively observed their work. As he read and watched, he began to "edit" the owner's booklet. To make a long store short, he subsequently sent his observations to General Motors, and they *revised* the manual!

My second personal remembrance had to do with golf. I often played golf at the University of Iowa's "Finkbine" course where Lindquist and the then retired former superintendent of the Iowa City school system always played together in a regular weekly match. Dr. Lindquist was "hooked" on golf, and on a number of occasions, I joined with these two old "geezers," who, by the way, played quite well. What shouldn't have surprised me, I guess, was the way they scored their games. Since they played together often, Lindquist kept a "running score" of their matches. He had calculated their scores on each and every hole for however long they had played and had determined the standard deviations and variances for their performances! Thus, rather than allow that they had earned, say, a 96 for the eighteen holes they had played on a particular day, Lindquist would say, "Well, in our nine rounds so far this year, you have 864 strokes, and you are 216 over par! I am 212 over par, so you owe me fifty cents!" (Moreover, he would allow as to how their "variance" on particular holes had been 1.2 strokes this way or that, and the standard deviation was 0.06 or something like that!) It was just amazing to me! Yet, whenever I might have hit the ball decently or have done something reasonably well, they were both most complimentary. All in all, they were marvelous company on the golf course, and we *never* talked "shop": no mention of work or problems or issues of politics, or what was wrong with Education in the country—just hit the ball and calculate the square root of the deviation from the established variance of that last nine rounds!

Lindquist's protégé (not much younger in years than himself by any means) was a professor of statistics named Blommers.[171] The latter was also the co-author with Lindquist in one of those statistics textbooks, probably the best of them. Professor Blommers had earned a bit of professorial fame in his own right as a marvelous but exacting instructor, though certainly just a bit eccentric. For example, it is well known that in his classes, he would begin to write a long formula on the chalkboard with his left hand and end writing it with his right hand! Dr. Blommers had little regard for any of those students in his many statistics classes who majored in Educational Adminstration. In truth he considered most of them to be somewhat lacking in intellectual strength, to say the least! Yet, at Iowa of course, one simply could not achieve a Ph.D. without at least six to nine semester hours of statistics, and *most* of that had to be with Blommers.

In about 1968 or '69, we were able to secure a generous federal grant that allowed us to recruit graduate students from throughout the United States in a program that was known in those days by the acronym PAERIS, which stood for "Programs in the Administration of Educational Research and Information Systems." The essence of this program was that we would prepare potential administrators who would be particularly knowledgeable and competent in the *management* of educational research. The rationale of our grant application was that school systems were, at that time, much more engagingly involved in the necessity of doing a lot of their own research, and that they required administrators who knew the ins and outs of design and analysis. The U.S. Office of Education thought that was a good idea, and they provided us funding to provide fellowships to qualified students that turned out to be quite generous, and this permitted us to recruit nationally.[172] As a consequence, we were able to bring in a group of graduate students who were extremely bright, aggressive, and reasonably sophisticated. We required higher than

---

[171] Paul J. Blommers's name graced the "Measurement Resources Library" in the new Lindquist building at the university. I have been unable to locate a photograph of him.

[172] The "Office of Education" was folded into the new U.S. Department of Education when it was established in 1979 under President Carter.

From Cabbage to Cauliflower

average test scores, and particularly in mathematics, since a large portion of their work would require considerable work in statistics.

It was my privilege to have served as Director of the PAERIS program during my last two years at Iowa, and that experience was of some significance on my "CV" [Curriculum Vita—academic form of a resume] when I later interviewed for the Deanship at WVU. Our first group of PAERIS students included people from New York City, Connecticut, California, Kentucky, and Texas as I recall. (Among these, incidentally, was a chap from Brooklyn named Fred Ignatovich who turned out to be one of the best graduate students I'd ever worked with and who subsequently joined the faculty at Michigan State University, my own alma mater, and who is presently a full professor there.)[173]

Those young men turned out to be real stars in Professor Blommer's classes, and on a number of occasions, he would ask me at this or that college social function (with a kind of quizzical and unbelieving look on his face), "where are you getting these people?" It just totally turned around his notions about Ed Ad students, and to give him due credit, he bent over backward to accommodate our PAERIS guys by even offering special sections of some of his courses in the summer terms just for their benefit. In truth, these were very special students, and almost all of them have gone on to notable careers, and some have made significant contributions to our field. I particularly remember them because they challenged those of us who tried to teach them since most of them could just as easily have taught us![174] But the PAERIS program didn't begin until after we'd moved from the old EE building over into the hotel, so that gets a bit ahead of my story. My office in that old EE building was indeed spacious, and since we had only recently moved to that old building, no one really knew that we were there, so life was reasonably pleasant and uninterrupted! Moreover, we enjoyed ample space for our full-time graduate students to have their own relatively private "domain," and we

---

[173] Dr. Frederick Ignatovich, aged 79, is still living as of this writing, though he is now retired from the university, where he was a full professor.

[174] It is interesting to note, first, that they were all men, not unusual in the late 1960s/early 70s, but bizarre by today's standards, *and* that, to a man, they were deeply devoted to and had immense respect for my father.

had about four or five *very* spacious classrooms that were totally at our disposal, and no more than a short walk from any of our offices. For all practical purposes, and for almost two years, our programs were the only occupants in the upper floor of that old building.

That said, to suggest that the old EE building was a source of genuine pride would be overstating the case. We were not all that happy with it, and in truth, neither was the university itself. In point of fact, there is a tale—probably true—that sometime previously when the president of the University of Iowa was a chap named Hancher, the old EE building apparently caught fire. Sometime in the late evening, someone called President Hancher and advised that the EE building was on fire, but not to worry because the fire department was there, and he is reported to have said, "why don't they mind their own business?!"[175]

As I've said, I particularly enjoyed my time in the EE building because, new to the faculty, it took a while before I began to be caught up in the general "flow" of student advising and committee stuff, so for about one year, I had little responsibility other than my teaching. Thus, at that time, I was contacted by Lloyd Chilton, an executive editor with Macmillan (and whom I've mentioned previously) to consider reworking a textbook that my colleague Bill Lane and a Sociologist at Ohio State, Ron Corwin, had begun to develop, but who had reached a stalemate in terms of what to do next. Lloyd thought the book had promise, but the other authors couldn't agree on a lot of things, and the book had gotten to be too long and too repetitive. He asked whether I'd be interested in coming in as a "third" author to see if I could rescue it. I had little else to do and told him that if he could work it out with the other two guys, I'd be willing to give it a shot. Lane was eager and Corwin was willing, so I took the huge manuscript and began to work on it. I wrote a completely new introductory chapter, slashed out a zillion pages of other stuff, and rewrote just about every chapter in it and wrote a couple of other new chapters by revising some of those extant and changed the title. In late Fall or early Winter of 1966, I had a manuscript ready for review. That book turned out to be quite good. We called it *Foundations of Educational*

---

[175] The name "Hancher" is principally known today for the large Music/Performance building constructed beside the Iowa River that is named for him.

Administration: A Behavioral Analysis, and it was selected as one of the three best books in Education in 1967. Needless to say, that book also established my own reputation as an up and coming professor in our field.

Jefferson Hotel building in downtown Iowa City

Let me merely observe that the nicest thing about moving into the old Jefferson Hotel in Iowa City after having completed the book, and having been around long enough by then to have taken on a good load of doctoral advisees, committee assignments, and so forth, was the remarkable nicety that each member of our faculty in that "new" facility had our own *private bathrooms complete with workable showers!*—which, of course, we never used—the showers, that is. And after less than a year, the university's physical plant folks came in and eliminated our private "johns." Tsk, tsk. It was great while it lasted, bizarre carpeting and inadequate lighting notwithstanding.

Adding Up the Iowa Score

My father in 1967, his second year at Iowa

The seven years we lived and worked in Iowa City added up to a succession of very positive experiences. After my first book, written with Bill Lane and Ron Corwin (Ohio State) was published in 1967, I made full professor in 1970.[176] I had a succession of really bright and productive graduate students, many of whom went on to notable achievement in their own right.

And I worked closely with some of the really best school administrators anywhere in the world. I think I earned their respect, and many of them whom I would occasionally meet at a national meeting here and there still seemed to remember me with affection. All in all, it was just great.

In 1972, in February, I was offered the deanship of the newly established College of Human Resources and Education at West Virginia University in Morgantown and accepted with eager anticipation. That series of events follows.

---

[176] It was actually his second book, following the small, locally-published work he co-wrote with Robert Ohm, but this one, co-written as he notes with Willard Lane and Ronald Corwin, *Foundations of Educational Administration: A Behavioral Analysis* (New York: Macmillan, 1967)—became a very popular textbook in Educational Administration courses and sealed my father's relationship with Macmillan, resulting in two more books with that Press.

CHAPTER VIII

West Virginia University (1972-1996)

My appointment as Dean of the College of Human Resources and Education (HRE) at West Virginia University was a curious scenario, and some of the circumstances remain a bit clouded (ie., I think I was not the first choice). Anyway, sometime in the fall of 1971, I received a phone call from my old friend Claude Kelley who was, at that time, Vice President for Administrative Affairs at WVU. Claude had left Oklahoma University in 1967 to accompany Jim Harlow when the latter had assumed the presidency at West Virginia University. At the time of his phone call, Claude had apparently already indicated that he had planned to relinquish his role in the President's office and resume a full-time faculty appointment in the HRE College at West Virginia University. He'd had some difficulty in reaching me since we'd all been involved in a series of moves at Iowa which were sort of like "musical chairs" and which were not all that uncommon in those days of rapid expansion and growth.

Now, as I mentioned some time previously, Claude Kelley had joined Mr. Harlow at WVU when the latter had assumed its presidency in about 1967. Claude had previously served as an associate dean in OU's College of Education, but when I had first met him, he was "merely" a professor, though certainly the titular head of educational administration. I say "titular" simply because in those times at OU, we did not really have "departments" in the normal organizational sense of the idea. We were rather a small college at Oklahoma University, although we had quite large numbers of undergraduate students. But when I joined the faculty in OU's College of Education, we were not particularly known for our graduate programs, and, except for Special Education and "Counselor" Education (which were, at that time sort of in the ascendancy in terms of graduate programs), we did not enroll very many people in our doctoral programs. To some extent, this was owing to the fact that we applied quite restrictive requirements on advanced graduate students, and, abiding by OU's Graduate School requirements, we required our advanced graduate students, regardless of field, to spend at least one full semester in "residence."

Needless to say, this was a practice that was increasingly abrogated in many of even the very best universities, for it was becoming increasingly difficult to expect school administrators—already, even in those years, beginning to earn salaries far in excess of even some tenured "full" professors in good universities—to give up a reasonably secure and comfortable lifestyle to come back to their universities and pursue doctoral degrees with little or almost no financial support. But, remarkably, some of them did, and among these, were many of the future leaders in their profession. At OU in those days, and for that matter, at many other first-rate universities, there were no accommodations made for many ambitious young school administrators who wanted to better themselves, though there certainly were a few who thought that merely by virtue of their achievements, they ought to be granted some sort of special privilege in pursuit of an advanced degree. Certainly, there were some of those who just came along, and, by virtue of exaggerated notions of their own importance, presumed that we would just pave the way for them to sail through a doctoral program, but, typically, they fell by the wayside. Dr. Kelley always cautioned those of us in those days at OU to remember that the doctoral degree was a very special privilege and that, as advisors, our responsibility was to ensure that our candidates did first-rate work, and, if they did not, we as advisors would be held accountable! There were several of us at that time who were "new" to the faculty, and it was enough for us, given Dr. Kelley's admonition, to be sure that our thesis candidates did us proud. I can so easily remember how many times I went over a thesis draft of a candidate to be *absolutely* certain that everything was just so! And even yet, I still remember how I went into some of those Orals with a great sense of trepidation.

Dr Keith Esch

Dr. Keith Esch later in life

My very first doctoral student at OU was a young man from Wichita, Kansas. His name was Keith Esch. We worked very hard together to make certain that his work was ok. He'd reworked the thesis half a dozen times, and we were finally convinced that we were, together, ready for the Orals.

Now, in those days at OU, doctoral orals were significantly announced and publicized throughout the university with a rather nice little brochure that was sent out by faculty mail throughout the entire university community. This little statement was also included in a student's final portfolio upon his or her graduation and included not only a little summary of the doctoral paper, but also a little biographical statement. This practice was discontinued some years ago, but, in those years—the 60s—it was an invitation for *anyone* in the university community to come in to the Oral and have a clear "shot" at the candidate, and, remarkably, a surprising number of faculty from just about *anywhere* in the university did occasionally show up to ask very *dangerous* questions! Incidentally, even in this day, these little publications are prized by those folks who earned their degrees in those years. But Keith Esch and I weathered our first doctoral oral together. His paper was well received, and the examination, though rigorous, was rewarding and fair. We have remained more or less in touch ever since, and he has enjoyed a long and apparently satisfying career as a senior administrator in the Wichita, Kansas public schools. Even still, we occasionally share some correspondence.[177]

---

[177] Unhappily, Dr. Arwyn "Keith" Esch died in February, 2010, in Wichita at age 80.

"Mr." Harlow and "Mr." Kelley

When he called me, Claude told me that the dean of the College of Human Resources and Education at WVU—Dr. Stanley Ikenberry—had resigned to accept an appointment in a vice-presidency at Penn State.[178] Interestingly, this man had been a contemporary of mine when we were graduate students at Michigan State, and we had met in those days, though only very casually. At that time, he was in the Higher Education Program, and I was in the Educational Administration program.

Dr. Stanley Ikenberry as President of the University of Illinois

Thus, our paths had little basis to cross, but both of us had been students of Dr. Paul Miller, who was an internationally recognized Sociologist, and, at that time was also Michigan State's Provost. "Stan" finished his Ph.D. about a year before me, and during his last year, had served an internship in the Provost's Office at MSU. Thus, he'd come significantly to the attention of Paul Miller, and when the latter assumed the presidency of WVU, he'd brought Stan with him. During

---

[178] Ikenberry later served two terms as president of the University of Illinois before returning to Penn State in a part-time position in that university's Center for Higher Education. He was still alive at the time of this writing.

my final term at MSU, I'd also participated in Dr. Miller's seminar in the Sociology of Higher Education, and although he subsequently probably had no real idea who I was, our rather generalized relationship at MSU apparently turned out to be of some influence. Ikenberry had remembered me, and with Mr. Harlow's and Claude Kelley's prodding, I was brought down to WVU for an interview.

Now, one must realize that moving from a professorship to a deanship was in that time beginning to be increasingly rare. University deans (in at least some of the better institutions) had managed to persuade their superiors that even deans required staff. Consequently, deanships were increasingly more likely to be filled by associate deans from other places. Thus, to presume that one might be appointed to such a post out of the professorship, even with "friends at court," was a long shot. Nevertheless, I went out to Morgantown for my first interview in early December, 1971. My wife was not all that enthusiastic about the prospects in any case, and anyone who has ever visited Morgantown, West Virginia in December can't possibly have a very sanguine perception of its vicissitudes.[179] Among the most beautiful places in the world in spring and autumn, Morgantown is among the most dismal in winter. The city is laid out, seemingly pell-mell, and its hills and turns (of which there are many) persuade any visitor that this is the most accidental of cities, where this road and that street all have seemed to have been designed at random. Of course, for one who'd spent the last twelve years in Oklahoma and Iowa—places whose history reaches back only to the early twentieth century for all practical purposes—coming to a part of the country where pioneers tread about as early as the late seventeenth century, one should have known that things were not laid out in other than "metes and bounds."[180] I mean, this was *old* America!

---

[179] The city has improved considerably over the last half century or so, but even now, it is not the most attractive of cities, regardless of the season, and in 1971, my father was being far too kind!

[180] An old English way of defining boundaries, used extensively in the original thirteen colonies, of which West Virginia was originally part. According to Wikipedia, "Typically the system uses physical features of the local geography, along with directions and distances, to define and describe the boundaries of a parcel of land." (https://en.wikipedia.org/wiki/Metes_and_bounds)

Yet, in truth, I never really thought too much about that or any other aspect of Morgantown as a place to live since I truly did not believe that I had much of a chance to be selected as dean, even though I did know that I had considerable support within the central administration. I thought my two or three days there went reasonably well. I thought that I had said enough of the "right" things to be considered, but since I *really* did not believe that I had much chance, I was probably much more candid than I might otherwise have been had I thought I was a top choice. I had done a good bit of homework about the place, and I knew a good bit about the prospects and problems of the College, and at least some of those with whom I interacted were apparently both a bit surprised and impressed by that. So, low and behold, I was advised about two weeks later that I was, indeed, a top choice, and then the fun began!

When I returned to Iowa City, Jane was understandably curious about the place. I told her that I had been particularly impressed by the people, but that Morgantown was, well, a bit unimpressive. Now, Jane was never *at all* enthusiastic about the prospects of being a "dean's wife," and had endured enough experiences otherwise to know that such a role was not to her liking. I assured her that she had little to be anxious about, for it was more than a little likely that I would *never* be considered. In late December, I was advised that I was under consideration. But nothing much happened afterwards, and then, in late January when I was preparing to attend the American Association of School Administrators annual meeting in Atlantic City, N. J., I received another call from Mr. Harlow. He said that I was their "final" choice, and what would it take for me to come down to Morgantown to assume the position. He told me that the best they could do on salary was about $27,000. I thought about that a lot. Now, at that time, considering that I was then a full professor at Iowa, and considering my extension income and my consulting income (though that was indeed rather modest), I indicated to him that there was just no way that I could come down to WVU for that kind of money. "Ok," he said, "what would you come down here for?" I told him that there was no way I would assume that job for less than $30,000, and that, moreover, I wouldn't come unless I could bring in my own assistant dean (for finance and administration). I'd already thought about all this stuff, and I knew that the only way I could *really* function effectively was if I were able to bring in my own people in key roles. Needless to say, I surely presumed that such demands would end the issue then and there. As a matter of fact, I had a bet with our long-time office manager in our research bureau at Iowa to the effect that I would not go to WVU. She bet otherwise that I would go.

I'd heard nothing more from WVU, and in February, Bill Lane and I went off to the convention of the AASA in Atlantic City, looking forward to fun and frolic. My responsibility was to secure our rooms and make arrangements for our own university's hospitality suite, such that we could welcome our many graduates and enjoy the respite of a week off from the routine of the winter term. We arrived late and found our rooms were not ready, but the harassed hotel desk personnel just finally tossed us keys to rooms not made up and said we could sleep in, and that we could make our proper arrangements the following day. That next day, I arose early and went off to attend a couple of meetings, planning to complete my hotel registration thereafter, thus not having officially registered, so no one really knew where the hell I was. When I returned about 11 am and took care of registration, I had a couple of "urgent" messages. One was from my wife, and the other was from "President James Harlow at West Virginia University." I had a pretty good idea what all of that was about. First, I called Jane. She said that she had talked with Jim Harlow the previous evening, and she told me, "I think that he's going to offer you that job!" Next, I called Mr. Harlow. (And incidentally, he was always "Mr." Harlow and didn't like to be addressed as "Dr." even when, as president of the university, he would call any of the deans or anyone else for that matter, he always indicated that it was "Mr." Harlow.) When I reached him on the phone, he said that he'd been able to find a little extra money, and that, were I still willing, I could have the deanship on my terms. I thought about it for about a full minute, and then I told him that I'd be delighted to come!

Interestingly, I went over after that to another meeting, this one a UCEA session, and sitting just in front of me was a WVU professor,

Dr. "Bud" Goodwin, who was at that time Chairman of Educational Administration at WVU, and he leaned back in his chair and said to me, "Well, from what I hear, you are going to be my new dean!" I had no idea how he knew that since I'd just accepted the position ten minutes earlier. I have no idea what went on at that UCEA meeting, for, needless to say, I was a bit preoccupied. An hour later, I went back to my room and called Jane. "I'm not at all sure you feel very good about all this, but I have to tell you that you are the new dean's wife at West Virginia University!" She was neither particularly surprised nor enthusiastic about this news. But I have to tell you that Jane was the best dean's wife ever. Throughout our ten years in the deanship at WVU, she was an always superb hostess and worked very hard, and successfully, to make the dean's work effective and productive. She is still well remembered for having organized many social activities in a college that had done little otherwise in that regard, and many faculty members and their wives still look back fondly on the Gourmet Dinner Group that she organized and planned, our marvelous College Christmas parties, and various other social activities that became a kind of hallmark of our years in the deanship. Those activities were great fun and particularly our Gourmet group. Though the group never counted more than about twenty members, some of those very elaborate dinner evenings were "wild and wonderful."[181] Moreover, and much more importantly, those participants (and a few others) represented the core of faculty who supported most of my changes in policies and procedures as we took over a college not all that enthusiastic about *any* kind of change! Jane's work was every bit as significant as my own.

The Easter Visit

Anticipating a move across country under any circumstances is always challenging, and although we'd been through it a couple of times before, in this case, things were a little different. After all, we were

---

[181] My father here makes a reference to the signs then posted on the state border: "Welcome to Wild, Wonderful West Virginia!"

assuming different kinds of roles and ones we were neither familiar nor all that comfortable with. We had a kind of hazy idea that our new status would require a more visible social responsibility, and we knew that we'd need a house that was at least somewhat disposed to modest entertainment. Accordingly, during the University of Iowa's several days of Easter Vacation (now generally known abroad as "Spring Break") in late April, 1972, we loaded up our 1971 Oldsmobile with our two boys and took off for Morgantown. Now, it is a long trek from Iowa to West Virginia. We enjoyed interstate highways almost all the way except that the last twenty or thirty miles of the present Interstate 79 (from Waynesburg, PA into Morgantown) were unfinished, and we had to proceed on the most hideous, winding, terribly narrow, and "curvy" highway one could imagine. Moreover, it had begun to rain, and those last miles were seemingly unending! I had tried to buoy up the spirits of my family, but US 19 from Waynesburg to Morgantown would have tried anyone's optimism, and by the time we'd arrived at the Holiday Inn in Morgantown, everyone had already begun to wonder (*aloud*!) what in heaven's name we were doing here!

It was particularly helpful that when we arrived, a marvelous bouquet of flowers were awaiting us compliments of WVU's provost, Dr. Jay Barton, and that helped enormously!

Our search for housing was depressing. While I attended to some business of the college, Jane and the boys toured about with a local realtor looking at everything that was available and that might suit us. Unfortunately, it began to look like we were not going to find anything really suitable. We had been most fortunate that our house in Iowa City had sold rather quickly and for a rather nice profit, so, at least we were in a fairly good position financially. Finally, after three or four days of disappointment, and after Jane had looked at just about everything in Morgantown that was remotely available in our price range, we were told of an older house in a section of Morgantown known as "South Park." South Park was (and still is) a kind of genteel area of well-kept older homes originally developed

Dr. Jay Barton, later President of the University of Alaska system

by "old" money and targeted at people who had some considerable wealth in the coal business. The Morgantown High School had been sited there and was still the prestige high school in the community, and the older houses were spacious and well-kept. Even to this day, South Park is a good address, and some of the houses there are genuine landmarks. The particular house we looked at had an interesting history of its own, though we didn't learn of that until later.

Our house on Allison Street in Morgantown

At that time, the house was owned by the widow of a nearby funeral home owner, and having subsequently remarried, she and her new husband had *completely* renovated the place. They had redone the plumbing, installed a sophisticated central air conditioning system, refurbished the house inside and out, but had retained its original character. She was an eccentric lady, and in fact, when we looked at the house, she had specified that no more than *two* persons could look at it simultaneously. Thus, only Jane and the real estate agent went in while I sat in the car with Greg and Joe. She came out presently and said that I ought to have a look, so in I went, too. As soon as I saw the house, I knew it was what we wanted, so we closed a deal on that very last day and almost at the very last moment before having to return to Iowa City. Fortunately, too, we were able to buy the house at a most reasonable price, and, of course, that is where we still live today even as I write this more than two decades later.[182]

Interestingly too, Morgantown is such a city of curious turns and street patterns that after we had made arrangements to buy the house, we decided to go and have a final look at it and take a photograph to show our friends in Iowa City, and we almost couldn't find our way back to it! That old house has become such a special friend, and we can't imagine living anywhere that is more pleasant nor more comfortable, but during our first year or so, when Jane began to make "modest" changes (!!!) with the help of a "handy man" (who almost became a member of our family!), our older son Greg, who during his occasional vacations from the University of Iowa was drafted as a helper, christened the old house as "the kidney." His notion was that the house was not unlike a human organism badly always in need of a transplant.[183] Jane's changes were not significant. We needed a closet here and there, changed some doors, did some painting, and recarpeted. But, in general, the house had been so completely redone otherwise that little really needed to be done. With a spacious dining room and a lovely "den" off an equally inviting living room, a small "morning room" near the back of the house, and a large master bedroom upstairs, the house "entertains" easily, and it has certainly made our lives in Morgantown all that more satisfying. During our "deaning" years, that old house endured some marvelous and memorable dinner parties and "open houses," and everyone who ever came there always commented on the special charm of "the kidney."

There were two rooms on the third floor, the more inviting of which became Joe's room, and the other, he and we used as a work and

---

[182] They would move next door to a newer one-level house at the end of 1999, only a few months before my mother's death.

[183] Actually, I gave it that name because it always seemed to be trying to "reject" us like a transplanted organ. "Mr. Martin" was the handy man, whose favorite reaction when something inevitably went wrong was to shake his head sadly and intone "trouble, trouble, trouble."

catch-all place. Curiously, there was also a closet in that other room that the owner had used to store a couple of French doors no longer used and some carpet and ceramic tile remnants, and wherein, on a visit there by Jane's folks, her father had found an old porcelain basin that had been used in embalming. He off-handedly joked that there were probably one or two bodies in there too. Thereafter, we always referred to that place as "the body closet." Telling Joe about this discovery was a mistake! He'd just endured the genuinely frightening experience of seeing the movie *The Exorcist*, and I finally *had* to put a lock on that closet door before he could sleep peacefully at night! Even to this day, I don't think Joe would go up to that place without a sense of dread![184]

The Decanal Years

Allen Hall, home of WVU's College of Human Resources and Education

---

[184] He never much liked the closet, but he got over it since he spent countless hours in that room designing and redesigning plastic car models, a hobby that later expanded to working on real automobiles.

When I came to the deanship in "HRE" [the College of Human Resources and Education at WVU], it was second only to the College of Arts and Sciences in size. We had about 2,500 students and 120 faculty members. The college had not had consistent leadership for a couple of years. Following the departure of Dean Ikenberry, his immediate successor was Dr. Delmas Miller, who at the time held a professorship and had previously served most notably as principal of WVU's University High School. In 1969 or '70, following a national trend, WVU relinquished its control of this "Lab" school and turned its ownership over to the county system. HRE had in turn to absorb most of the staff in the University School who wanted to maintain their attachment to the university. Most of the faculty decided to remain on the staff at the school and became employees of the county system, but those who decided otherwise became important practitioners in our teacher education program, although none of them held degrees beyond the MA. These arrangements had already been made prior to my arrival. Dr. Miller's full professorship was in secondary school administration, and he had enjoyed considerable status.

Dr. Delmas Miller, 1907-1986[185]

[185] This photo of former Dean Miller from "West Virginia History OnView" is reproduced with permission of the West Virginia and Regional History Center, West Virginia University Libraries.

He was named acting dean for one year when Stan Ikenberry moved to Penn State, and then was named dean for his final year before retiring from the university. Accordingly, Dean Miller had no mandate to do very much, since everyone knew that a new dean would have his or her own notions about things.

When I came to the deanship, I had little real knowledge of what a dean did nor what really needed to be done. In that regard, the best advice I had was from my dean at Iowa, Howard Jones. I had great respect for Howard Jones, and when I'd finally decided to take on the deanship at WVU, I went in to see him and to solicit his counsel. He said, "Look, ask for what you think you need, and not for what you think someone is willing just to give you. Be particularly careful in your personnel decisions—hiring and firing—because whether you're good or not, it's the quality of your staff that will determine whether you're effective." It was advice that I learned to treasure. He was exactly right! I had been away from undergraduate education for more than seven years, and even during my OU years, my familiarity with undergraduate teacher education was superficial. I knew that I had a lot of catching up to do. I also knew that there were lots of things about the general administration of a college that I *didn't* want to know. I was particularly weak in financial affairs. Thus, I insisted that the university allow me to bring in my own Assistant Dean for Fiscal Affairs. In this regard, the central administration was reluctantly agreeable, and I was able to persuade a young man whom I'd come to know at Iowa to join me in that position.

Ernest Goeres had been in a couple of my classes at Iowa while he was completing his own Ph.D. and had served previously as a successful business manager in the Dubuque, Iowa public schools. I knew that his general grasp of fiscal issues was a real strength, and that even though his experiences had been in public schools, I was confident that he would quickly adapt to the higher education environment.

Dr. Ernest "Ernie" Goeres, far right, his wife Sharon, center, and my father, left

Now, even though the West Virginia situation was (and remains) a state centralized bureaucratic nightmare, Ernie did indeed manage well. It took both of us a year or so to really get a handle on the ways things had to be done, but he was a jewel. Today, he still "runs" the place, for all practical purposes, has earned a promotion to full professor, and no one in the labyrinth of WVU procedures and complexities is more respected nor more knowledgeable.[186]

A second issue I had to confront was my significant lack of familiarity with undergraduate education and curriculum issues, so I badgered Mr. Harlow and the Provost for Instruction, Dr. Jay Barton, to get me an Associate Dean for Academic Affairs. Again, fortune smiled. Only about a year or so before I arrived on the scene in Morgantown, the state had restructured the entire system of governance of higher education. Previously, WVU had operated under its own Board of Governance (Trustees), and all other state colleges were under the auspices of the State Board of Education. The new system consolidated *all* higher education under a statewide Board of Regents with its own Chancellor. This had become a rather popular trend throughout the country, and the idea—generally supported early

---

[186] Ernest "Ernie" Goeres is today retired from WVU and still living in Morgantown.

on, by the way, by President Harlow—was merely to effect greater efficiency and centralized management. Unfortunately, it turned out to be a great disadvantage to the "flagship" university. In any case, WVU had previously managed an elaborate off-campus operation in the Charleston area that had grown and prospered and had included a variety of programs such as Business, Engineering, and Education. So much had this operation grown that, in fact, just before I arrived on the scene, the new Board of Regents, with legislative approval, had decided that this Charleston operation deserved a measure of autonomous independence from WVU and had made it into a free-standing institution called COGS (College of Graduate Studies).

The man who had been dean of the operation when it was under the auspices of WVU was Dr. Arthur "Jiggs" Hostetter. He had been very effective and enjoyed great respect in Morgantown, and when the Charleston operation was established as an independent institution, he had to confront a choice: stay with the newly formed unit or return to the faculty at WVU.

Arthur "Jiggs" Hostetter (at left) at work in Charleston before he joined WVU's College of Human Resources and Education as Associate Dean[187]

---

[187] I am grateful to WVU Libraries for locating this photograph of Dr. Hostetter (reprinted, courtesy of A&M 5188, West Virginia University, News Service, Photographs, West Virginia and Regional History Center, West Virginia University Libraries).

Since he'd engaged in more than a number of touchy conflicts with the new system's chancellor, a headstrong martinet kind of man named Prince Woodard (and who had once indicated that his favorite movie was *Patton* and that he'd seen it ten times!), Dean Hostetter decided he'd have little chance to be named President of COGS, so he opted to return to the Morgantown campus.

As is often the case in such a circumstance, there was not a readily available slot for a full professorship for a resigning dean, and Mr. Harlow suggested I investigate the possibility of his assuming my needed associate dean position. I did that and Dean Hostetter agreed. (Actually, neither he nor I had much choice in the matter, truth be told.) Of course, Mr. Harlow, who was always sensitive to maintaining closeness between faculties and deans, didn't like my proposed title, so we named him "Associate Dean for Teacher Education," which, as it turned out, was a more accurate description of his role. It was a year or so after he'd come aboard that he became more familiar to me as "Jiggs," a nickname he'd picked up because of his likeness to a comic strip character in a long discontinued but once popular strip called "Jiggs and Maggie." When he first came to work, we talked a bit about what I thought would be appropriate for him to do, and both of us were understandably a bit tentative. I was particularly sensitive to the fact that here was a man who'd been dean of an operation more complex and more involved than HRE. After all, the COGS thing had included not just Education, but Engineering and Business Administration, and was, for all practical purposes, a "branch college." Yet, he was subordinate to me in his new role, and I wasn't real sure that he might have felt all that good about it.

Then one day not long after he joined us, I received a book in the mail that was entirely in Chinese. Even the page numbers were in Chinese, so I dashed off an inter-office memo to Dean Hostetter on one of those little pink forms that are ubiquitous around offices everywhere (or were then) and attached it to the Chinese book with this message: "Please read this and give me your opinion." When I returned from a long lunch that day, the book was back in my in-basket with a similar pink memo attached. It was to me from him, and the entire message was *handwritten in Chinese*. I still don't know how he did that, and I have no notion even to this day as to what his message said. I suspect that he entered into a conspiracy with one of our distinguished full professors who just happened to be Chinese. But, however and no matter what his "opinion" was, after that small bit of foolishness, "Jiggs" Hostetter and I got along famously, and until his retirement from the university in about 1976, he was as important to my success as anyone else, and he was a good friend until he passed away in 1992. Incidentally, I later learned that the book that prompted all this nonsense was my own co-authored book with Bill Lane and Ron Corwin, *Foundations of Educational Administration*, which had been reprinted in Taiwan, there being no copyright requirements for the Taiwanese. I guess in retrospect, I should be complimented that they'd even provided me with a copy!

Problems, Solutions, and Successes

In planning for my first several years in the deanship, I had indicated to the faculty and administration that there were a number of particular goals that I wanted to pursue. After that period, my intention was to establish some new goals, and that's the way I worked across two five-year periods in the deanship. (And, for what it's worth to any prospective administrator, that's not a bad way to plan one's long-range efforts: Set some goals and periodically reassess and revise them.) Without detailing it, I wanted to gain some significant improvement in college morale and felt that the best way to this was, first, to be sure we could get meritorious people properly promoted; second, to get a better handle on and control of an almost chaotic off-campus program in the college (we were taking courses all over the state without any seeming system or reason); and third, I wanted to achieve more efficiency in the structure of the college's overall organization.

Promotion and Tenure: On the first issue, I had scanned the university catalogue and had recognized that, while the Engineering College (next to our own in the "Listings") had a much smaller faculty, it had many more senior professors. In our case, in 1972, we had only six full professors in an entire staff and not too many more associate professors. I felt that this was either due to some kind of obvious discrimination, or else the College had done a very poor job in presenting its candidates for promotion. It was, in retrospect, a bit of both. I then did something almost revolutionary. I initiated a "merit peer assessment" system whereby the lion's share of the work in promotion and tenure decisions would rest on the faculty itself. This was a three-tiered system involving the faculty, department chairs, and dean. We provided a rather systematized portfolio pattern and publicized it so that all faculty understood the format, and we encouraged an individually-initiated promotion procedure based on the portfolio. In other words, if *any* faculty member met the minimum criteria, he/she could initiate their own promotion. It then went to department chairs and screened there again, and then to me. *But*, if any portfolio "passed" the faculty committee, it went automatically to me whether or not the department chair approved or disapproved.[188]

It was more elaborate than this, but that provides the gist of it. Utilizing this process, when I went "downtown" to argue with the central administration's Promotion and Tenure Committee, which was composed mostly of all of the five provosts (Mr. Harlow had no vice-presidents, only provosts for each significant piece of the university's concerns.), I had a compelling presentation. I still remember with much satisfaction that of seventeen candidates for promotion to either associate or to full professor, I came away with sixteen of them! The faculty were appropriately impressed, and that system we initiated (with some considerable amendments, of course) was subsequently installed throughout WVU and is still used more or less similarly even up to the present. Prior to that, a dean just went downtown with a pocket full of hopes and with only superficial documentation, and played a kind of swap-out game. Naturally, those colleges with very visible scholarship came off well. In our case, our own system and the portfolios we provided, all nicely bound in a neat and impressive package, made it difficult to turn us down.

---

[188] Interestingly, the process described here is now fairly standard throughout much of the American college and university system.

"Official" picture of my father as dean, sporting a slightly longer hair style typical of the early 1970s

Off-Campus Programs: I was also successful in restructuring our chaotic off-campus continuing education procedures. Since faculty were not compensated for off-campus teaching (Mr. Harlow referred to faculty "load" as 100% of effort, whatever the hell *that* meant), most of our off-campus instruction had been subtly shifted to "adjunct" people who could be compensated at a rate of about $1,200 per course, and most of whom held full-time positions in public schools. Most of these also were preferential graduates or graduate students in our various programs, and these "nuggets" were nicely used by faculty as quid-pro-quos for…whatever. In any case, almost *no* senior faculty *ever* taught off-campus if they could avoid it, and most of them were able to do so with aplomb!

Accordingly, HRE's reputation off-campus was "spotty" to say the least. And one must remember that of *all* courses offered off-campus by WVU in those times, "Education" represented about 90% since there was a state requirement that, in order to maintain one's certification as a teacher, one *had* to accumulate at least six semester hours of additional course work about every other year, and except for COGS (and, in some fields, Marshall University), only WVU could offer the graduate-level courses required. Moreover, to earn an administrator's certificate, there were explicit course requirements, most of which could be earned off-campus, but at that time, *only* WVU could offer that work. So this was a very lucrative market for our College's wares. Some of our "adjuncts" certainly did a very good job, but others, too many in truth, did poorly. Moreover, there was just a little sentiment to the effect that off-campus work was considered "beneath" the dignity of our full-time professoriate staff.

I worked out an arrangement with the Provost for Continuing Education, a chap named Ralph Nelson, who became a life-long friend by the way, whereby, following Mr. Harlow's notion, the "full load" of any faculty member would indeed include off-campus teaching, but I adjusted the overall load to compensate. Thus, I was able to require regular faculty to teach off-campus by reducing their overall instructional requirements accordingly. In other words, if a full professor was to teach an off-campus graduate course in a particular term, his/her overall load was only, say, six semester hours rather than the nine hours that was the norm. I made sure that my department chairs understood this pattern and strictly abided by it. Accordingly, no professor could really complain since loads were adjusted. Some did, of course, but they quickly began to learn that such complaints were not looked upon with much sympathy in the dean's office![189]

Secondly, we arranged for four specific sites where *all* off-campus courses would be provided, and thus, no longer were we expected to teach a class *anywhere* if twenty people signed up for it. To coordinate these efforts, we successfully lobbied our state Board of Regents to provide funding for four full-time off-campus coordinators. These persons then made all arrangements for sites, facilities, registration, etc. Accordingly, no longer could anyone in our regular faculty beg off from teaching off-campus. At the same time, I knew that these programs could not withstand the increasingly severe accreditation requirement that we would soon have to endure with NCATE (National Council for the Accreditation of Teacher Education) which we were scheduled for in about 1975 unless we could also demonstrate adequate library holdings in each of these so-called "Centers." Thus, I also lobbied successfully for significantly increased holdings in each of the Centers. This latter effort was only marginally adequate—actually, of course, almost *totally* inadequate—but it was enough to get us by NCATE without sanctions. More importantly, we were able to really justify the presumption that, for once, the courses we were offering off-campus were comparable to the same courses offered at the Morgantown campus, and perhaps even more importantly, by the same people! Finally, to further establish that reality, I insisted that our off-campus courses carry the same numbers and course descriptions as our on-campus curricula.

And, all in all, that whole restructuring of HRE's off-campus system reflects one of my most significant accomplishments as a dean. Certainly, I couldn't have done that without significant cooperation and assistance from a lot of other administrators here and there throughout

---

[189] Later, after my father left the deanship and entered the regular faculty, he taught off-campus like everyone else.

the university. Off-campus personnel were instrumental, and we had marvelous support in the president's offices, but we did it! Although, after all these years, I'm sure no one really appreciates what a really remarkable achievement that turned out to be, it was, in retrospect, almost revolutionary. Only a new sitting dean could have pulled that off. That program remains in force even to this day, and our programs off-campus now have the same status and quality of our regular Morgantown programs, although since then, there has been a significant decline in the total teaching force, and due to the relative immobility of instructional personnel generally, most of our teachers in West Virginia now already hold MA degrees. Thus, our off-campus programs have declined a bit over the years. Still, our off-campus coordinators continue to function, and courses are still offered, and with adjustments here and there, we still maintain the same system.

Reorganizing the College: Regarding restructuring of the College, I was less successful, or maybe I was, in retrospect. I'd presumed that our overall pattern could be much more efficient. We had too many very small departments, and my notion was that we could consolidate a lot of our effort. To pursue this notion appropriately, I appointed a "blue ribbon" committee of professors and charged them to examine our structure and provide me with some recommendations. The upshot? After more than two months of deliberate and intensive study, they came back to me with a quite impressive written report, with much detail, but which, in essence, told me that there was nothing all that wrong about the structure and to just leave it alone.

Which, I did.

Summarizing the Role

My first five years in the deanship were certainly the most satisfying. Although I'd had some painful decisions to make regarding personnel (I'm fundamentally a bit too soft-hearted to be a really first-rate administrator), I'd made several of those, and our staff had recognized that

I was capable of that kind of decisiveness.[190] More importantly, those early years were managed when I *knew* where I stood in the so-called "head shed." I worked well with my president and with his executive staff. I respected and was respected by my major superior, the provost for instruction, and I had a good grasp of our planning and budgeting procedures. What I had really not thought all that much about was the fact that Mr. Harlow would reach mandatory retirement age at just about the end of my first five years in the deanship.

And what none of us had anticipated was the significant change in the fiscal environment that was to occur in about 1975. Up until then, we'd pretty much operated on a kind of "growth" system whereby *all* of our budget and operational planning was based on the familiar linear pattern of growth and financial accretion. In other words, from 1972 until 1976, we enjoyed about an average of 7% yearly increases in our overall budgets. Naturally, we all thought this was far less than we needed, but, all in all, those were really quite good years, and we had a little fiscal elbow-room to do some things that needed to be done. We could match the salary of a gifted professor being wooed away, and we could buy some needed equipment and pay expenses of staff who wanted to attend some national meeting here or there.

Then, in about 1976, that all went out the proverbial window. Suddenly, the costs of energy skyrocketed, our enrollments began to decline, and the state started asking us to assume costs that we'd never had to assume previously. A lot of "new" notions began to pervade our deliberations. We began to talk about "down-sizing" and "programmed budgeting" and "shortfalls." In 1977, all of the colleges were almost suddenly asked to "remit" a percentage of budgets in mid-year. In our own case, our "target" was about $186,000, and for a college like ours, with an overall total budget of just over $2 million (excluding our "soft" dollars from federal and other contracts), that was a significant blow. At first, the pattern was what came to be known as the "shotgun" approach. Each unit was expected to cut a standard proportion. Then, we went to the "rifle," whereby specific programs were targeted. During

---

[190] He attempted to fire two tenured professors, leading to a drawn-out process of appeals. One left, the other managed to stay.

these years, we received almost no additional funds for promotions' and merit increases, and even though we were "legislated" to provide mandated salary increases, we were provided no additional funds to support them. This was a new world for those of us in higher education administrative roles. We'd had no experience in so-called "decremental management." All we knew was how to chart growth and to make our budgets on that basis. All this budget reduction stuff was totally foreign to us, and we didn't know how to do it. It was painful, and it was not well managed. Many decisions were made that pitted college against college, and it sort of became a free-for-all.

It was about in the middle of this new environment that I decided to give up the deanship. I simply knew that this was an administrative environment for which I was just totally unsuited. Moreover, I'd become very tired of dealing with recurrent personnel issues and new faculty whose lifestyles were just totally different from my own notions of what the academic morality *should* have been. We had entered an era in which there was no longer much of a demand for our good people since higher education faced a general malaise, and there was no more expansion in the old sense of that idea. People wanted long-standing positions and were thus much more concerned about tenure and promotion issues, and we found ourselves caught up in almost unrealistic requirements for publishing and research-based reputations.

It was an increasingly anxious environment, and, in truth, I no longer had much of a stomach for it, so at the beginning of the fall term in 1981, as had always been my custom, I went before the faculty for my annual decanal address, and at that time, I told them that 1981 would be my final year. Between 1977 and 1982, I'd worked with three new and different presidents, and three different Vice-Presidents for Academic Affairs, most of whom were not in their jobs one month before they began to think about where they would be next, and some of them were openly hostile toward capital "E" education and presumed that whatever it was that we did, it probably did not belong in a major research university.

Pictured toward the end of his deanship and suffering the ravages of stress-induced Rheumatoid Arthritis

I had always made it a practice to begin each academic year with a dean's address to the faculty. My longtime secretary and great personal friend, Ms. Donna Moore, had always referred to me as a "writing" dean, and she had always labored through my almost undecipherable penmanship to get my words in typed form in those days before word-processors. I'd always provided these papers to the faculty and encouraged their reactions. On that occasion, I told the faculty that I'd done about all I could do, and that the college now needed new and different leadership, and that, joining the faculty fulltime once again, that we should all get together and make some demands on the new college administration!

Dean's staff pictured at my father's farewell party as dean. Standing Left to Right: Laddie Bell, Ernie Goeres, Evelyn Reeder (office manager), my father, John Carline (Jiggs Hostetter's replacement when he retired). Sitting Left to Right: My father's personal secretary Donna Moore, Mary Zoe Bowlby, and Jenny Ammons

Family Matters in the WVU Years

When we moved to Morgantown, son Greg was already an undergraduate at the University of Iowa. He subsequently completed his degree there, and among several institutions that had accepted him for graduate study in European history, he'd decided on the University of North Carolina at Chapel Hill.[191] It had a most prestigious faculty in his field, and (perhaps more importantly to him at the time) was in a part of the country where winters such as those he'd endured in Iowa were unknown! His mother and I helped him to get situated there in a graduate dormitory. It was a much more difficult circumstance for him than we could have known, but he braved it through. In the meantime, he'd met a young woman nursing student at Iowa, and it was clear that this was a relationship that

---

[191] Alas, my father is incorrect here. I aimed too high in my applications, and UNC was in fact the *only* institution to which I was accepted for graduate study.

was considerably more than casual. When Rita Short graduated from Iowa a year later, she and Greg made plans to be married, and in early June 1976, they were married in Rita's home town at Independence, Iowa. More's the pity, that event conflicted with son Joe's commencement at St. Francis High School in Morgantown, and Joe never enjoyed that special pleasure.[192] (He made up for it in a little way when he subsequently attended *two* commencements at WVU—his BS degree and his MA in Special Education, the latter with a straight 4.0 GPA!)

Rita and Greg made a new home in Chapel Hill living in a student apartment. Later, after Rita had entered Duke University's prestigious School of Nursing, they moved again, this time to an apartment off campus.[193] Jane and I particularly enjoyed our several trips to Chapel Hill, although Greg's experiences there in pursuit of his MA degree were not all that pleasant. After a couple of years, and as Rita was completing her own graduate work at Duke, I made some discreet inquiries about prospects for these young people at WVU. It turned out that there was a faculty vacancy in Nursing, and Rita was persuaded to interview for it. At the same time, I'd learned that Greg might be welcomed for Ph.D. work in European history at WVU, and although he'd been pretty much "soured" on any prospects for still further graduate work, I knew that he was an absolutely incurable academic, and his mother and I persuaded him to give it a shot.[194]

As it turned out, that was all most fortuitous. Rita was a "star" in the WVU nursing faculty, and Greg found a comfortable and respectful faculty within which to pursue his own studies. As a graduate instructor, even to this day, I still occasionally meet someone who doesn't *remember* me as dean, but who does remember either Rita or Greg: "Are you related to Greg Monahan, who taught History 101?" "Yes, he

---

[192] Actually, Joe did go through commencement at St. Francis, but he and my parents had to leave the next day to drive out to Iowa. I blame myself for not helping to choose a better marriage date!

[193] This sentence obviously conceals a substantial story that belongs in my own memoir.

[194] Again, this is not exactly as I remember it, but that's not surprising, since two people will often remember something differently. I'll deal with the "move" to Morgantown in my own memoir.

is my son." "Goodness, he was the best teacher I ever had!" Or: "are you related to Rita Monahan who taught nursing here?" "Well, yes, she is my daughter-in-law." "Really. She was first-rate, you know!" (Well, heck, I was the dean of HRE. Do you remember that? No? Umm.) Greg and Rita not only did very well at WVU, he subsequently won a Fulbright Scholarship to study in France, where he completed his Ph.D. research, and, though American inflation was such that being paid in francs, he actually took a cut in salary just about every month, he somehow managed. His French was only marginal when he departed, but by the time he came home, he was nicely fluent. He almost literally starved himself but managed to put away enough money so that Rita and their infant son Andy could join him in Europe at the end of his term for a grand tour. How they ever did all that with a baby in a stroller is beyond my comprehension!

When Greg and Rita moved to Morgantown, what with Rita rather gainfully employed, they decided to buy a house and were able to secure a modest though quite nice place. Greg did much of the finishing work himself, though where he *ever* learned how to hammer a nail is beyond me—it is *certainly* not in the genes! It is almost impossible to realize that, as this is being written, little Andy is almost sixteen years old and has just completed requirements as an Eagle Scout. My, my![195] And then, after Rita and Greg had been appointed to faculty positions at Eastern Oregon State College in La Grande, we were advised that another one was on the way. Thus came little Cathy, and now she's going on seven! Where does the time go?

During these West Virginia Years, life was really rather difficult for Joe. We enrolled him at St. Francis because its curriculum was somewhat more like what we'd presumed he was used to in Iowa City. Perhaps that was a mistake, but who knows? We don't think Joe enjoyed his high school years all that much, but he is surely a genuine

---

[195] Actually, Andy was fourteen in 1996, but he had indeed completed the requirements and become an Eagle Scout.

survivor, and he made it ok.[196] His freshman year at WVU was not all that productive, at least so far as scholarship was concerned. He lived in the dorm, partied a lot (apparently) and had a beat-up car that only his consummate skill as a shade-tree mechanic kept running. But during the summer after his rather disastrous freshman year, he worked in a fast-food place in Ocean City, Maryland, and there he met a young woman who changed his life, in more ways than one.

He and Judy married the following year, and he went back to school with a vengeance. He worked part-time at a gas station, and he made himself work at college. Although his and Judy's relationship couldn't quite withstand the pressures of work and want, he did subsequently graduate from WVU with a degree in teacher education and then went on for an MA in Special Education (with a concentration in Behavior Disorders) and has taught for the past almost ten years in Bridgeport, West Virginia.[197] His special pride just this past year was the purchase of a brand new Dodge Avenger, a lovely car. So Joe is doing ok, and Greg and Rita are just about permanently situated at Eastern Oregon State. Their simultaneous sabbaticals, spent last year in Paris, and then, for Greg and Andy, another term in Montpellier, were most productive, and Jane and I particularly enjoyed being able to spend some time with them first in Paris in the fall of 1993 and then with Greg and Andy in the south of France (and in Italy) in the spring of 1994. Last year—1995—we all spent Christmas together in Orlando, Florida, compliments of Jane and I.

[EDITOR'S NOTE: In the last chapter, my father briefly mentioned that my mother went to work in the late-70s for Pat Stewart Real Estate. Pat and Guy Stewart became great friends of my parents, and they saw them socially for some years.

---

[196] This is an odd argument. I remember distinctly that they chose St. Francis because they lacked confidence in the quality of Morgantown's public school system. The difficulties my brother and I both had with changing schools in the family's moves determined me not to move once my own children entered school.

[197] He switched from Special Education to become a fine history teacher and retired prior to the Fall Semester of 2020.

Guy and Pat Stewart

My mother finally tired of the odd hours and endless pressures of the job, but not before she had made a great success of it. It was while she worked for Pat Stewart that she helped my wife and I find our house in Morgantown, and when we left to move to Oregon, she helped us sell that same house.]

West Virginia University has been good to all of us, but so have all the other places we have lived. But, as my favorite philosopher Alfred North Whitehead once observed when, at the age of 60, he left England to assume a professorship at Harvard, "We have had a succession of lovely dwelling places, each one of which meant everything to us at the time, but not one of which we have ever regretted leaving."[198] So, indeed, it is the same with us. We've lived all over the country, have enjoyed every place and every move, but have finally learned that it is the friendly hills and valleys of this melancholy Mountain State that holds us firmly in its grasp. We live and die with our mighty "Mountaineers" whether in football, basketball, or in a succession of remarkable Rhodes scholars that this most underrated university has produced.

HOW SWEET IT IS!

---

[198] My father comes pretty close to getting this quotation from the *Dialogues*, p. 51, correct: "We have left behind us the most extraordinary succession of daylight dwelling-houses each of which in turn once meant everything to us, but not one of which we now regret having left."

CHAPTER IX

Rewards and Recognition

As I write these sort-of ending comments in early autumn in 1996, I have been officially retired from the academy for more than five years. Through the influence of two old friends and colleagues, Dr. Ranjit Majumder, who is now the director of HRE's Rehabilitation Research and Training Unit, and Dr. Ernest Goeres, the long-time Associate Dean in HRE whom I managed to bring with me from the University of Iowa when I came to this institution as dean in 1972, I have recently been allocated new office space in WVU's College of Human Resources and Education after having relinquished the office space that I sort of "carved out" for myself when I quit the deanship in 1982. These two men have been particularly close to me across my years at WVU, and they have known that I still enjoy having a place to hang my hat, and, between them, have made it possible for me to continue, literally, to hang it!

Dr. Ranjit Majumder

Office space is an always important concern in colleges and universities. Accordingly, when I decided to quit the deanship, I also gave much thought to where I might find a place to work thereafter. Thus, I went over across the hall on the eighth floor of HRE and decided that a fairly ample space over there no longer well-served the work of some of our Educational Psychology staff and told them to "clean it out." I contacted our university Physical Plant people and told them that I wanted that space partitioned off appropriately (for it was too large for a single office). Ernie Goeres was then able to secure surplus carpeting from the Medical School (he was very good at this sort of thing), and since the Physical Plant folks owed me a favor or two, we were able to completely refit that space with built in bookshelves, fresh paint, and the "works" without costing the university a single dime, and they made into a really first-rate office.

In truth, as it turned out, it was much more spacious and pleasant even than the dean's office that I'd previously occupied, but I thought that was altogether appropriate for one who'd given so *much* to the place (chuckle, chuckle!). Nevertheless, the space was so pleasant and spacious that I was just a little uncomfortable with the possible reaction to it by our new dean, Diane Reinhard, who had come to us from the University of Oregon.

Thus, one day about a month after we'd enjoyed a pleasant lunch and a glass of wine, we came back to Allen Hall, and I said, "Diane, I want to show you something." And I escorted her into my new office over across the hall on the eighth floor.

She had never seen this space, and I knew that it would impress her, so when I showed it to her, I said, "Now look, there are going to be days when you are going to be under all kinds of pressures from the chairs about how inadequate their space is. And you'll be going home after a trying day, and, after a couple of relaxing drinks, you're going to say to yourself, 'Hey! Monahan's got all that space over there!' And when that thought occurs to you, I just want you to remember that someday, *this will*

Diane Reinhard as President of Clarion University

be yours!" Diane Reinhard was, and is, a very savvy lady. She knew immediately what I meant, and there were many days across her own years at dean of HRE when she would come over to my office, bare her soul about this problem or that, and then look about with a sort of wistful look on her face and say, "you know, this is starting to look awfully good to me!" And we'd laugh about it, but it was true. That space was, indeed her own at any time she might have decided to take it. Fortunately for me, at least, she'd had a bit of a taste of what it's like to be a university president during a short period when she served as WVU's interim president, and a couple of years later, was appointed as president of Pennsylvania's Clarion University. So far as I know, she's done very well there, but I'd guess there are times even yet when at least the symbolic aspects of my old 803 Allen Hall office must still look awfully good to her.

Thus, I managed to retain that office until the fall of 1995 even though I shared it for the final couple of years with my good friend and colleague, Dr. Ed Smith. Ed had served for many years as the Associate Provost for University Administration, but had finally decided to assume his professorial status in HRE's Educational Administration department, and since space in our Ed-Ad department was scarce, and neither of us got along all that well with other members of the department, I agreed for him to move in with me. It worked out beautifully, and especially since, by that time, I had officially retired from the university and spent only a few days each week in the place. So, all in all, it worked out well, and then in 1995, Ed was instrumental in securing a major National Science Foundation grant for several million dollars involving computerization of public schools with HRE management, and I was willing to relinquish my space in the old office to make room for the computer whiz kids that the new grant supported. Ed himself, after having got the whole thing up and going, decided also to retire, so our long-standing pleasant and collaborative relationship ended.

It was collaborative in many ways, not the least of which was that during our office-together years, we managed to do a small co-authored book which summarized a most enjoyable case study research effort whereby we studied the ways the U.S. Army develops its leadership activities.[199] Ed at that time had been a full colonel in the U.S. Army reserve, and through his connections, we were able to gain access to installations and high-level personnel that we could not probably have gotten otherwise. We tried to see how we could apply that stuff to the preparation of school and collegiate administrative leaders, and the book was subsequently published by Scholastic, Inc. All in all, my and Ed's years together in 803 Allen Hall turned out to be not only very compatible, but more or less productive, all things considered.

Interestingly, the office I now occupy is tiny by any standards, but I'm delighted to have it. Dr. Majumder has made it possible, and I'm grateful to him. I should hope that I'll be able to continue to come in here and "fool around" until I die, for the routine of having a place to come in and work, even though the "work" doesn't amount to much, is a very important aspect of my kind of lifestyle. In that, and in so many other ways, I have been very fortunate. I enjoy telling colleagues here and there that it's a great feeling to come in for work and have no work to do. I think some of them might feel that has been my case all along![200]

Recognition and Reward

All of that is merely by way of suggesting that my very long career in higher education has been quite satisfying. I think that I did some good things during my ten years as a dean at WVU, though much of that sort of effort went more or less un-noticed. In truth, though, effective administrative work is like that. It's the sort of thing one just ought to be able to do when one engages in organizational leadership, and the day-by-day stuff is the real measure of accomplishment. As some forgotten observer once said, the days teach much that the years

---

[199] I referenced this book in my preface to this work.

[200] My father gave up going to his little office not long after the death of my mother in 2000 when his arthritis began to worsen. His use of the term "come in here" would seem to indicate that he composed much of this memoir in that office.

never know.²⁰¹ So, over the longer term, far less important things are typically remembered because they have a sort of a "big deal" feeling about them, but a meeting here, a decision there, a letter written (or not written), and an occasional acknowledgment of some faculty member who might happen to have done something notable—those kinds of things are the measures of effective administrative life.

The WVU "Personal Rapid Transit" system is still very much in operation

That is particularly true, for example, in the case of President James G. Harlow, who, as I have elsewhere mentioned, was instrumental in my appointment at WVU in the first place. Mr. Harlow completely restructured WVU's internal budgetary and accounting systems, created effective administrative procedures, and restructured the total staff patterns for more efficient management and promotion of grants and contracts for outside funding. Furthermore, he was instrumental in professionalizing our entire curriculum and instructional patterns, and consolidated the university's significant research and service activities. Additionally, he almost single-handedly established our university's

---

²⁰¹ Here my father actually reverses a quote from Ralph Waldo Emerson's *Essays, Second Series:* "Experience," in which the essayist wrote "The years teach much that the days never know."

rapid transit, or "People Mover" technology that, even today, remains a model for automated systems of its kind. Yet, it is almost as if Mr. Harlow was never even here.

Almost nothing has been done to recognize his efforts, and probably because most of those efforts were devoted merely to doing one hell of a good day-to-day job.

In my own case, as examples of deaning efforts that go largely unheralded, we were able to consolidate and control our chaotic off-campus operations by establishing four off-campus centers for coordination of all off-campus work. We adjusted the teaching loads of all faculty to ensure that even "full" professors taught off-campus work, and we developed fairly good library holdings to insure that off-campus work was at least a little more than somewhat equitable to similar efforts on campus. To make that even more the case, we engineered a proposal through our faculty senate to use the same course numbers and syllabi so that any off-campus course was treated in exactly the same way as any on-campus course, and this made it possible for many of our students to complete almost all of their work for M.A. degrees in the off-campus centers.

In that same area, with considerable help from a number of people in our staff and the university's central administration, we were able to head off a big push by Marshall University to gain permission from our State Board of Regents for doctoral-level work in education fields by our successful effort in developing a "cooperative doctoral program" with the College of Graduate Studies and Marshall. The degree has remained a WVU degree, and that effort has effectively prevented either COGS or Marshall from offering their own doctoral degrees across these many years.

I was also able to completely professionalize and standardize our entire promotion and tenure procedures.[202] When I first came into the deanship, I was particularly chagrined to note that, in the College of Engineering (which was next to us in the university catalog), that that college had many more senior professors even though their faculty was considerably smaller. I made it one of my initial objectives to get more promotions, but I knew we couldn't do that without a very tight system

---

[202] My father obviously felt this particular accomplishment to be especially noteworthy since he already discussed it in some detail in the previous chapter.

of peer review. The system we installed not only resulted in sixteen out of seventeen successful initial recommendations, but, albeit with considerable subsequent modifications since that time, still remains as this university's procedural pattern for peer review. Only two years after HRE initiated the pattern, the entire university began to utilize it. I'm not all that sure that even a few of those people we managed to get promoted between 1972 and 1982 appreciate the process we developed that made it possible for their meritorious work to be appropriately recognized, but those of us in the dean's office celebrated our achievement!

The Convocation and the Alumni Association

Regardless of those unsung administrative achievements, the two accomplishments for which my deanship years are probably most remembered were more or less ritualistic. In 1974 or thereabouts, I decided that having our graduates merely stand up and be recognized "in toto" at our annual big year-end spring commencement exercises was pretty much anticlimactic. After all, these young people had endured us for four or five years, and to merely have me, as dean, recite a little speech to the effect that "…will the graduates of HRE please stand and be recognized…" or something like that, seemed to me as if their work sort of ended with a semicolon. So, despite the fact that many of our faculty at that time were products of the turbulent 60s and had considerable distaste for any kind of ritual since they tended to feel, still, that all such university ritual reflected some kind of institutional paternalism or authoritarian symbolism, I felt that the world had changed and that our students were much more interested in some kind of recognition. Accordingly, I initiated our own HRE convocation. I appointed a committee to organize such an affair, and I told them that I wanted every graduate's name listed in a program, and that we would read every graduate's name and have them stand and be recognized. At the same time, I indicated that I wanted this convocation to recognize our "Outstanding Teachers" (which was an internal, university awards program that had been ongoing for many years) and that we would send out invitations to all parents of our graduates so that they might attend. I also instructed my long-time (very efficient) Office

Manager, Ms. Evelyn Reeder [pictured in the last chapter with others of the dean's staff] to purchase silver mugs with appropriate inscriptions thereon to present to recognized faculty and students.

The idea was greeted with considerable indifference, and I could not require faculty to attend. We simply invited them. But I did insist that all faculty who attended should wear full academic regalia. The first of these convocations was held in a couple of large rooms in the basement of Towers Dormitories. We had about two hundred people there, and, happily, quite a number of our faculty showed up. We enjoyed a kind of faculty/student processional whereby we all marched in to the music of Pomp and Circumstance with the faculty leading and all of our graduates in caps and gowns following. It turned out to be a very nice affair. Last year, in 1996, it was held in the large combined ballrooms at the university's Mountainlair Student Union—its nineteenth or twentieth year—and we had more than 2,500 in attendance! The ceremony itself is little changed. In that initial session, it was my requirement that we choose one "outstanding" student, and he or she would be commissioned to deliver *the* convocation address, and that has been the pattern ever since. Some of those short talks (we limited them to twenty minutes, for I wanted us to be in and out of there in no more than one hour) have been most notable.[203]

The Alumni Association

Another sort of ritualistic idea that developed into reality was my initiation of our own HRE Alumni Association. Now that was very hard work. First of all, we had real difficulty in merely trying to determine who our graduates were! But with diligent effort and pouring through records and then computerizing those, thanks to a taciturn faculty member in our Counseling programs named Tom Blascovics (known

Thomas Blascovics

---

[203] I had the privilege to take part in one of these convocations in 1985 when my wife was awarded an Ed.D. and I received my Ph.D. in History at WVU. Arts and Sciences had no such convocation at that time, so my father got special permission from the then deans of both colleges to "hood" both my wife and me at this very special ceremony.

affectionately around our shop as "Blast-Off"), who was very good in those early days with computers at a time when computers were rather primitive, we were able to develop a reasonably accurate initial list.[204]

We then invited alumni to join us and began publication of a very small newsletter. We encouraged all graduates to join us and persuaded the university association to let us charge alumni an extra dollar for joining our association when they joined the university's. It has taken much effort and much work, but now, in 1996, we have an active and supportive alumni association. And just this year, we have initiated our own alumni journal! Quite an accomplishment, all things considered.

Our HRE Alumni Association has always struggled with its financial support, which is typical of all such endeavors. And along the way, Jane and I have contributed several hundred dollars to its work, but the largest grant, and which has insured the Association's survival, was from a marvelous old West Virginia native who went off to Oklahoma after many years as a public school and collegiate instructor in West Virginia, a chap named Berlin Basil Chapman.

Berlin Basil Chapman at his desk

---

[204] Thomas Blaskovics was indeed a pioneer of early computers as well as the internet. He died at age 84 in December 2017.

From Cabbage to Cauliflower

He'd written a delightful book chronicling the development of the first real public high schools in West Virginia, *The Webster Springs High School*, and I was asked to review the book for our WVU Alumni magazine sometime in the middle 70s, which I did.[205] It was a pleasant memoir, and I gave it a most positive review, and subsequently, one day this chap showed up at my office! We had a pleasant visit and renewed remembrances of Oklahoma and so forth, but I didn't give it all that much significance. But when he learned that we'd begun our own Alumni Association, he was intrigued. To make a long story short, he became an enthusiastic supporter of those efforts, and when he passed away a couple of years ago at 90 years old, he bequeathed $5000 to our HRE Alumni Association.[206] Needless to say, that has assured its survival.

So, among a lot of more significant kinds of achievements that I thought I ought best be remembered for (at least in my view), the Convocation and the Alumni Association seem to have prominence. Certainly, too, the fact that the Alumni Association established a Convocation award in my name—the William G Monahan Outstanding Student Award—which is presented each year, and the recipient now delivers the annual convocation address, will have managed to keep those early efforts alive. Obviously, this is flattering, but some of the other things that I tried to do, or did, as a dean weigh much more in my own personal remembrances of accomplishment.[207]

---

[205] My father neglects to mention that the book was published *by* the WVU Foundation: Berlin Basil Chapman, *Education in Central West Virginia, 1910-1975* (Morgantown: West Virginia University Foundation, 1974). Chapman subsequently published extensively on Oklahoma history.

[206] $5000 in 1996 would be worth a little over $8,200 in 2020, which is not all that much money. The HRE Alumni Association must indeed have been a shoestring operation!

[207] That may be, but my father was the main contributor to the award in his name, and my brother and I have continued occasionally to donate money in support of that award since my father's death.

Some National Recognitions

During my ten years in the deanship, I enjoyed considerable visibility and prestige in other areas. I served for most of those years (and for several years after I'd retired from the deanship) on the Appalachian Educational Laboratory's Board of Directors. AEL was a federally funded "Educational Laboratory" situated in Charleston, West Virginia that served all or parts of a half dozen Appalachian states. As dean of HRE, I originally served on its board by kind of automatic tender since its corporate charter required participation by the "dean of the major doctoral-granting institution in the region" and which was similarly the case for all the other twelve or so Ed Labs across the United States. In any case, my work with AEL reunited me with an old friend from UCEA days, Dr. Terry Eidell, who was appointed Executive Director of AEL not long after I came to West Virginia.

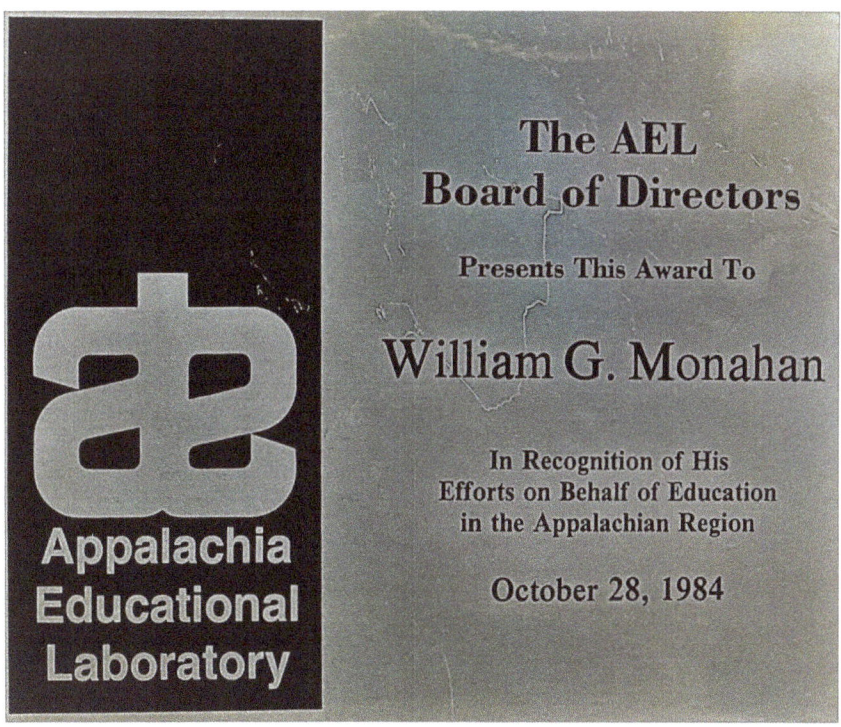

AEL Service Award

I subsequently served AEL as its board president for two unprecedented terms, and not too many years after I'd retired from active university work, AEL presented me with its highest award, its "Distinguished Service Award." It had previously been presented to such persons as Congressman Bill Natcher (D-Ky) and to U.S. Senator Jennings Randolph. I was also the very first recipient of the State of West Virginia's "Leaders of Learning" Award. That honor is now considered among the highest recognitions that any educator in West Virginia can achieve, and I was particularly pleased to be the first.

And Other Things

During my dean years, I was also elected to the Board of Directors of the American Association of Colleges for Teacher Education. That was particularly satisfying because I was elected by my peers across the country. And I also was honored by being elected as president of the Association of Schools and Colleges of Education in Land-Grant and State Universities. This association was composed of all of those of us who served in deanships in major institutions, and my association with those men and women was a high point of my long career. Jane and I particularly enjoyed attending several of that group's national meetings which took us to many pleasant places and established friendships which have lasted all these years.

In West Virginia itself, I was named to the state's Advisory Commission on Teacher Education and served with a number of distinguished West Virginians in revising our teacher education certification standards in the early 70s and served on two different occasions as president of this important State Department of Education body. Perhaps more importantly, I helped to initiate our own West Virginia Association of Colleges of Teacher Education chapter of the national AACTE and served two terms as president of that organization.

The Preston County Award

But, in some ways, my most pleasant recognition was from Preston County, West Virginia. A large and mountainous county bordering our own Monongalia County, Preston had endured a long period of significant difficulties in providing its children with high quality education for all of the familiar reasons: It is even still a poor county, very mountainous, and it is terribly spread out. In the 70s there were, and still are, strong sentiments on behalf of highly localized schools, and there remain, even still, strong loyalties for local communities and equally strong antagonisms toward any idea for consolidating any kind of services, much less education. Yet, it became obvious to some progressive Prestonians that their county simply could no longer sustain any genuine curricular quality without restructuring their old system of many small and inefficient schools.

Accordingly, a movement began to eliminate some of their many very small, rural high schools and move toward the development of more centralized and therefore, more enriched instructional programs. This became a very emotional issue, and after several years of critical and determined efforts to successfully consolidate schools, a counter effort emerged to *de-consolidate*! As this movement gained some momentum, a couple of the school board members asked me if I would be willing to consult with them in the effort to head it off, and this I was willing to do, and fortunately (for some still unknown reason) I indicated that in virtue of my position at WVU, I would do so without compensation! As I've noted—I'm not sure why I did it that way—perhaps Mr. Harlow so advised me, but in truth, I just don't remember. It turned out to be most fortuitous, however, since those who opposed any kind of consolidation contracted a professor at Boston University (a former native of Preston County who'd gone on to better things) to represent their interests and paid him rather handsomely.

To make a long story short, we were successful in persuading the State Board of Education (at a very emotional and standing-room-only meeting in Charleston one cold winter day) that consolidation of several high schools was the only ultimate option. I can well remember one or two occasions when I went up to Kingwood, West Virginia to meet with my "group" and rocks were thrown at my car as I departed. But we were able to pull it off. Today, many years later, there is now only one Central Preston County High School, and the fact that its football team won our state championship this past year is, at least, some measure of the extent to which the old opposition has significantly subsided.

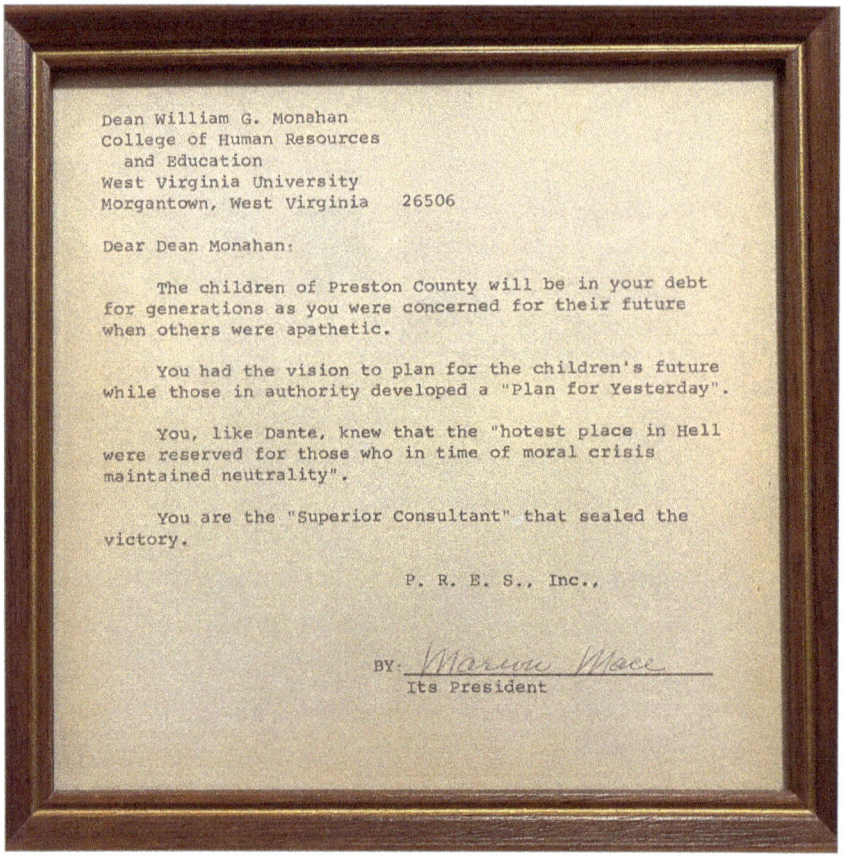

Preston County Letter of Appreciation

On behalf of my work with those marvelous "Prestonians," they presented me with a nice, specially designed "plaque" and a special note of appreciation, and it hangs on the wall of our little sitting room in our house on Allison Street with my very prized caricature of myself presented to me by Ernie Goeres and my then department chairs upon my retirement from the deanship in 1982.

Caricature poster commissioned for my father on the occasion of his retirement from the deanship at WVU

So, all in all...

It is altogether remarkable that I have done so well. I still think of myself primarily as a teacher. I think that I have been an effective teacher, if not always so diligent, i.e., I certainly could have been more attentive to testing, marking, and more exact in my assignments and in tracking my students' work. Moreover, I always tended to talk too much and engage my students in dialogue too little. But, by the same token, if my marks were a bit above the norm, then, like Whitehead, "I never wanted it said of me that I discouraged an incipient talent!"[208] But, almost universally, my students reported that they enjoyed my courses and claimed that they learned much in the process, so I'd guess that, beyond that, much less could have been expected.[209] I have a little to be proud of and a little to be ashamed of, but that is probably the case with just about anyone who looks back on long life.

The Fortunes of a "Good Life"

Much more importantly, mine and Jane's lives have been spared from major tragedy or serious misfortune. We have endured no life-threatening diseases, no tragic accidents, no criminal felonies, no accidents of circumstance, nor terrible ordeals. We can only hope that all of those who come after us are equally fortunate.

Now, if we can just get our golf swing tempo down pat and putt just a little better....

---

[208] My father here paraphrases a section of Price's *Dialogues of Alfred North Whitehead*, p. 46: "I reflect that I would rather not have it on my head that I was the one who discouraged an incipient talent." This sentence comes at the end of a section previously cited in this memoir in which Whitehead extolls the attributes of B students over A students because A students only tell one what one wants to hear.

[209] Indeed, my father was always a popular teacher at all the institutions with which he was associated. I once attended a lecture at the University of Iowa and was impressed. He was easy, informative, entertaining, and interesting. Of course, I may have suffered ever so slightly from a certain bias!

CHAPTER X

The Later Years (1996-2011)

by Greg Monahan

As I wrote in my preface to these memoirs, my father indicated once that he had written further about his life after the deanship, but if he did, I was never able to find any of those writings. It thus falls to me to write some words about his later years leading up to his death in 2011.

Dad doesn't have much to say in his final chapters about his years teaching after he left the deanship in 1981-82, but he continued to be active as a teacher, giving, as he indicated earlier in this memoir, a *lot* of "A" grades! He even took his one and only sabbatical in spring and summer,1985, when he and my mother journeyed to Athens, Greece to spend a semester abroad.

Visiting some ruins during their sabbatical in Greece

They enjoyed themselves during that term, and while I'm not sure Dad did much work beyond some summer teaching, they did see the sights and, for the only time in their lives, immersed themselves in another culture.

The arthritis that had plagued him during the last years of his deanship abated somewhat with the help of regular "gold" treatments, and he and my mother were able to play golf at The Pines Country Club regularly, where they maintained a membership and a large coterie of good friends. They also continued to attend football and basketball games where they made friends with those who sat around them. Both were popular with their friends, and Dad in particular was always a very gregarious man, full of good stories told with wit, verve, and healthy self-deprecation.

Likewise, the decision of my wife and I to move to Morgantown in 1980 and the subsequent birth of our son Andy in 1982 meant that both of my parents got to exercise the joys of grandparenting "close up." Dad adopted the name he had always used for his own father and became "Pop" to his grandchildren, especially Andy, and the two became very close before our move to Oregon in 1986 (my daughter was not born until 1990).

My parents with one-year-old Andy in 1983

Andy provided them with a number of stories, one of which Dad particularly adored. We had taught Andy to say "excuse me" when he burped or farted, and one time he was at a restaurant with his grandparents at a mall south of Morgantown when my father inadvertently bumped my mother's feet under the table. "Excuse me," he said. Andy, then all of three years old, piped up in a loud voice: "What's wrong Pop? Did you pass gas?" Other diners thought it was pretty funny, and Dad never tired of telling the story.

Once Dad had retired definitively from teaching in 1992, he and my mother embarked on a number of trips, often with other West Virginia retired faculty. These journeys took them to the Caribbean, Ireland, Spain, and Portugal, as well as back to France when I took my first sabbatical there in 1993-94. They celebrated their fiftieth wedding anniversary with a trip to Las Vegas in 1995 and must have looked back in considerable wonder that they had managed so well, considering that they started so young.

Traveling in Lisbon, left, and aboard a cruise ship, right

Thus, as Dad wrote at the end of his memoir, the 90s were largely a happy time for them both, but his last paragraph about not suffering any serious crises or illnesses in the family proved sadly prophetic. In 1997, only a year after he had finished his autobiography, my own wife Rita was diagnosed with metastatic colon cancer. During the year and a half that we fought that disease, my parents were tireless in their support and aid. They flew out to Oregon several times to help out, and when we traveled to West Virginia in the summer of 1998 to get a PET scan at WVU (the equipment for which was fairly rare then), they watched our eight-year-old daughter Cathy for us while we took a short "vacation" trip to Washington, D.C. with Andy. After Rita's death in July 1999, they invited us to come back to West Virginia for Christmas for what we all hoped would be a "healing" holiday.

Alas, that was not to be. That October, on their way back from an annual golfing holiday at Myrtle Beach, my mother suddenly lost half of her vision. A rapid trip to West Virginia University's medical center revealed that she was suffering from an aggressive brain tumor. While an operation removed most of the tumor, it could not remove all of it, and my mother elected to undergo radiation treatments that resulted in aphasia and occasional bouts of paranoia. What made it even more difficult was that, the previous summer, they had purchased the property next door to them as a permanent retirement home. Their first house at 316 Allison Street was an older multi-floor house, and the stairs were gradually proving difficult for my father with his arthritis. The new house had the master bedroom and living space on one floor, while still providing ample bedrooms upstairs for visitors (as well as a real urinal in the master bathroom, which my father adored!). Thus, my mother's diagnosis came as they were preparing to move into the new house and while she was supervising improvements to it.

My parents' last house at 310 Allison St in Morgantown, next to their former one

They accomplished the move, but that Christmas visit proved difficult. There were occasional happy moments, as when a song came on the radio and my brother watched in delight as my parents performed an impromptu dance in the kitchen! But my mother had difficulties with focus and attention, often seeming very far away. It was hard for all of us to witness her decline, especially since she had always been an incredibly sharp and "in charge" individual. What is more, dealing with this terrible illness brought on massive stress for my father, who started smoking again to deal with it. We always suspected he had been a "secret smoker" (one of the reasons he liked that little "get away" office so much!), but now he resorted to it far more often, and my mother was terribly upset by that. In the end, no matter how heroically she struggled, she could not defeat this disease, and she died on February 19, 2000, six months shy of their 55th wedding anniversary.

Despite occasional crises in their over half-century of marriage, they had remained deeply in love with each other, and my mother's loss was a tough one for my father. His friends and especially my brother Joe certainly helped get him through it.

The Pines Country Club

He continued to play golf and enjoy a certain degree of social life at the Pines Country Club, winning its Senior Club Championship in 2001, writing and editing its popular newsletter for seventeen years, and dining at its excellent restaurant.

This may have been my father's favorite award!

Then, in 2005, he suffered a bad fall on one hole that resulted in several cracked ribs. He concluded that the rheumatoid arthritis that had returned to bedevil him at the end of the 1990s made playing golf at the hilly course too dangerous and gradually withdrew into his recliner in his den of the new house. He still attended football games until accessing his seat also became too difficult. Basketball games, on the other hand, were still possible for a few more years. The university maintained handicapped parking spaces close to the Colisseum, and his seats were fairly easy to access. As he mentions in the previous chapter, he also funded a "prize" in his own name to be awarded to the outstanding student in his former college and was later happy to be one of the first recipients of the College's "Hall of Fame" honor.

My brother Joe, living only 35 miles south of Morgantown in Bridgeport, West Virginia, made it a habit to drive up to Morgantown on Wednesday and Sunday evenings where he and my father would share a meal at any number of local restaurants and watch shows and movies on television.

My father and my brother Joe at dinner

Those weekly visits became vitally important for both of them, and they became even closer than they had been before. I was deeply grateful for those visits because they enabled Joe to "check up" on Dad, something I could not do because I lived so far away. They also continued to attend Mountaineer basketball games together until two years before my father's death when the university started charging $20 per game to use the handicapped parking spaces. Having already paid a lot of money for tickets, my father concluded that was one nickle-and-dime too much. Likewise, my father joined Facebook and used a laptop computer to stay in regular touch with me and with some of his older friends such as Stan Hecker and Herb Hengst from his years at Michigan State and Oklahoma. He often managed to mess up the computer (how exactly, we could never quite figure out!), but luckily, my brother's stepson Miguel, who had come to love "Pop" very much, was able and willing to fix it whenever he came up to Morgantown for a visit. Dad also traveled a few times to Grenada, Mississippi to visit his sister Joan where he even managed to play a few rounds of golf on a course that was comfortably flat and on which he could drive a cart right up to his ball.

He finally quit smoking for good in 2006 when my brother also quit that habit (a promise made to his new wife Cathy, whom he married that year). Until then Dad could regularly be seen sitting out on his front porch during warm weather with a cigarette, a cup of coffee, and his crossword puzzles.

In his usual spot on his front porch

I visited him twice a year, at Christmas and in August for his birthday, and we talked every Sunday on the phone, when I would hear about various doctor's appointments, tv shows, and we'd discuss that week's events. He read newspapers from cover to cover, subscribed to the *New York Review of Books* and *The New Yorker*, and stayed up on what was going on. Despite my occasional suggestions, he was not inclined to attempt much of a social life. He largely confined his social interactions to Wednesdays and Sundays with Joe, flirting (innocently!) with young waitresses at his lunch spots, and very occasional visits from friends like his old colleague Ernie Goeres, who lived close by.

He did travel four times back to Oregon after my mother's death, first to attend his grandson Andy's high school graduation in 2000, then Andy's wedding to his wife Laura in 2004 (where Dad delivered the traditional Irish blessing), then in 2006 to meet his first great grandson Isaiah, and, for the last time, in 2008, to attend his granddaugher Cathy's high school graduation and to meet his second great grandson Liam. He also traveled with my brother, my son, and Andy's then future wife Laura to visit my daughter and me in France at Christmas time during my second sabbatical there in 2001. I had lured him to travel that time by promising to visit the cemetery in Belgium where his eldest brother Sonny was buried, a promise we all fulfilled together.[210]

With grandson Andy at his high school graduation

---

[210] On Sonny's service and death in the Second World War, see Appendix B.

At Sonny's grave

Toasting Andy and Laura with the Irish blessing at their wedding

Meeting great grandson Isaiah

With granddaughter Cathy at her high school graduation

In 2010, I prepared to take my last sabbatical before my planned retirement, and a plan came together for the entire family—my daughter, my son and his family, and me—to convene at my father's house for Christmas that year. Dad was excited, even though it would mean that his house would be overrun by three little boys (my son and daughter-in-law had produced a third son, Owen, the year before), but he was unconcerned. "I just plan to sit in my chair—you, Andy, and Laura will do all the work!" The details proved challenging. I would be flying back from France while Cathy, Andy, Laura, and the boys would all be flying from Portland. In addition, Cathy, who had begun college at Willamette University in the fall of 2008, was to begin a semester of study-abroad in Morocco that spring, and would be accompanying me back to France after Christmas!

Remarkably, it all came together. Flights arrived more or less on time, and we celebrated with Dad for Christmas, where my brother Joe, his wife Cathy, and her children Miguel and Eliana also joined us. It was quite a gathering.

With his three great grandsons Liam, Owen, and Isaiah at Christmas 2010

My father was overjoyed, not least because he also got to meet his third and, in the event, last great grandson Owen. What we did not realize was that this almost perfect Christmas would be his last, so that made it, in hindsight, a particularly rewarding and delightful one.

In June 2011, as my last sabbatical in France came to a conclusion, I offered to accompany my father on a trip to visit his ailing sister in Mississippi. He had not been able to drive to see her for a few years, and he was excited that he might get to see her again, so we flew down to Mississippi that month. Joan was suffering from a slow-growing cancer that would end her life in 2013, but she was still fairly healthy then and delighted to spend some time with her brother. While we were there, I posed them for a photo very much like the one they had taken in 1931, eighty years before. That earlier one was the first photo to survive of my father:

While we were visiting his sister, my father suffered what doctors later called a "Transient Ischemic Attack," or mini-stroke. Suddenly, sitting at the dinner table, he started babbling, repeating himself, and was unresponsive. We forced him to go to the hospital, but since he didn't remember having suffered the attack, he was furious with us for taking him there! After our return to Morgantown, he scheduled an appointment with his doctor, but I am fairly sure he continued to suffer these attacks. My brother and I witnessed another small one when I returned to Morgantown in August to celebrate his 84th birthday with him. I could tell there had been some decline, but rationalized it with the fairly logical assumption that anyone is going to suffer some decline at age 84. Yet, when my aunt Joan and her daughter and granddaughter journeyed north to visit him one last time in the fall, they all felt there had been a very noticeable decline. Nevertheless, my daughter and I planned to fly back for Christmas, as was our custom, and moreover, directly into Morgantown, where Dad, my brother, and his family would join us for a meal at a restaurant in the airport. We arrived more or less on time and found Dad sitting at the table with a martini. He had ordered his favorite meal there—a prime rib. We now think he may have suffered another T.I.A. while he was trying to eat a large bit of meat, but whatever the cause, he choked, and we were unable to dislodge the meat.[211] Deprived of oxygen for too long a time, his heart was revived by EMT's, but he died the next day without ever regaining consciousness, his family at his side.

As sad as that end was, we took some measure of comfort from the fact that his family had been with him, he had just had his favorite drink, and he was sitting down to a good meal. He loved all three of those things very much! Of course, his death made for a very different Christmas for all of us, but not, surprisingly, as sad a one as might be imagined. My son Andy and his wife Laura flew to West Virginia for the service, as did my father's sister Joan, her daughter Nan and granddaughter Katie, and we celebrated the holiday with memories and stories of him. His memorial service on New Year's Eve was well attended by friends and colleagues despite the fact that it was a holiday. Indeed, the reception at his house after the service morphed into a New Year's Eve party with just the family drinking champagne, telling stories, and generally acting kind of silly. We all agreed that he would have laughed and joked and offered more than his share of great stories had he been there.

---

[211] The Heimlich Maneuver was unsuccessful.

*Family gathered for my father's memorial service.
Left to right: Laura Villani Monahan, married to grandson
Andy Monahan, granddaughter Cathy Monahan,
Niece Nan Westin Parnell, sister Joan Monahan Westin,
son Greg Monahan, daughter-in-law Cathy Ervin Monahan,
son Joe Monahan, grandson and granddaughter by marriage
Miguel Fortney-Henriquez and Eliana Henriquez,
grandniece Katie Parnell*

My father was not a believer. Of course, given his Irish-American background, he was born and raised a Catholic, but as his letters from Japan show (see Appendix A), he gradually abandoned that church for the simpler service (and more attractive hymns, which he enjoyed!) of my mother's Methodist church, and while he served briefly as a deacon of a Methodist church in Oklahoma, I now wonder to what extent that was a matter of maintaining appearances. When they moved to Iowa, my parents occasionally attended the nearby Presbyterian church there, largely because they enjoyed the intellectual sermons of the minister, but after that minister left to transfer to another church, they didn't go back, and they never, to my knowledge, attended a church during all their years in West Virginia. Indeed, my father interviewed for a number of small college presidencies while he was a dean, but he once told me that questions about his beliefs—which were legal then—usually elicited a response about how "his

Sundays were important to him," resulting, no doubt, in his not being offered the job if the college were religiously affiliated! (Also, having moved so much in his career, he was just disinclined to do it again. As he notes in the previous chapter, he and my mother had come to like living in Morgantown.) Before his death, he made it clear that he did not want "any preachers" near his memorial service, and my brother and I honored that wish, allowing only my son Andy (who is a believer) to lead those attending in the Lord's Prayer. Interestingly, I had asked Dad at one point if that would be ok, and he reluctantly agreed, entirely for the sake of his beloved grandson.[212]

A few months before he died, we were sitting together, and I told him that he was a wonderful father—warm, supportive, tolerant, and funny—and that he had served as a marvelous example for me as I pursued my own life as an academic, a husband, and a father. He was touched and grateful, and after he died, I was profoundly glad I had told him that while he lived. That sentiment still stands. Indeed, now, as I approach the age he was when he wrote this work, I look back on his life and that of my brother and marvel that we should have had such wonderful and loving parents. While he was by no means perfect—none of us are—he was a good man, an ethical man, and a man of accomplishment. He came from a humble background and made an extraordinary career, enjoyed a loving family, and had a long and eventful life, a classic American life. I miss him. I miss those weekly phone calls, those occasional goofy emails, laughing with him while watching a funny show, sharing our mutual hostility to ignorant conservative politicians, and just remembering together the lives we led together. Of course, in some ways, he's not gone. He lives in his professional books and articles, in the memories of his students and his friends, in the genetic inheritance of his grandson, granddaughter, and great grandsons, in my brother, and, also, of course, in me. I will not forget him, and if others read this book, then perhaps they will have some cause not to forget him either. He didn't believe in an afterlife. We are his afterlife, and so, finally, is this book.

---

[212] He also loved the singing voice of his grand-niece Katie, and so we asked her to sing "Amazing Grace" at the service. We didn't think Dad would have minded too much!

*Photo chosen by my father to be published
with his printed obituary*

APPENDIX A

Your Billy: Letters From A Nineteen-Year-Old Soldier

From the time he first enlisted in the army in mid-1946, my father wrote to his new wife nearly every day. Remarkably, my mother kept every one of his letters. He never mentioned them to me, but, interestingly, he did discuss them in an email to my friend Gordon Golding, who was then at work on his own father's war letters: "There is still a big box of all the letters I wrote to Jane while I was in service, but since we had sort of a 'deal' that we would try to write daily, there's probably not much in mine that anyone other than she at the time would be interested in. I realize now of course that trying to write daily letters becomes a pattern, and finding things of interest to write under that regimen is not likely. Still, I was only eighteen and barely literate!" After my father's death, I discovered the box. My mother had kept the letters in their original air mail envelopes and tied them in packets with ribbons. Unhappily, only two letters from her to my father survive, and those only because he sent them back to her in one of his letters. During the war, soldiers were required to destroy letters from home, lest they fall into the hands of the enemy and reveal where American forces were stationed at any given time. Whether that rule still held during the Occupation, or whether my father simply did not have space to keep them, only two have come down to us. Thus, we have only one half of what was certainly a lively correspondence.

My original intent was to do with these what I did with those he wrote to her from the Merchant Marine and basic training in the army, which was to use them to supplement his own account with occasional asides and footnotes, but I think the letters from Japan merit a separate appendix to his work for two reasons. First, there are a lot of them, and they thus constitute an almost daily chronicle of his life during the eventful year that he was in the service. Second, and more importantly, they offer a fascinating contrast to his perspective on the period when he wrote the second chapter of his memoir fifty years further on. Here was a very young man leaving his wife to embark on an adventure. As he makes clear in that chapter, he had enlisted in part to avoid being drafted so that he could enjoy the benefits of the G.I. Bill, but his service did take him to a foreign country in a post-war world that was just beginning to evolve.

Sample letter with envelope below

Because of the sheer volume of the letters, I have chosen to exercise my role as editor in choosing passages and sections of those that seemed of most interest. Dad usually dated the letters, so keeping them straight is fairly easy. He also often signed the early ones "Your Billy," thus the title of this appendix to his autobiography. We begin with a letter written while he was on a train bound for California, from where he would sail across the Pacific to Japan.

Saturday, November 24, 1946 aboard the Santa Fe and Topeka railroad on the Grand Canyon Limited bound for California: "I started missing you before I left you and I suppose that, if I let myself think about how long it is going to be before I see you again, well, I'd probably never live through it. Realizing what is ahead of me, it causes me to miss and long for you more than ever."

Friday, November 29 from Camp Stoneman in Pittsburg, California: "Well, this is our last evening in the good old U.S.A. We're leaving at 3:30 AM tomorrow morning. I don't feel a bit bad about it somehow because I'm beginning to realize that when I come back, I'll be ready for a discharge. That will mean that we'll be together for the rest of our days. We'll make it a great and glorious lifetime Jane, one that we will be proud of someday…. I wish you could see this gang of mine. They all come up to me every ten minutes with a new question about going aboard ship, about how rough the Pacific is, etc. Honey, I'm really having a field day (except for the fact that I lost five bucks in a blackjack game). I'll stick to poker from now on. But don't scold me, I'm still a little winner."

Sunday, December 1, aboard ship bound for Japan: "The sea is the roughest that I've ever seen and has been that way ever since we left. We're awfully cramped for space as we're all down here in holds. I grant you that it's nothing like going to sea the way I did the first time. We sleep four high in destroyer bunks which consist of a strip of canvas roped and steel rims and held up by chains. We have no portholes at all and boy does it get hot down here. This ship is a converted tanker, and she rocks and tosses like a box. Everywhere you look you see guys puking their guts out. I've made the trip ok although I don't know how. It's awfully hard to write because you actually have no room. I'm standing up now and if it wasn't for this writing kit I probably couldn't even write at all."

Tuesday December 3rd, aboard ship bound for Japan: "We were pleasantly surprised today with a packet from the Red Cross. Mine contained a sewing kit, deck of cards, pocket book "the Magnificent Obsession," a roll of life savers (mints), soap and container and shoe strings. It also had stationery and envelopes. It almost seemed like Christmas around here. At least we knew they were thinking of us. You know hon, most of our service men today have the idea that the American public has forgotten them, and they're just about right. That little gesture seemed to pep everybody up a lot…. There is still a lot of talk about us going to technician school when we get overseas. I'm sure looking forward to that because I think I might make a good Dentist. You'll never see a poor one."[213]

---

[213] This is the first of several mentions of plans to enter Dentistry. When I first read of these plans, I shared them with my brother, and we had a good time speculating how different our lives would have been had we been the sons of a Kentucky dentist!

Thursday, December 5, aboard ship bound for Japan: "I long for you so terrible much sometimes that it makes me weak all over. I don't have any idea how I'll exist without you for this whole year to come."[214]

December 9, 1946: He had written on the 8th about rehearsing for a show on board ship. On this date: "Well the show went over quite well. We intend putting one on every day with, of course, slight variations. I sang "Body and Soul" and "Embraceable You" as an encore. They seemed to like me fine. I got more applause than all the other soloists put together. We had all sort of acts, a ventriloquist, a negro vocal sextet with spirituals, a ten-piece orchestra and a five-piece hillbilly band. We had an accordion soloist and a mouth-organ soloist, a negro 'jam session' complete with a jitterbugging team. And we'll probably have more tomorrow.... Tomorrow I'm going to do a couple of Irish tunes for the vocals instead of the popular. We think that most of the men will really go for that."[215]

Thursday December 12, still aboard ship: "My buddies ask me to tell them about you and how we came to be married and how married life functions. I stick out my nice little chest and tell them all about how we met, what we liked and disliked, and how glad I was that I was married to you. I've told them, I guess, a dozen times but they say they love to hear me tell about it, and that I seem so proud every time I tell it that it even makes them feel good. They envy me Jane. They envy me a lot and I don't blame them for it."

---

[214] I should note that most of my father's letters from this period included a great deal of language like this, some of it just a bit risqué, but I haven't included that much of it because it would frankly be repetitive. Likewise, some of it might also embarrass him a bit, and it is useful to remember that this is effectively his book and not mine! I should add that, based on his summaries of her letters, my mother apparently wrote similar things to him. They were, after all, still very young, he nineteen and she twenty.

[215] Alas, the weather took another turn for the worst, and they couldn't put on further shows until the 13th when he wrote that he was once again a hit. It is interesting to note the presence of African-American servicemen on board.

Friday, December 13, aboard ship: "I shaved this evening for the first time since I left Stoneman and I had become quite attached to those whiskers. I had a pretty nice beard and would have kept it only my Compartment officer asked me to shave it off."[216]

The ship arrived in Korea on December 17 and soon left for Japan. He next wrote my mother on Christmas Day evening from Camp Chickamauga, Beppu, Japan: "It has been a quiet Christmas Day here. I went to mass at 9:15 this A.M. then did nothing for the rest of the day.... Last night was the first time I had slept in a bed with springs in it since I left California. It was all anybody could do to get up this morning.... We had quite an earthquake here the past week. It was felt here but damage was slight. On Honshu, however, it was another story. There were numerous deaths and injuries there and property damage was high.[217] We weren't here then but we felt it through tidal waves at sea.... I met a company sergeant here who…said that this company is in need of a clerk, so I went to their Captain and told him that I had experience in that field (F.B.I.). He asked me if I could type and when I said yes he took my name and serial number. I talked with him about twenty minutes and I'm pretty sure that I will get the job. I will probably get a rating out of it pretty quick also so I think it's quite a deal."[218]

Thursday, December 26: He was excited about the job he had gotten: "I think this is the deal I've been waiting for. Our barracks are more like mansions and the food is far better than it ever was in the States. I'm good buddies with every non-com from the First Sergeant to the mess sergeant and they all seem to like me." He was soon to make $160 per month, from which he hoped to send as much as $30 home per month.

---

[216] This is the only time I know of that my father ever grew a beard, or even a mustache, for that matter. There are no photos of him with it, alas!

[217] This was the Nankai earthquake, which measured 8.7 on the Richter scale and made world news.

[218] Interestingly, he had apparently given up on getting into some kind of medical school and pursuing Dentistry!

December 27, 1946: "I like this job mainly because the time passes quickly." He also mentioned it was pretty easy duty, with not that much to do, but having work was nice: "Boy, for a while there, when we were doing nothing at all, it was beginning to get me down thinking about not seeing you for maybe a year, maybe more." But the work did pick up occasionally, and he wrote on January 1, 1947 "I pounded that typewriter until my fingers were immovable. It was harder work than digging a ditch."

January 5, 1947: "I went on sick call this morning and guess what was wrong. I've got malaria. Sergeant Cuthbert, the medic who checked me, said that I had evidently had it sometime before because it isn't the kind one gets for the first time. He said that if I start having chills to have someone call up. He also gave me some quinine which I must take every four hours for five days."[219] On that same date he noted: "I went into town today and boy if that dump is a town I'm an elephant. Its people are the dirtiest, filthiest creatures I've ever seen." He noted the lack of plumbing and the use of what "American personnel aptly named 'honeybuckets'. They use these for toilets and when the bucket is full, they use its contents for fertilizer for their gardens. When anyone eats the vegetables raised off human fertilizer, they contract all sorts of diseases…. All military personnel are strictly forbidden to eat any Japanese food and anyone caught eating food outside the camp is dealt with severely."[220]

January 8, 1947: He has gotten his first stripe and is now a private first class. Interestingly, there is often a P.S. in his letters wishing "Mr. and Mrs. Newcom" well. He does not appear to have started referring to his in-laws by their first names until the 1950s.

---

[219] This was the first I had ever heard of his having malaria. He apparently recovered from it, since I have no memory of his ever suffering from it.

[220] Later in life, when he recalled his time in Japan, my father showed considerably more understanding and compassion than his teenaged self for that country and its people, struggling to recover from a devastating war that they had, it is true, brought on themselves. Treated human waste, by the way, is used in modern agriculture, but there is continuing debate about the efficacy of "night soil," or untreated human waste, especially for growing food.

January 10, 1947: He writes, as he has in almost every letter, bemoaning the fact that he had yet to receive any mail from my mother—or from anyone. "It's very hard to keep up my good spirits. It was in November that I left for Stoneman. It has been two months almost, since I have seen or heard from any of you. So many things can happen in that span of time. I'm frantic sometimes, wandering if you are well and happy. I do hope I hear from you soon…. Every night, as I lie in bed, I bring out of the depths of memory those many wonderful moments we've spent together."

January 13, 1947: All is well as he has finally received his first letter, labeled "#28" and causing him to be excited at the prospect of receiving the first twenty-seven! Most of the letter was spent telling stories he had heard about the earthquake which had understandably worried my mother and other family members of servicemen stationed in Japan.

January 21, 1947: "I think you should see a doctor about your headaches sugar, cause you have them a lot and I know how you suffer with them. Will you honey? For me."[221]

January 24, 1947: He has learned that his departure date would be November 28th, causing him to hope he would be home for Christmas. Thinking of his future career, he mentioned writing to someone at "U.K.," presumably the University of Kentucky: "I've definitely decided on Journalism with English and English Lit as my major. My mind can't be changed." [Of course, it did change!] "Since I've been overseas, I have reached a point of mature reasoning. For the first time in my life I can actually sit and make accurate and proper decisions. My job

---

[221] My mother later suffered from chronic headaches, and it is striking—and more than a little sad—to hear that they might have started this early in her life. In the event, she continued to have them. She had to have some kind of operation in September 1948, and he wrote her from college in Bowling Green on the 25th "I hope those headaches vanish. That worries hell out of me. I've asked lots of people if they've ever heard of migraines appearing because of a spinal anesthetic but no one has, thank God." What kind of operation she had that required such an anesthetic, none of the three surviving letters in this later period tell us.

From Cabbage to Cauliflower

has helped me in that respect a lot because three fourths of the time, everything is left up to me."

January 30, 1947: "I had chills last night with my malaria but I took a lot of quinine today and I feel just as though nothing was ever wrong. They told me at the dispensary that it wasn't a type of malaria that would ever cause me a lot of trouble but that it would probably be aggravating."

February 3, 1947: Apparently responding to much talk in my mother's letters: "When you talk about having a baby it makes me proud as a peacock. I guess I sort of feel like a father at those times. I pray it isn't a boy now Jane because there will be another war, I know. If it doesn't come in fifteen years it will before another twenty-five. We're preparing for it now. Yes, it's true… That's why I want a girl. I know you will spoil her terribly but you would spoil a boy just as bad."[222]

February 6, 1947: He wrote he had finally received his Christmas presents in a box, including a new lighter he liked from my mother's parents. My mother had apparently written him that she had started teaching. "I'm thrilled to death to hear that you are teaching.… But baby, that's exactly what I'm doing over here only under different conditions, and I find that it is easy to get roaring mad at my class [as chief clerk, he helped in training recruits with "lectures" on various subjects]. With your temper you will get awfully P.O'd at the kids so don't lose your patience with them angel. Boy, I would sure enjoy being in your class."[223]

---

[222] His prediction proved correct. There was a war twenty years later, though not the one for which he thought he was preparing! And he fathered two boys. Luckily, I had a fairly high draft number, avoiding the fate he presciently predicted, and my brother was too young to enter the draft.

[223] Here another reference to my mother's temper. She had inherited the "Howerton Temper" from her father, who in turn got it from his mother, born Henrie Howerton. It was explosive, but, luckily, burned itself out fairly quickly! (I know because I inherited it too.) That said, further letters indicated she was teaching at Marion High School. They do not hint at the subject, but a yearbook photo printed in Chapter I indicates that she was teaching stenography, typing, and office management, perfectly logical given that she had attended business school.

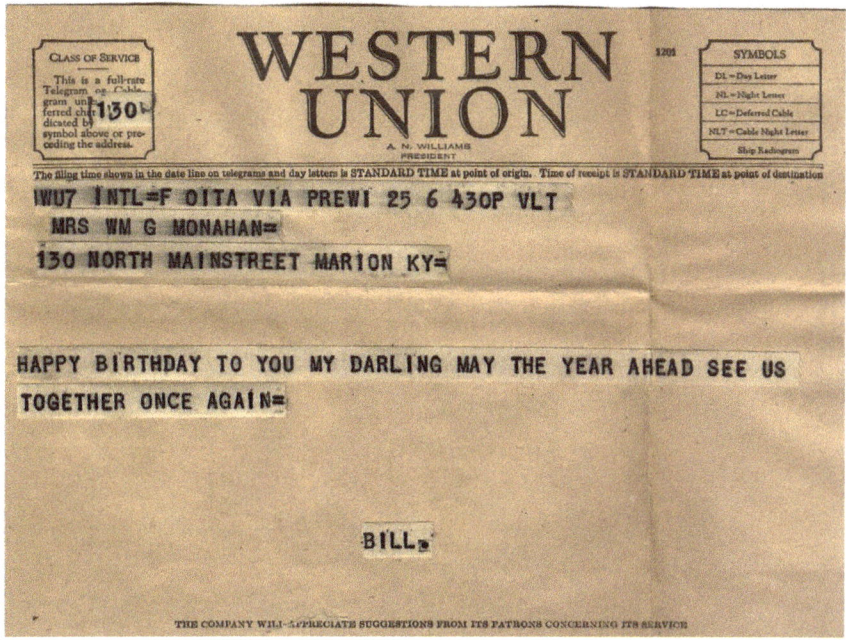

One of the very few telegrams my father sent my mother during his service, wishing her happy birthday

February 7, 1947: "I've been studying all afternoon on my lecture. This morning I was told that it must last at least an hour and a half. I had planned about an hour's talk so I spent the morning adding to it. I've decided that ninety minutes is entirely too long to conduct a lecture so I've divided my material so as to make it half discussion. It will not only be better for myself but I actually think the men will get more out of it."[224] On the 9th, he again noted my mother's teaching and wrote "I've always said that teaching is a good life, and that I wouldn't mind it myself." And on the 12th: "This lecturing to troops in training is valuable to me as experience. I've found that I can now talk easier to large groups and that my sentences also come more readily than at first. The men have come to respect my word and I notice that, through definite effort to make my classes interesting, the men are more attentive than before. I think I'm succeeding."

March 2, 1947: "I'm going to the movie rain or shine. On the way up we are going to stop in at the Sister's Orphanage and give them our rations for the week. They are in a pitiful state there. They have nothing to eat but what rice they can raise in their meager gardens. The government doesn't help them at all."

March 9, 1947: "I've started smoking a pipe again and I think I'm gradually acquiring the habit. You should see the pipe I have now. It is one of those curved stem jobs and I really look like an old man with that thing in my mouth."[225]

March 16, 1947: In the aftermath of Truman's famous "Truman Doctrine" speech of March 12 effectively declaring the Cold War and asking Congress for aid against Communist insurgencies in Turkey and Greece, there was a war scare. "We here in Japan are concerned more than anyone else. We were put on alert tonight. If we do go to war soon, we know that we will be the very first to see action…. I'm scared Janie…. I don't want you to worry over this letter baby, but I do want you to be prepared for any news. If there is a war, I pray to

---

[224] At only nineteen, this showed a fine awareness of student attention spans, and as he notes, all the teaching he was doing in the army surely influenced him to consider it as a future career.

[225] My father smoked a pipe for many years until we finally hounded him into quitting in the late 1960s. We suspected him of sneaking cigarettes occasionally after that, but, as I noted in my own last chapter of this memoir, he didn't take up that habit again on a regular basis until my mother's illness in late 1999.

God that I see you before it actually starts. I do believe that it will start soon." But by the next day, things had quickly calmed down: "First don't pay any attention to that letter I wrote you last night.... It is nothing like being a crisis yet." He did mention he had started training that day on radios, something he discusses in his memoir.

On March 26, he reported "This damned malaria is with me again and when it hits you it leaves you so tired." But he also noted that training was soon to be cut to a half day. "I have put in an application to teach English Literature, high school level. Mr. Crawford, the I&E chief here, told me that I had a good chance of getting the job. I sure hope that I do because I will not only be teaching others but in a way I'll be teaching myself a few things."[226]

March 28, 1947: Complaining of the lack of news of the U.S.: "It has gotten to the point where we wonder if there *is* really a United States or whether or not it was all a realistic dream.... True, we get the Stars and Stripes every day but that damn thing is only 'the printed mind of General Doug' [MacArthur]. I sometimes believe he writes, prints, and distributes it all by himself. Boy, they sure 'brown-nose' him with it."[227]

April 3, 1947: He responded to my mother's news that she had consumed two bottles of beer per day for the last week. "I don't care if you drink a case as long as it isn't with some guy. I'm kinda glad you are beginning to like it because we can drink beer together when I come home and have a hell of a time. Of course, there will be another thing we will have one hell of a time doing too."

---

[226] There is no more mention in his letters of this possibility, so it apparently did not happen. It is interesting as yet another indication of his future career, even though he still planned throughout his time in Japan to be a journalist.

[227] Douglas MacArthur, General of the Armies, commanded in Japan from the end of the war in 1945 until the beginning of the Korean conflict in 1950, when he took command of United Nations forces there. He was not renowned for modesty.

From Cabbage to Cauliflower

April 10, 1947: "I didn't write last night. We graduated from commo [Communications] training yesterday so we celebrated it last night at the beer hall. I got gloriously drunk and we sang and sang all night long. Excuse me for it baby but that communications was rough and we just let ourselves go. I'm a full-fledged radio, telephone and line man now and I'll give you two to one that I could get a job with Bell Telephone simply because of my army training. It may come in handy someday."

April 18, 1947: His former assistant (who became the clerk) had left, and he had double duty until he could find and train a new one. He reports that the new man is catching on quick, and he's anxious to get back to "commo." He also reports in this letter that he has been promoted to corporal. He writes that his captain [Captain Keyes] wants to send him to West Point, but Dad has put him off saying he is "waiting for your letter." He obviously wanted my mother to veto the idea for him!

Late April brought their first (and only) "fight by mail." My father had apparently sent a cheap gemstone to his brother Spencer to give to a girl and had also written a lot of letters to people in Bowling Green without writing to my mother's parents. She let him have it in a letter, accusing him of "making a fool of himself." He sent that letter back to her along with an earlier, much sweeter one. Thus, we actually do have two letters she wrote to him. The nicer one is similar to his, full of longing and a few ordinary details of life.

Dated April 15, 1947: "Dearest Billy, If I don't get to see you pretty soon and kiss you and hold you close I will just die. I never dreamed that I could ever miss anyone and long for them as I do you. I am simply living in the past. Everything that I do or say or that I hear reminds me of something we did. If I didn't have my dreams of our future I couldn't live." He sent this one back as an example of the letters he liked to get (!) and wrote a response to the angry one, but chose to send it to her with a cover letter apologizing for anything he had done and let her know how hurt he was. The exchange shows just how difficult it was to maintain a relationship over such a long distance when the mails were not often very slow.

May 2, 1947: "You have been to B.G. [Bowling Green] and you will know. How is Dad? You see baby, Mother doesn't tell me too much, I suppose because she fears that I will worry. Actually I worry more because I don't know the truth. Dad wrote me a letter. Tears sort of swelled up inside me as I read it. He said nothing except that he missed me terribly. Over and over he repeated that. I'm entitled to know the truth and I know that Mom will never tell me. Please won't you?"[228]

May 4, 1947: "Janie, I think I will just die if I don't see you soon. Every thought, every word, is you. I breathe you and I eat you, work you and sleep you. Every damn thing I do is you. I'm not exaggerating one little bit either." His letters are always full of such longing, and it would be inaccurate in summarizing them not to quote an occasional passage like this one!

May 9, 1947, on maneuvers in Kyushu: "I didn't write last night but I was so very tired. I'm not quite used to these 14 hour days. We go all day and every minute from 4:30 till 6:30 and I mean every minute. They just about run me to death out there because wires go "out" about every half an hour and I no sooner finish the establishment on one line before I'm called for repair on another. All that and I must fire too. My scores so far are not so good as they were at Polk but we didn't fire the 300 yard range there. I fire for record tomorrow and you can bet that I will be working hard to get "expert" again this year."

---

[228] Robert "Pop" Monahan was suffering from serious heart disease. He would die two years later in 1949, by which time, my father had left the service and was back in Kentucky. His emotional response to his father's letter mirrors the great affection for "Pop" he displays in this memoir.

Captain Keyes from my father's military photo album

May 12, 1947: "I found another recording of "My Old Flame" and one of the fellows is playing it for my benefit now. It's no secret around "I" Company that it's my favorite tune and whenever somebody catches me writing you, they run to the Vic [Victrola: record player] and put the record on for me. I really have these characters trained around here."

May 22, 1947: He announces he has made "buck sergeant." "I had no idea that I would make it this soon but I'm sure not kicking about it." He also reports continuing pressure from "Captain Keyes" to go to West Point. He was very complimented and occasionally even tempted.[229]

Sunday, June 15, 1947: "I spent the evening drinking cokes, eating donuts and thinking a lot about you and me and little Bill. You know sweets, the three of us are going to make a wonderful trio."[230]

---

[229] As my father notes sadly in the second chapter of his memoir, Captain Keyes, who so admired him, was killed early in the Korean War along with many other members of "I" Company.

[230] Now, apparently, he's wanting a boy—a "little Bill"! When I was born six years later, I was in fact named for my father—"William Gregory Monahan, Jr."—though from the beginning, they called me by my middle name.

June 17, 1947: After an exhausting day on maneuvers carrying a 40-pound radio: "I'm terribly happy for Ann and Harvey [my mother's sister Ann had just gotten married]. As for West Point, well, Captain Keyes will be out here with us, his wife back at camp worrying and wondering. That's not for us Janie, and besides, if it weren't for the army I could have attended my sister-in-law's wedding. I've decided against the Point." Several subsequent letters complained of incessant rain with leaky tents and wet clothes! "This is the infantry at its roughest."

Photo taken while on maneuvers

June 28, 1947: The effect of getting a letter: "When he handed it to me, I was standing in mud up to my ankles, my feet and socks were soaked and I was completely miserable. Then as I read that first page about what you and I were going to do, well, the mud, blisters, rain, mountains—nothing mattered anymore. When the going got rough I'd read that page and take right off like a rejuvenated man."

July 10, 1947: "I fixed five electric fans today and that involved taking them completely apart and reassembling them. Believe it or not but they all work like a charm. I guess I'm just a little genius (but don't tell anybody that I said so)." He complains about the extreme heat, noting he's sweating so much, he's having to change his underwear twice a day!

August 2, 1947: "I have a guitar now. It's nip made and I got it for a carton of cigarettes. Believe it or not but I can play almost anything.[231] 'Prisoner of Love' and 'Falling in Love is Wonderful' are my specialties. If I improve just a little more, I'm going to take a shot at a job at the club playing and singing. I'm also in a review scheduled for the 5th of September here in the Regiment. It's something to pass away the time with."

August 9, 1947: His 20th birthday, and he reports that "The fellows here in the cadre room went in together—pooled all their Black Market yen in other words—and presented me with a guitar.... They have evidently been watching my—er—um—progress, shall we say, on the guitar and they said that they wanted me to have my very own so I could 'serenade' them to sleep at nights. They made a big 'to do' over it and presented it to me at dinner.... I was tickled pink because I know they were sincere. It isn't an elaborate guitar but it has a good tone, is small and durable and it has an easy finger board. I think by the time I get home I'll be able to play anything."[232]

---

[231] It was common practice during and after the war to refer to the Japanese as "nips" and "Japs." He also occasionally used the term "gooks" in his letters, a derogatory term that was also used by American soldiers during the Vietnam War for the Vietnamese.

[232] He bought another guitar many years later after we moved to Iowa and would play on it now and then.

August 21, 1947: "I got a pretty interesting book at the library last night. It's 'The Marriage Reader'. It is awfully thorough and covers the works. According to statistics—so the book says—our marriage is a very great risk and will probably bounce off the rocks in less than five years. I had to laugh at that. I firmly believe that this is one time statistics will not concern me."[233]

August 25, 1947: "All of a sudden there seems to be a pretty bad epidemic of polio here in Japan. I've read where several children and three sergeants have died of it up north. Tonight, Company "A" was quarantined because of it and a child who lives in the same apt. building with Sgt. Layne was stricken late last night. There seems to be no way of stopping the spread of it. The least ache or pain and a guy begins to get panicky. It's pretty bad I guess. Tomorrow we get some kind of shot for it."[234]

August 30, 1947: "Well, they've cut transfer orders on me. I'll be going to Regimental Headquarters Company around Monday or Tuesday. I imagine I'll get a good deal out of it though who knows…. One good thing about that company is that they always ride. I'm glad of that anyway."

September 3, 1947: My mother was apparently quite the skater: "I hope that skating rink doesn't close because it at least affords you a little entertainment while we're 'sweating out' these last twelve weeks. You know, angel, you can probably out-skate me all over the place but with the experience I've had in the Infantry I'll bet I can out walk you."

September 8, 1947: "They've really messed up "I" Company. In one part of the barracks they have put the rehabilitations and Isolation troops, or, in other words, the Clapp Shack; VD ward.

---

[233] The book proved prescient. My parents briefly separated for two months in the summer of 1952—five years after this letter was written—but they weathered that crisis as they did so many in their lives.

[234] Since the polio vaccine was not available until 1955, I have no idea what kind of "shot" the army planned to give its soldiers—perhaps penicillin in hopes of warding off infection or vitamins of some kind?

Those few of the old gang who are left there are plenty burned up about it too."

September 12, 1947: "I'm in Kumamoto, Kyushu now.... I'm here with the Glee Club. How I came to be with the Club is quite a story. One night several weeks ago I met the Director of the Glee Club and he said that Sgt. Plonta (with whom I was stationed in I Co.) had told him I could sing.

Plonta was a boxer as well as a fine tenor

He said that there was a probability of an opening for a 2nd tenor and wondered if I would consider taking it. I told him yes but frankly I didn't expect to hear from it again. Wednesday afternoon he called me and told me to pack up because I was leaving with the show Thursday. I almost fell over. I had to pack that afternoon and catch the last show they gave in Beppu that night. The next morning I went on the range and fired; came back in at ten o'clock, took a shower, shaved, changed clothes and caught [transport] at 10:45.... I'm going into the show tonight. I know none of the music so I'll be working all afternoon picking up what I can about it. I'm a TDY [transfer of duty] with 24 Div Spec. Serv but my address will remain the same."[235]

September 14, 1947: He is preparing for a ten-hour train ride. "I've played bridge almost all day. These fellows are pretty good and I can tell that my game is improving. Maybe by the time I get home I will have stopped trumping your Aces."[236]

Nagasaki church before the bomb

---

[235] For a photograph of him singing while with the Glee Club, see Chapter II.

[236] He didn't. Indeed, he so frustrated my mother in bridge that she seldom teamed with him. They laughed about it, but when they played with my grandparents on our trips to Kentucky, my mother often made him partner with her father! Dad's bidding mystified my grandfather, who would shake his head and look at me with a sweet "I can't believe he did that" smile, but my grandparents had come to adore him, so they put up with his occasionally "challenging" play in bridge!

From Cabbage to Cauliflower

Nagasaki church after the bomb

September 21, 1947: "Friday [September 19] we went to Nagasaki.... That is one of the cities that was hit by the atomic bomb. We got some wonderful pictures of the devastation too. It was beyond description angel. Everything was blown away from the bomb—by that I mean that the debris lay quite a ways from the original location. Most of the damage was from the terrific heat. I got one very good souvenir—there was a hospital and medical college quite close to the place where the bomb went off and it was in the hospital that I got it. It was, or rather, it is four or five laboratory slides that were fused together by the heat and within them there is a smear. It was all ready for the microscope when the bomb hit. I've already been offered a lot of dough for it but I want to keep it and have it analyzed."[237] "The show is still gaining momentum and we're still as good as always (bragging)."

September 22, 1947: "We've worked pretty hard here if you can call rehearsals work. We're getting in shape for the new show and so

---

[237] If he brought this artifact back home, there is no sign of it anymore. This is all he wrote at the time about visiting Nagasaki.

far it is shaping up ok. And guess what—I'm going to get to sing my own song in it. I wrote it on the spur and I call it 'Working Man'. Don Stout is writing the music. I talk most of it with rhythm background. The producer liked it so I guess it's in."

October 5, 1947: He's beginning to think of switching from Catholicism to Protestantism. He had attended a Protestant service. "I've got to know if I would be in danger of losing my soul should I desire to change my denomination. According to the laws of my church I am at present nothing. It has been close to a year since I have received Holy Communion Jane and so I am automatically 'fallen away' as the phrase goes. I'd appreciate it if you wouldn't say anything about this to anybody. I say that because there are those—both Protestant as well as Catholic—who could put it to bad use—gossip, you know…. I've got a lot of deep thinking to do and I'm not kidding. It would kill Mom and Dad were they to know of these thoughts. Makes me shudder."

October 10, 1947: "We did the show last nite and it went over grand. Colonel Yancey came back stage and congratulated all of us. He was so excited he could hardly talk…. My tune, 'Chao, Chao Refrain' was a hit as well as 'Lost Love' by Plonta and myself. The song 'Long Gone' (with my own more appropriate lyrics 'Long Gone from Beppu') went over great and I got an encore."

October 12, 1947: A second show has gone even better, and he got three encores. "This afternoon I worked out at the gym. I weigh 162 now and I'm lifting weights to put it in the right places." He notes he can press 110 lbs "over my head" [military press].

October 19, 1947, Tokyo, Japan: As planned he used the "telephone exchange" to call my mother for their second anniversary. "It's almost 6 pm now, yet it still seems as though I have just finished talking to you. I didn't say anything that I had planned but that was beside the point anyway. The important thing was that I talked to you ten thousand miles away on our 2nd anniversary…. Tomorrow we have the entire day off. No rehearsals and no show. We've planned to go to the War Crimes Trial. I wouldn't miss that for anything either."

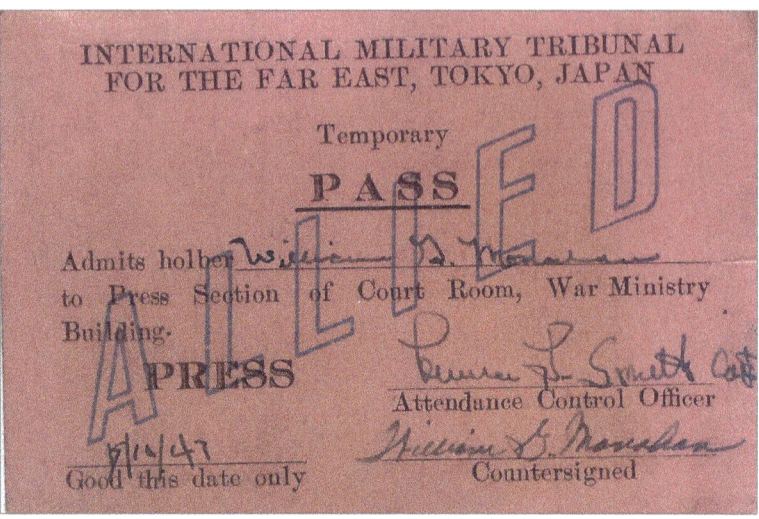

My father's war crimes trial press pass

October 21, 1947: He had a great time the previous evening celebrating his wedding anniversary in swanky surroundings of the Tokyo Non-Com Club. Then he reports attending the trial: "This morning we sat in on the War Crimes trials and the court room is right down the hall from where we slept. (We have fun bragging about how we walked through the court room in our underwear to take a leak—our room was something too—two fellows sleep in each room). We had Allied Press Passes. I took notes on the prosecution and defense but you don't care anything about that. It was very interesting to me because I had a chance to see how these big wheel journalists work. I sat alongside of some of America's greatest reporters this morning and I 'ate it right up'. We left there about 10:45 am and went down to the Pyle for coffee and a bite to eat before coming back here to the hotel…. We are leaving Tokyo about 8 o'clock in the morning and we'll sure hate to leave. This is so much like the states here. They have everything."[238]

---

[238] Interestingly, he says nothing about attending the trials in his memoir, but he did preserve the press pass. This passage is all he had to say about it in his letters.

October 22, 1947: "We're in Kyoto now and we play here tomorrow nite. It has taken us ten hours by train—these damned trains are so slow and also stop every fifteen or twenty minutes.[239]

Picture of a Japanese train from my father's military photo album

We're staying at the Recreation Center here and it is without doubt the nicest place we've been billeted…. We have Japanese house boys to make our beds and wait on us while we're here. They just came and turned our beds down."

November 10, 1947: His talent had unintended results, when an officer apparently requested he be transferred to a special entertainment group that would delay his getting to go home. He martialed support from friendly officers to reverse that request and writes that he will leave in three weeks. The Glee Club gig has ended and he'll be happy to go back to communications. "I know I won't be declared essential or anything like that. I'll be going home in, roughly, three more weeks."

---

[239] Today, the incredibly efficient and fast Japanese bullet trains, the Shinkansen, can make the 319 miles between Tokyo and Kyoto in two hours and fifteen minutes.

November 15, 1947: "My Janie I love you so much—never doubt that love sweetheart for it will never die. It is more powerful than it was and it will always increase. Always remember that Janie hon, always." Most of his last letters from Japan are filled with lovely sentiments like these, though he also continued to struggle thinking about religion, as his next letter showed.

November 16, 1947: It's obvious that he prefers what he calls the "simplicity and honesty" of Protestant services (and he appears to like singing the hymns!), but he worries about being an "outcast" if he abandons Catholicism. He wants my mother to convince him! "Catholicism, even though I am not devout in its practice, is yet instilled so very deeply in me that it has a very direct bearing on my conscience.... I know that religious harmony is the key to a pleasant, happy and formulative family life.... You've got to talk me into that which will very probably make both of us outcasts to hundreds, perhaps even more."[240]

November 7, 1947: He's enjoyed his radio training. "It's good practice for college physics and chemistry which I'm sure I can't get out of taking when I get to school." As for electrical engineering: "it requires quite a bit of mathematics. I'm not too quick in higher math problems." Otherwise, morale is high because everyone is excited to go home, talking about "girls, milk and sundaes"!

November 22, 1947: Last letter from Japan. "I'll wire you when I'm leaving and you'll know long before you get this. By that time I'll be half way across the ocean on my way to fresh milk, hamburgers and chocolate milk shakes and…well, you know all about that!!!!" The end of the letter: "Signing off, Your loving husband over and out—Your own Bill."

---

[240] In the event, my father did leave Catholicism for my mother's Methodist church, a decision that created substantial tension in his family. My grandmother may have blamed my mother for my father abandoning the Catholic Church, but these letters make clear that he was giving it serious consideration all by himself.

Telegram dated December 22, 1947 from Camp Stoneman, California: "Called but received no answer. Will not make it for Xmas. Expect to be discharged Friday. Will take plane to Evansville if reservations are not delayed otherwise train to same city will write as to time and date of expected arrival. Merry Christmas to all of you. Love Bill."

WHILE THERE ARE SOME LETTERS SURVIVING FROM THE FEW other times they were apart, including during the brief separation in 1952, the "military" letters constitute the vast majority of them. Yet, whenever they were written, whether from Japan in 1946 and 1947, from Maryland when he was traveling for Southern States in 1951, from his mother's house in Houston, Mississippi in 1952, or a few from George Peabody College when he embarked upon the studies for his Master's degree in the summer of 1953, they universally testify to the deep love he had for my mother, a love he continued to cherish after her death in 2000 all the way up to the end of his own life eleven years later. She was always his "Janie," and as the few letters we have from her testify, even when he irritated her about one thing or another, he was always, and to the last, her "Billy."

APPENDIX B

The Death of Robert "Sonny" Monahan, Jr.

The Ploiesti oil fields and refineries in Romania provided at least 30% of the total fuel used by the Axis powers in the Second World War. The first effort by American bombers to damage them occurred in June 1942, when thirteen B-24 Liberator bombers launched a mission from British-held territory in Egypt, inflicting only light damage. German General Alfred Gerstenberg then constructed substantial defenses around the fields, including some 200 deadly 88-mm anti-aircraft guns. When the German offensive against Stalingrad in the Soviet Union failed in 1943, the Ploiesti fields became even more important to Hitler's war effort. In August of that year, the USAAF (United States Army Air Force) tried again, with Operation Tidal Wave, sending 177 B-24s from allied-held fields around Benghazi, Libya manned by some 1,750 crew members. The large formation had to fly a long way at very low altitude, trying at the same time to maintain cohesion vital to a large group of bombers trying to defend themselves without fighter support. German and Axis fighters and anti-aircraft inflicted heavy damage, and 53 aircraft and 660 crew were lost.[241] Damage to the fields and refineries was greater than in 1942, but much of that damage was repaired fairly quickly, and the Germans reinforced their defenses even further. The attack was considered a failure, and American bombers did not return to Ploiesti until early 1944, once the Americans had gained a foothold in Italy and could support their bombers with accompanying P-51 fighters.

---

[241] An excellent account of this raid as well as the entire American bomber campaign against Ploesti can be found in Jay A. Stout, *Fortress Ploesti: The Campaign to Destroy Hitler's Oil* (Havertown, PA: Casemate, 2003), reprinted in paperback in 2017.

As my father notes in his memoir, Robert "Sonny" Monahan had always wanted to fly, and even if, due to some unnamed physical condition, he could not become a pilot, he could still join the Army Air Force as a gunner.

Patch of the 718th squadron

Sometime in the early spring of 1944, he shipped out to Italy, where he became part of the 718th Squadron of the 449th Bomb Group. In his war diary, written before he left for Italy, he quoted an anonymously written piece titled "The Gunner's Poem":

"I wish to be a pilot, and you along with me, but if we were all pilots, where would the air forces be.
It takes guts to be a gunner, and sit out in the tail, when the Messerschmitts are coming and the slugs begin to wail.
The pilot's just the chauffeur, it's his job to fly the plane, although we do the fighting, we may not get the fame.
If we must all be gunners, then let us make this bet, we'll be the best damn gunners that have left this station yet."

One letter from him while stationed in Italy survives, written on Wednesday, April 5th, 1944, only eleven days before his fatal mission. In it he wrote "I'm now a veteran of 7 combat missions over enemy territory. I shot down one ME 109 G. He partly blew up and went down in flames. When I fly 43 more I'll be through."[242] The remainder of the letter referenced various family members and friends, either wondering how they were or reacting to the kinds of small events in their lives that achieved out-sized importance to soldiers overseas. For example, "I was surprised to hear about Joan and her date. I guess she's really growing up" or this: "I'm still looking forward to getting Spencer's address so I can look him up."[243] Or here, the only indication of the pressures of war: "I wrote Buddy a letter while I was in California, I hope he got it. If I was him, I certainly wouldn't want to come over here." And finally, he added a P.S. with his only reference to his youngest brother: "Tell everyone at home hello. Tell Billy to keep on singing with the Red and Gray Band." He signed it "All my love, Sonny."

The flight crew

---

[242] The Messerschmitt Bf-109, popularly known as the 109-G, was the backbone of the Luftwaffe's fighter force.

[243] His brother Frank Spencer Monahan was fighting in the Infantry in Italy. Injured and briefly missing in action, he survived the Second World War to fight again in Korea.

His flight crew nicknamed their plane "Hellzapoppin'," taken from a 1941 musical film adapted from a Broadway play. One picture survives of at least part of that crew, showing only eight men of what would have been a crew of ten or more for a B-24 Liberator bomber. Sonny is obscured in the picture, and on the back, someone has scrawled "Can't see him plainly". None of the men in the photograph are identified by name but are listed below:

> The total crew:
> - Frank Temchulla, Jr., pilot, taken prisoner, 16 April 1944
> - Frederick Royalty, co-pilot, not on board for this mission
> - George D. Daniels, Navigator, taken prisoner, 16 April 1944
> - Charles J. Orrico, Flight Engineer, killed in action, 16 April 1944
> - Irwin Salovitz, Radio Operator, taken prisoner, 16 April 1944
> - Dennin J. Bauers, Ball Gunner, killed in action, 16 April 1944
> - Harold J. Mayers, Assistant Radio Operator/Nose Gunner, taken prisoner, 16 April 1944
> - Robert E. Monahan, Jr., Tail Gunner, killed in action, 16 April 1944
> - Lucius Carter, Waist Gunner, Assistant Engineer, taken prisoner, 16 April 1944

Remarkably, two aerial photographs have survived from the April 16 mission. Is one of the planes shown in the photos the "Hellzapoppin'"? It is impossible to be sure, but if so, one or both of these photos would represent the last ones taken of that plane, and, by extension, of its crew:

After their plane went down, five survivors were taken prisoner and not liberated until Spring 1945. On March 14 of that year, after his own liberation and nearly eleven months after the event, the radio man on his mission, Irwin Salovitz, wrote a remarkable letter to Sonny's father detailing what had happened.[244] That letter came into my father's hands, and he kept and treasured it as a last testament to his heroic brother. Here it is in its entirety, reproduced exactly as written:

---

[244] I have been unable to locate any record indicating what happened to Mr. Salovitz after he wrote this letter.

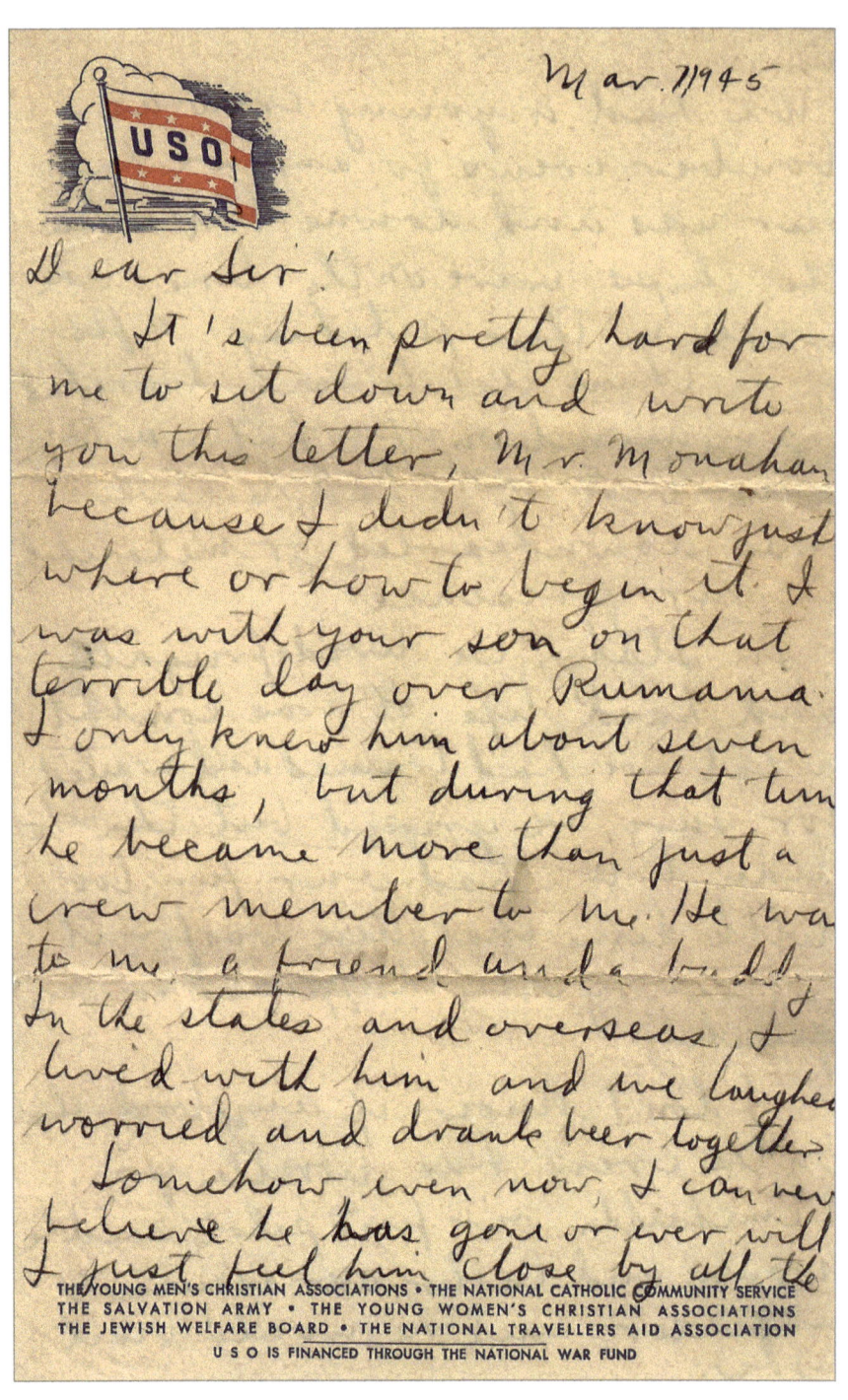

First page of Irwin Salowitz's letter

"Dear Sir, It's been pretty hard for me to sit down and write you this letter, Mr. Monahan, because I didn't know just where or how to begin it. I was with your son on that terrible day over Rumania. I only knew him about seven months, but during that time he became more than just a crew member to me. He was to me a friend and a buddy. In the states and overseas, I lived with him and we laughed, worried and drank beer together. Somehow even now, I can never believe he has gone or ever will. I just feel him close by all the time.

We had a young crew as bomber crews go and we had our ups and downs but when the chips were on the line we were in there pitching. A few of us think that he may have had a premonition of what was to come but if he had, he never was downhearted or melancholy in our presence.

In Italy, we lived a frugal and hard life. It was combat, what we had trained and waited for. Sure, we griped but then who didn't. We had our fun, too, little time that there was for it. But everything happened so very quickly.

I don't know if anybody else on the crew has written you. Temchulla our first pilot, said he would and Carter, our assistant engineer, said he would visit you.[245] But I thought you might like to know just how it all happened. I had just come back from a hospital further north in Italy, after recuperating from a wound received on a mission in March.

They wanted to ground me for a couple of weeks, which would have meant some green replacement flying in my place (not that I was a veteran by any means). But I liked the boys and I didn't want to fly with any other crew and if anything happened I wanted to be along to try and do my bit.

Then on that day in April, I think it was the 17th we took off for a target in Rumania.[246] We were flying the high element

---

[245] My father mentioned in an email to me in 2001 that he and his family had journeyed to Cincinnati to meet a member of the crew in 1945, but he could not recall the name. Presumably, it was Lucius Carter, though it could also have been the pilot, Frank Temchulla, Jr.

[246] He was close, but records show it was the 16th of April.

of our formation. Soon after passing over the Adriatic Sea, we hit a solid overcast. Since we were the high element, we stayed above the overcast while the rest of the formation flew either in or below the overcast.

The weather grew steadily worse. We were separated from our formation, which turned about and bombed some target in the rear. We didn't make communication with them. Finally, when we got within 10 minutes of the target we broke out of the overcast and saw the target but our squadron and group was nowhere to be seen. The pilot of our 3 plane element decided since we were so close, to go in and bomb the target. Our fighter cover had long since left us. So all we had was a prayer and some guns.

After bombing the target, we turned back and had been on course about 10 minutes when we spotted about 35-50 enemy fighter planes. This was it. I guess we all knew that we didn't have a ghost of a chance of getting back.

The first attacks came from the tail. The other two ships got it first. One ship went up in flames almost immediately and the other fell out in a steep dive, which left us all alone. They hit us from every position but mostly from the tail. About 8 of the bastards got on the tail. You know that Bob was our tail gunner. Well, he kept 'em plenty busy but there were just too many. Carter and myself were back in the waist firing our flexible machine guns. Suddenly I heard Bob's guns stop firing. I looked back and saw him sprawled over in the turret. The turret had been shot to pieces and I know he had no pain, Mr. Monahan. Just then, I got a slug in the lower part of my left leg. It knocked me off my feet. The entire tail and waist of the ship were riddled. Two engines were feathered, one was on fire, there was a fire on the flight deck, and a fire in the bomb bay.

About this time we got the signal to bail out and I motioned Carter to jump. He did. I couldn't reach my chute because of my leg and all the smoke in the rear of the plane. I believe they were still shooting at us. Then Bauer, our new ball gunner, came out. I thought they'd got him and he put my chute on. I tried to get him to go and look at Bob first but he literally threw me out of the plane's camera hatch.

I have never seen Bob or Bauer since. I do know that he could have gotten out since he was right behind me when he booted me out but I am pretty sure that he went back to see if Bob was still alive. I spoke to Rumanian officials a few months afterwards and they told me that they had found both of them dead in the wreckage of our plane. Bob and Bauer were both given decent Christian burials. A Rumanian woman, who tried to help the American prisoners in the hospital the best she could, told me all this. I think Lt. Temchulla has all the rest of the information, if he hasn't already written you about it. I'm pretty sure Bob got a couple of the bastards.

That's all I know, Sir, except that I must be living on borrowed time myself. I will probably go back again if they'll let me. I shall never, never forget anything about Bob as I knew him.

I can only say, Mr. Monahan, that I was honored to live and fight with the man, Robert Monahan, your son and my buddy.

Sincerely,
Irwin Salovitz"

Sonny's parents at far left, standing in line at the airport to receive their son's Air Medal with clusters

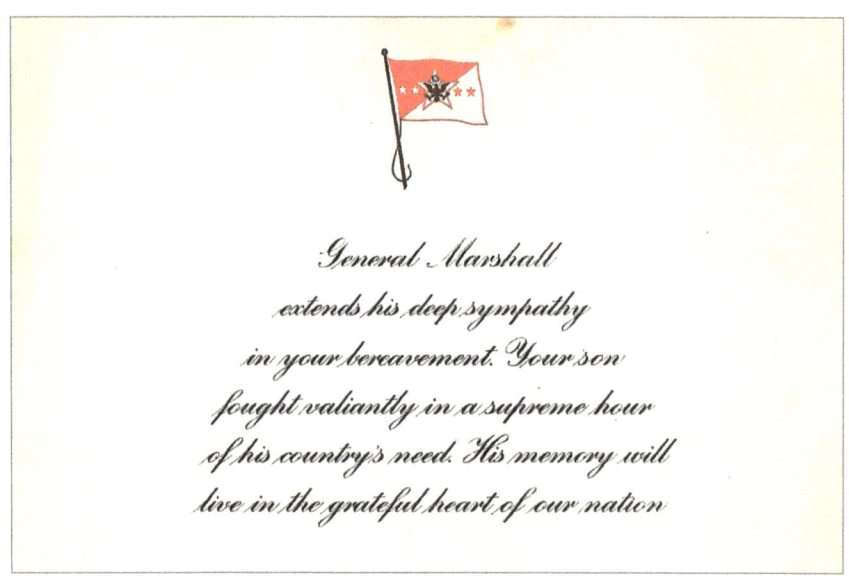

Standard form letter sent by the American chief of staff to my father's parents, as it was to so many gold star parents

*Ardennes American military cemetery in Belgium
where Sonny is buried*

Index

A

AACTE (American Association of Colleges for Teacher Education), 282

AASA (American Association of School Administrators), 245

ACT (American College Testing), 233

AEL (Appalachian Educational Laboratory), 281-282

Alumni Association, College of Human Resources and Education, West Virginia University, 278-280

Anderson, Jack (Professor, George Peabody College for Teachers), 147

Association of Schools and Colleges of Education in Land Grant and State Universities, 282

Atterbury, Camp (military installation), 81

B

Barton, Jay (Provost, West Virginia University), 248, 254

Bauserman, John, 230, 231

Benjamin, Harold (Professor, George Peabody College for Teachers), 146

Benjamin Harrison, Fort (military installation), 81

Beppu (Kyushu, Japan), 84, 85, 87, 204, 309, 322, 325

Berlo, David (Professor, Michigan State University), 195

Blascovics, Thomas (Professor, West Virginia University), 278-279

Blommers, Paul J. (Professor, University of Iowa), 235, 236

Bowling Green Business University, 53, 124, 203

Bowling Green, Kentucky, ix, 10, 13, 18, 20, 23, 27, 35, 40, 53, 58-61, 62, 79, 80, 84, 105, 119, 121, 126, 185, 203, 205, 311, 316, 317

Breckinridge, Camp (military installation), 139

C

Campbell, Clyde (Professor, Michigan State University), 195

Carter, Lucius, 333, 337, 338

Chandler, Albert B. "Happy" (Governor of Kentucky), 180-181

Chapman, Berlin Basil, 279-280

Cherry, Henry Hardin (President, Western Kentucky State College), 128-129

Chicamauga, Camp (Japan) (military installation), 87, 94, 95, 309

Chilton, Lloyd (Editor, Macmillan Press), 220-221, 237

Cincinnati, USS warship, 70

Coombs, Bertram "Bert" (Governor of Kentucky), 180, 189

Cooper, Ann: See Newcom, Ann.

Corwin, Ronald "Ron" (Professor, Ohio State University) 237, 239, 257

Coughlin, "Father" Charles, 34-35

Counts, George (Professor, Michigan State University), 194, 200-201

Coward, Noel, 1

Cowles, Joseph "J. H.," 121-123

D

Daugherty, Mary Ann, 35

Deutschmann, Paul (Professor, Michigan State University), 195

Dixie Bell Roadhouse, 124, 125

E

EE (Electrical Engineering) Building, University of Iowa, 231, 232, 236-237

Eidell, Terry, 281

Emerson, Ralph Waldo, 161, 174, 275

Esch, Keith (doctoral student), 212-213, 242

F

Filer, Lloyd "Jack," 228

Fisher, Leslie (doctoral student, then Superintendent of Schools, Moore, Oklahoma, later Oklahoma State Superintendent of Schools), 213-215

Fisk University (Nashville, TN), 148

Flatt, Adrian, 227-228

Ford Ranch Wagon (1956 automobile), 126, 162-163, 184, 210

Fortney-Henriquez, Miguel (grandson), 293, 298, 301

Frankfort, Kentucky, 2, 155, 156, 157, 160, 162-164, 167, 180, 192, 203, 210

G

Gentry, Richard Lee (Crittenden County Superintendent of Schools, later Professor, Eastern Kentucky University), 154-155, 159

George Peabody College for Teachers (Nashville, Tennessee): See under Monahan, William G.

GI Bill (Servicemen's Readjustment Act), 4-6, 80, 104, 211, 305

Goeres, Ernest "Ernie" (Assistant Dean, then Associate Dean and Professor, College of Human Resources and Education, West Virginia University), 253-254, 266, 271, 272, 284, 294

Goodwin, "Bud" (Professor and Department Chair, West Virginia University), 247

Goslin, Willard (Professor, George Peabody College for Teachers), 146

Guam Island, 72, 73, 74

Guess, Neil (President, People's Bank of Marion, Kentucky), 162

H

Haak, Leo (Professor, Michigan State University), 194

Haller, Archibald "Archie" (Professor, Michigan State University), 194, 202

Hancher, Virgil M. (President, University of Iowa), 237

Harlow, James G. (Dean, College of Education, University of Oklahoma, later President, West Virginia University), 208, 216-218, 222, 243, 244, 245-246, 254-255, 260, 263, 275-276

Hecker, Stanley (Professor, Michigan State University), 167, 182-186, 293

Hellzapoppin' (B-24 bomber nickname), 333

Henriquez, Eliana (granddaughter), 298, 301

Henriquez, Miguel: See Fortney-Henriquez, Miguel

Hereford, Karl (Professor, Michigan State University), 195

Hill, Ann: See Newcom, Ann

Hill, Harvey (brother-in-law), 70, 319

Honolulu, Hawaii, 70

Hopper, Robert "Bob" (Professor, Michigan State University), 183, 186, 195, 207

Hostetter, Arthur "Jiggs" (Associate Dean, College of Human Resources, West Virginia University), 255-257

Howerton temper, 52, 312

I

Ice Box Refrigerator, 25-26

IEIC (Iowa Education Information Center, University of Iowa), 232

Ignatovich, Frederick (doctoral student, later Professor, Michigan State University), 236

Ikenberry, Stanley (Dean, College of Human Resources and Education, West Virginia University, later President, Michigan State University), 243-244, 252

Iowa tests of basic skills, 233

Iowa, University of (Iowa City, Iowa): See under Monahan, William G.

Irish Potato Famine, 6

J

Jefferson Hotel Building, Iowa City, Iowa, 231, 236, 238-239

Jones, Howard (Dean, College of Education, University of Iowa), 233, 234, 253

K

Kaiser (1951 automobile), 126, 127, 157, 162

Kelley Claude (Professor, University of Oklahoma, later Provost, West Virginia University), 208-209, 240-241, 243, 244

Keyes, Captain, 96, 316, 318, 319

Kumata, Hideya (Professor, Michigan State University), 195

L

Lane, Willard "Bill" (Professor and Department Chair, University of Iowa), 221, 233, 237, 239, 246, 257

Liberty ships, 65, 66, 69, 76, 110

Lindquist, Everett F. "E.F." (Professor, University of Iowa), 233-235

Louisville and Nashville Railroad ("L&N"), 10-13, 16, 56

M

Macarthur, Douglas, 315

MacLean, Malcolm (Professor, Michigan State University), 195

Majumder, Ranjit (Professor, West Virginia University), 271, 274

Marion Reporter (Newspaper), 151

Marker, Robert, 232, 233

Martin, Robert R. (Kentucky State Superintendent of Schools, later President, Eastern Kentucky University), 156-160, 166-170, 172, 174, 177, 179-182, 187-190

Measurement Research Center (University of Iowa), 233

Melby, Ernest (Professor, Michigan State University), 194, 201

Mertz, Judy (former daughter-in-law), 269

Michigan State University (East Lansing, Michigan): See under Monahan, William G.

Miller, Delmas (Dean, College of Human Resources and Education, West Virginia University), 252-253

Miller, Paul (Professor, Michigan State University), 194, 243-244

Monahan, Andrew G. (grandson), 268, 269, 288-290, 295, 298, 300, 301

Monahan, Anna Catherine (mother), 10, 16, 19, 23, 27, 29, 30, 31, 33, 35, 36, 43, 54, 317, 340

Monahan, Catherine E. (daughter-in-law), 294, 298, 301

Monahan, Catherine R (granddaughter), 268, 290, 295, 297, 298, 300, 301

Monahan, Dennis (great uncle), 10

Monahan, Frank Spencer (brother), 11, 38, 44, 54, 316, 332

Monahan, Isaiah G. (great grandson), 295, 297, 298

Monahan Jane (spouse), 95, 113, 135, 138, 141, 149, 156, 157, 161, 162, 163, 181, 184, 186, 193, 222-223, 226, 228-229, 267, 269, 279, 282, 286

    As Co-author, 1

    Family Background, 49-52

    Education, 53, 124, 203, 218-219

    Meets and marries William G. Monahan, 49, 64-65, 79-80

    Correspondence with William G. Monahan, 74, 82, 83, 88, 304-329

    In various jobs while married, 124, 139, 202-206

    Concerns about accepting political job in Frankfort, 160, 182

    Moving to Oklahoma, 209-211

    As high school teacher, 52, 312

    As shopping master, 164, 205

    In various jobs while married, 139, 200, 202, 205-206

    Miscarriage in 1962, 219-220

    Chronic headaches, 220, 311

    Moving to Morgantown, West Virginia, 245, 248-251

    As dean's wife, 245, 247

    As realtor, 206, 269-270

    Travel after retirement, 287-289

    Death of, 290-291

Monahan, Joan (sister), 9, 15, 16, 29, 31, 35-36, 38, 42-43, 293, 299-300, 301, 332

Monahan, John (uncle), 25, 29-32, 37

Monahan, John Joseph "J.J." (grandfather), 9, 10, 12, 16

Monahan, Joseph "Gus" (cousin), 10, 11

Monahan, Joseph "Joe" (son), 2, 156, 211, 223, 226, 229-230, 249, 250-251, 267, 268-269, 291, 292-294, 298, 300, 301, 302

Monahan, Laura V. (granddaughter-in-law), 295, 296, 298, 300, 301

Monahan, Liam A. (great grandson), 295, 298

Monahan, Owen (great grandson), 298, 299

Monahan, Rita S. (daughter-in-law), 2, 231, 266-268, 289-290

Monahan, Robert Eugene "Pop" (father), 32, 33, 36, 54, 340

    As Railroad Machinist, 10-14, 16

    As Park Superintendent, 17-20

    As police officer and Chief of Police, 21, 22, 29-30, 59, 62

    Sickness and death, 29, 317

Monahan, Robert Eugene Jr. "Sonny" (brother), 11, 21, 38, 40, 44-47, 60, 330-341

Monahan, W. Gregory "Greg" (son), 2, 126, 156, 163, 195-196, 211-212, 223, 225-226, 228-229, 230-231, 266-268, 288, 289-290, 293, 294, 295, 298-301

Monahan, William G. (author)

    Irish Background, 6-8

    Youth in Bowling Green, Kentucky, 8-48, 58, 61-62

    Meets and marries Jane Newcom, 49, 53-57, 64-65, 79-80

    Employed by Federal Bureau of Investigation, 62-64, 309

    Service in Merchant Marine, 44, 48, 64-79, 110

    Gets embarrassing tattoo, 74-75

    Service in the U. S. Army, mostly in Japan, 80-98, 111, 204-205, 304-329

    Sickened by malaria in Japan, 310, 312, 315

    Ambition to be Journalist, 105, 311, 326

    Attendance at Japanese War Crimes Trials, 90, 326

    Attendance and life at Western Kentucky State College, 105-130, 205

    As president of Western Kentucky State College Geography Club, 112

    As singer in Western Kentucky State College Red and Grey Orchestra, 116-117, 332

    Employed by Southern States Cooperative, 127, 134-136

    As high school teacher and coach at Marion High School, Marion, Kentucky, 137-140, 150, 176-177

    As graduate student at George Peabody College for Teachers, Nashville, Tennessee, 141-150, 193

    As newspaper writer, 150-153

    As Supervising Teacher at Murray State College, Murray, Kentucky, 155-156, 159

As Administrative Assistant (Public Affairs Officer) for Kentucky State Superintendent of Schools, Frankfort, Kentucky, 164-182

As graduate student at Michigan State University, East Lansing, Michigan, 184-185, 193-201, 210, 236

As faculty member at University of Oklahoma, Norman, Oklahoma, 131, 195, 207-222, 240-241, 242, 253

As faculty member at University of Iowa, Iowa City, Iowa, 222, 227-239

As Dean of the College of Human Resources and Education at West Virginia University, Morgantown, West Virginia, 61, 100, 131, 175, 190, 240, 252-266, 271, 274, 276-285

Reforms Promotion and Tenure Procedures in College of Human Resources and Education at West Virginia University, 257-258, 276-277

Reforms Off-Campus Programs in College of Human Resources and Education at West Virginia University, 260-262

Inaugurates Graduation Convocation in College of Human Resources and Education at West Virginia University, 277-278

Inaugurates Alumni Association in College of Human Resources and Education at West Virginia University, 278-280

As consultant to Preston County school consolidation campaign, 283-284

Retirement from deanship, 264-266, 271-273

Awards and honors, 191, 281-284

Sabbatical in Greece, 287-288

Travel after retirement, 289, 293-300

And Pines Country Club (Morgantown, West Virginia), 288, 291-292

Thoughts on the Academy, 99-103

Sickness and death, 299-300

Moore, Donna (Secretary to the Dean, College of Human Resources and Education, West Virginia University), 265-266

Morgantown, West Virginia, 2, 206, 218, 229, 239, 244, 245, 248-250, 254, 255, 256, 261, 262, 266, 267, 268, 270, 288, 289, 290, 292, 293, 300, 302

Murphy, William "Will" (grandfather), 21-23, 26-29

Murphy William "Bill" (uncle), 54, 56, 64

Murphy Brothers Stone Company, 23

Myles, William "Pig," 123

N

Nagasaki, Japan, 78, 84, 91-92, 323-324

Nankai Earthquake (1946), 309

NCATE (National Council for the Accreditation of Teacher Education), 261

Nelson, Ralph (Provost for Continuing Education, West Virginia University), 260

New Deal, 5

Newcom, Ann (sister-in-law), 51, 52, 54, 319

Newcom, Clarence J. (father-in-law), 49, 51, 52, 137-138, 156, 197, 310

Newcom, Clarence R., 52

Newcom, Henrie Howerton, 52

Newcom, Pearl (mother-in-law), 49-51, 52, 310

Newcom, Virginia Jane: See Monahan, Jane.

Nineteenth Infantry Regiment, U. S. Army, 84-87, 96-97, 204

Norfolk, Virginia, 67, 73

Norman, Oklahoma, 206, 208, 209-212, 215, 218, 226, 228, 229

O

Odum, Howard, 147

Ohm, Robert (Professor, University of Oklahoma), 218

Okinawa Typhoon (1945), 73, 76-78

Oklahoma, University of (Norman, Oklahoma): See under Monahan, William G.

Oldsmobile Dynamic 88 (1960 automobile), 210-211

P

PAERIS Program (Programs in the Administration of Educational Research), 235-236

Panama Canal, 69-70

Parker, Franklin (Professor, West Virginia University), 147

Parnell, Katie (grandniece), 300, 301, 302

Parnell, Nan Westin (niece), 9, 300, 301

Pearl Harbor, Hawaii, 70, 71, 78

Phelps, Jewell (Professor, George Peabody College for Teachers), 147

Ploiesti Oil Fields (Romania), 44-45, 330

Plonta, Sergeant, 322

Polk, Camp (military installation), 81-83

Potato Famine: See "Irish Potato Famine"

Preston County school consolidation campaign, 283-284

Proctor, Robert "Bob," 121-122, 127

PRT (Personal Rapid Transport system, West Virginia University), 275-276

R

Red Fox beer, 67

Reeder, Evelyn (Office Manager, Dean's Office, College of Human Resources and Education, West Virginia University), 266, 277

Reinhard, Diane (Dean, College of Human Resources and Education, West Virginia University, later president, Clarion College), 272-273

Reservoir Park (Bowling Green, Kentucky), 17-20

Rhodes, Dusty, 96

Riley, Matilda, 100

Roe, William "Bill" (Professor and Department Chair, Michigan State University), 183-184, 186, 187, 195

S

Saint Joseph's Catholic Church (Bowling Green, Kentucky), 20, 53, 80

Salovitz, Irwin, 333, 335-339

Sandel, Wesley, 96, 97

San Francisco, California, 78-79, 98, 110

Scott Street House (Residence, Bowling Green, Kentucky) 21, 22, 24-26

Seelbach Hotel (Louisville, Kentucky), 54, 56-57

Shreveport, Louisiana, 82

Simpson, Al, 123

Smith, Edwin R. (Professor, West Virginia University), ix, 85, 273-274

South Park Neighborhood (Morgantown, West Virginia), 248-249

Spartan Village (Michigan State University), 187, 192, 209

Spencer, Jennie (grandmother), 23

Stephen T. Mather (Liberty Ship), 67, 76

Stewart, Pat, 269-270

Stoneman, Camp (military installation), 98, 204, 306, 309, 311, 329

Sullivan, Johanna (grandmother), 10

T

Tabor, Pauline, 58-61

Tabor, William "Billy," 58-61

Talisman Ball, 117-118

Teacher Training Schools, 132-134, 211-212

Temchulla, Frank, Jr., 333, 337

Thirteeners (Student Club, Western Kentucky State College), 119-121

Thompson, Tommie Thornton, 49

Thornton, Adolphus J "A.J.," 49-50

Thornton, Kittye (born Mary Catherine Ballard), 49

Thornton, Pearl: See Newcom, Pearl.

Truman Doctrine speech, 314

Twain, Mark (Samuel Clemens), xi

Twenty-Fourth Infantry Division, U. S. Army, 84, 87, 96, 204

U

UCEA (University Council for Educational Administration), 221, 246-247, 281

Ulam, Robert, 175

V

Vanderbilt University (Nashville, Tennessee), 142, 144, 146, 147

Veterans Village at Western Kentucky State College, 114-115, 205

W

Ward, Barbara, 160

Wearden, Stanley (Dean of Graduate Studies, West Virginia University), 199

Weber, Max, 174

Western Kentucky State Teachers College (also called Western Kentucky

State College, now Western Kentucky University) (Bowling Green, Kentucky): See under Monahan, William G.

Westin, Joan. See Monahan, Joan.

West Virginia University (Morgantown, West Virginia): See under Monahan, William G.

Whitaker, J. Russell (Professor, George Peabody College for Teachers), 142-143, 145, 147, 192-193

Whitehead, Alfred North, 107, 161, 175, 270, 286

Willkie, Wendell, 48

Wirth, Fremont P. (Professor, George Peabody College for Teachers), 145, 147, 148, 193

Woodard, Prince, 256

www.ingramcontent.com/pod-product-compliance
Lightning Source LLC
LaVergne TN
LVHW051224070526
838200LV00057B/4600